the Other Germans

the Other Germans

Report from an East German Town

by Hans Axel Holm

Translated from the Swedish by
Thomas Teal

Pantheon Books
A Division of Random House
New York

Library of Congress Catalog Card Number: 73-113721
Manufactured in the United States of America
by Haddon Craftsmen, Scranton, Penn.
ISBN: 0-394-44263-6

9 8 7 6 5 4 3 2

First American Edition

✪ Reservations

You believe that you choose your material, but until the material is gathered, you have little idea where it will lead —you look for one thing and, despite good guidance, you time and again find the opposite. In the end, you hope these surprises will even each other out and all together result in something that resembles truth and justice. Which is not to say that you really know how either "truth" or "justice" should be defined—the truth about what? justice in relation to what? All you can do is choose examples. That you actually do choose the examples is a delusion, no matter how deliberately the selection takes place. But the exercise of selection within each separate example is unavoidable, no matter how unpremeditated the process may be. Completeness is impossible. I have tried to rework the material as little as possible, to manipulate it as little as possible, to interpret and control it, appraise and assess it, as little as possible—what I find good and what I find nonsense are for me to decide.

Finally, if anyone should wonder what the past has to do with the present, there are plenty of answers—particularly in that Germany from the past which no longer exists.

✪ Conditions of Time and Place

My visit to Neustadt-Glewe was in two installments: the end of May and beginning of June 1967, and the end of February and beginning of March 1968—seven weeks altogether.

My first visit coincided with the outbreak and conclusion of the six-day war between Israel and Egypt. My second visit took place at the same time as the student unrest in Warsaw, and while events in Czechoslovakia were reaching the point where, on March 25, the people of Neustadt heard that the Czech border had been closed.

In February and March 1968 the proposed new constitution was distributed to the citizens of the German Democratic Republic—one copy of the complete proposal to each household.

Had my visits occurred at other times, other events would have been reflected and discussed in the interviews I conducted. But the thrust of opinion would differ only in the rare case. In any event, the interviewer's task is not that of the pollster.

My intent has been to try to give a picture of people living together in a small East German town, of their individual and not purely political ambitions and problems. But, inevitably, even the most private aspirations and problems will often be emphatically political in a place where political events and political measures have as thoroughly altered the life style of each individual as they have in the GDR, and where one form of political solidarity has been exchanged for another, ideologically the opposite.

This would be no problem for the interviewer if so many of those interviewed did not experience it as a problem themselves. It all has to do, of course, with the surveillance of the private citizen. Such surveillance exists, though I won't touch here upon its extent or justification. What is crucial, particularly for an interviewer, is that people live in the knowledge that such surveillance exists. In this situation a tape recorder was as good as useless if I was after anything other than the kind of data which is just as easily entered in a notebook at once. Even a notebook and pencil can strike people dumb with distrust, even when the interviewer seems to be dealing with fairly neutral matters. I have also had my notebook and my pockets searched by the people I've been talking to.

This distrust was less annoying on conducting the interviews than it was in transcribing them. Since I had to rely chiefly on memory, I made notes as soon as each interview was completed. In most cases, the interviews in this book are taken directly from those notes.

In other cases, I've felt compelled to tamper with identities, and I've done so with two conflicting fears: the fear of falsifying, and the fear of not falsifying enough.

The way to avoid falsification is, primarily, to make no additions, and to avoid creating, by means of deletion and rearrangement, implications and possibilities of interpretation that have no relevance to the raw material. My method of disguising identities, on the other hand, has consisted chiefly in either deleting material or pulling out a given passage and placing it in some other spot in the book.

Another technique has been to use fictitious names. But to fabricate names in a description of a place as small as Neustadt is pointless unless you also fabricate the reality that surrounds the names—and then you're on dangerous ground if you want to give your account any journalistic authenticity.

That I am conscious of this danger and have worked with the caution this consciousness dictates is the only guarantee I can offer for the validity of the result. In no case is there any question of addition, only of revision.

Altogether I conducted about 100 interviews. Many lasted for several hours, and many were drawn out over several meetings. What interested me—besides such basics as living quarters, salaries, working conditions, school conditions, etc.—were the different relationships between people, and between people and the past. I was interested in the kinds of thought patterns that don't show up in answers to direct questions, just as I was interested in achieving a more or less clear conception of the causes of these thought patterns. Perhaps this approach is somewhat presumptuous, but to my way of thinking, it is still the most meaningful. And one way of succeeding at it is to acquaint yourself with the subject's life history, perhaps even with the history of his family.

The choice of Neustadt-Glewe was actually a personal one. I was already familiar with the place. I can't prove with figures that it is a "typical" or "average" East German small town. According to Neustadt's mayor, it is a fairly "active" and "progressive" place—a claim, however, which may be taken for what it is: a statement by the mayor, who represents Neustadt to the world.

The reader is hereby warned against taking any of the statements quoted in this book as anything more than quoted statements.

During my first visit, I stayed in a private home. I had not yet set out any definite plans for my work.

On my second, five-week visit, I had written the mayor in advance and let him in on my plans and wishes, and I stayed in a hotel. The mayor gave me complete freedom of the town, which in practice, naturally, didn't eliminate all the hurdles and difficulties, since after all the mayor was not the ultimate decision-maker in every instance. For statistical information, for example, you have to apply to the District Central Bureau of Statistics in the district capital, Ludwigslust. But at the bureau in Ludwigslust you are informed that certain statistics—such as population size and profile, emigration and immigration for particular periods, average salary scales, division of work force by sex and age—do not exist for the town separately, or else that these statistics, to the extent they do exist, cannot be divulged.

Permission to visit the town's leading industrial plant was not granted me, despite good references. Permission to visit the school was not granted, despite several invitations. Permission to visit the State Farm was not granted.

On the other hand, few difficulties presented themselves in getting (some) statistics through semiofficial channels. Nor was there any difficulty, without specific permission, in simply walking alongside an employee as he passed the gatekeeper on his way to work in the factory, and then accompanying him to his job. No problem arose, either, when I quite simply knocked at the door of the chairman of an agricultural collective other than the State Farm. And on such occasions I was always hospitably received.

According to the mayor, my failure to make any progress through official channels was the result of having the wrong visa. He thought I should have had a special journalist's visa, and he may have been right. On the other hand, I'm afraid a visa that would have opened more of the official doors might have meant that many of the unofficial ones would have closed.

During my first trip I didn't concern myself very much about the visa problem. Before and during my second trip, the different information I was given in different places on different visas was contradictory—from Stockholm, where I applied, to the Sassnitz–Trelleborg ferry, where the visa was stapled into my passport, to the police office in Ludwigslust, where I had to report to have the final corroborative validation stamped in. Among other things, I was informed in Ludwigslust that my visa could not be extended, a possibility I had earlier been assured of, and one which I had wanted to hold open.

❈ Location, Administration, Data

Neustadt-Glewe is situated 19 miles south of the regional capital of Schwerin, 5 miles northeast of the district capital of Ludwigslust, and 22 miles from the West German border and the border station at Dömitz. Neustadt is 92 miles northwest of Berlin.

As of the spring of 1968, Neustadt had 6,700 inhabitants, of whom 80 percent were employed.

The principal industries are leather and agriculture. VEB* August Apfelbaum Tannery employs 1,200 workers, roughly equal to the total number employed by the larger agricultural enterprises: the Lewitz State Farm, the Turkode LPG,** and the Fourth Party Meeting LPG.

In addition to the tannery, the town has two other large industrial plants: VEB Funkmechanik, which makes radio parts, and Hydraulik Nord, primarily a manufacturer of hydraulic couplings for automobiles. Each has about 600 employees.

Approximately 2,200 residents receive pensions, which is to say that approximately that many people are over the age of 65.

The schools, from the first to the tenth grade level, have 1,080 students altogether.

About ten percent of the inhabitants belong to one or another political party. Six hundred people belong to the German Socialist Unity Party (SED). Party representation on the town council is as follows: SED—17; CDU (Christlich-Demokratische Union—Christian-Democratic Union)—1; LDP(D) (Liberal-Demokratische Partei [Deutschlands]—Liberal Democratic Party)—1; NDP (D) (Nationaldemokratische Partei [Deutschlands]—National Democratic Party)—1.

Besides the larger industrial facilities, the town has a state-owned dairy, a state-owned concrete factory, a state-owned poultry-feed mill, and a privately-owned clog factory, with from 20 to 50 employees each.

The cooperative Konsum runs a shop for household utensils, a clothing store, a bakery, an electric shop, a delicatessen, a curtain and dry-goods store, and a grocery.

---

*VEB=Volkseigener Betrieb—people's enterprise.
**LPG=Landwirtschaftliche Produktionsgenossenschaft—agricultural collective.

The Handelsorganization (HO—the state retail organization) operates a furniture store, two milk shops, a book store, a bakery, a butcher shop and delicatessen, two restaurants (one with dancing), two hotels with restaurants, and one café. In addition to the HO book store, which sells mostly stationery, there is also a government book store.

There are about 20 private businesses in Neustadt, among them two painting contractors, a paint store, a shoemaker and shoe store, an upholstering and invisible-mending shop, a butcher, a shipping agent, a baker, a fish and vegetable store, a photographer, a seed store, and a summer café.

There is one automobile for every 120 inhabitants.

Neustadt has one taxi owner, with two cars. The driving is done by the owner and by her son, who works on a part-time basis for about a quarter of the work week.

Most common form of personal transport: the motorbike; most common form of freight transport: the tractor lug, plus, to some extent, the horse.

There is a post office (open from 9:30 to 12 and from 2 to 5), a drugstore (8–12 and 2–6), a savings bank (10–12 and 2–4), and a police station (one detective, two traffic policemen; office hours: 9–12 and 2–4).

There is one movie house, called the Friendship Theater, and a lending library.

The nearest law court is in Ludwigslust, as are, also, the nearest hospital (the private Stift Bethlehem), the nearest foreign exchange, SED party institute, travel bureau, and auto mechanic. The nearest legitimate theater is in Parchim.

Trains leave for Ludwigslust at 5:54 and 11:08 a.m. and at 2:00 and 6:32 p.m. Departures for Parchim: 6:41 a.m. and 1:04, 5:08, and 11:24 p.m. The trains to Parchim come from Ludwigslust, and the trains to Ludwigslust come from Parchim, which means that the departure times for Parchim also represent the arrival times from Ludwigslust, and vice versa. Travel time to Ludwigslust is 14 minutes. Travel time to Parchim, the nearest city of over 15,000 population, is 26 minutes. Bus connections to Ludwigslust: 5:57, 6:22, 7:27, 8:02, and 8:32 a.m. and 12:32, 2:28, 4:02, 4:22, and 5:17 p.m.

Normal shopping hours in both Neustadt and Ludwigslust are from 8:30 to 12 and from 2 to 4.

Private telephones in Neustadt: 150.

The leading newspaper of the area is the *Schweriner Volkszeitung ("Schwerin People's Times")*.

The town's largest organization is the association of allotment gardeners, with 800 members. The sport-fishing club is the second largest, with 400. Other organizations include the "Forward" Sporting Club, with soccer, boxing, track and field, swimming, and sail-planing. The tannery is responsible for maintenance of the athletic field. Swimming and diving practice is held in Neustadt Lake. The beach director is employed by the town.

The association of allotment gardeners organizes communal spraying and pruning, gives advice on fertilizing, and places large group seed orders through the private seed store. The poultry and small-animal organization organizes wholesale purchase of feed. Both gardeners and bird and small-animal owners have the right to sell what they raise.

The philatelists society has about 100 members, and the chess club around 50. The latter meets every Thursday in the meeting room of Theodor Körner Hotel.*

At the eastern edge of town lies an airfield that was built in 1942 for the shops of the Dornier aircraft factory, which Hitler established in Neustadt-Glewe. This airfield is now used for sail-planing, and there is a sail-planing club with

---

*Named for the poet Theodor Körner (1791–1813), known for his songs celebrating nationalism and liberty.

nine members, each with his own glider. The planes were purchased by the club, but the individual members are responsible for their maintenance. The municipality pays the sail-planers an allowance during competitions.

The culture club has about 50 members and arranges bus trips to the theater in Schwerin roughly once every three weeks. There is also a monthly meeting, with a lecture— a member who has made a trip to some foreign country, for example, or a Ph.D. from Leipzig who shows slides and discusses the art treasures of Cracow. The average age of the members is higher than that in any of the other organizations.

On Breitscheidstrasse,* the main thoroughfare, stands the Veterans Club, where those over 65 can sit from morning to evening and read newspapers, drink coffee, and take their meals.

Both of the youth organizations, the Young Pioneers and the Freie Deutsche Jugend (Free German Youth— FDJ), hold their meetings in the party headquarters on Geschwister Scholl Platz,** opposite the old castle, which now serves as a primary school. The party headquarters was also the party headquarters under the Nazis.

The young people's club rooms are officially open from 4 to 10 every weekday evening. But they are open less often during the coldest part of the winter because of higher fuel consumption and relatively fewer visitors, and when the weather grows warmer, they are open less often because there is then thought to be less need for them. The club rooms are furnished with TV, radio, and games.

The Pioneers have a Friendship Club, whose members exchange letters with Pioneers in other countries.

---

*Named for Rudolf Breitscheid, a Social Democratic Party leader in pre-Hitler Germany who later, while in exile in Paris, collaborated with the Communists in the Popular Front.
**Hans and Sophie Scholl, brother and sister, were Munich university students who were leaders in the anti-Nazi underground during World War II.

According to a survey made in 1967 by W. Weinholdt, one of the schoolteachers, 352 Neustadt Pioneers were then corresponding with Lenin Pioneers in the Soviet Union.

FDJ members in the three highest grades take part in Hans Beimler* competitions, which, for boys, include hand-grenade throwing, shooting, and an obstacle course, and for girls, shooting only. According to Weinholdt, all 231 of the eligible FDJ members took part in the 1967 Beimler competitions.

Overall, participation by members of the two youth organizations in their various activities broke down in 1967 as follows: sports, 420; culture, 105; natural sciences, 120; miscellaneous (e.g., gardening), 100. Seven students attended voluntary extra sessions in mathematics.

The FDJ's responsibilities include fulfillment of their quota of National Construction Work (Nationales Aufbauwerk—NAW). During 1967 the FDJ completed 2,500 hours of NAW, consisting principally of supervision of the town parks: lawn mowing, litter gathering, cleaning up of the paths. Average contribution per member: three hours. For work purposes the members are divided into 20 brigades.

Pioneer and FDJ activities are pursued in close conjunction with schoolwork.

During the spring the school took up a collection for Vietnam, which yielded the sum of 451.28 marks.

The school has 36 classes. In 1966, 3.2 percent of the pupils failed to pass on to the next higher grade; in 1967, 2.2 percent. "Our goal for next year [1968]," says Weinholdt, "is 1.2 percent."

The Parents Committee has 32 members, of whom 11 are laborers, 11 office workers, and 10 intellectuals.

*Beimler was a veteran Communist leader who escaped from Nazi imprisonment and subsequently fought and was killed in the Spanish Civil War.

The FDJ and Young Pioneer club rooms are on the second floor of the party headquarters. On the first floor is one of the communal kindergartens, Geschwister Scholl.

CAPACITY OF THE TOWN'S KINDERGARTENS

Geschwister Scholl	84 children in 6 groups
Klara Zetkin,* Breitscheidstrasse	54 children in 3 groups
Tannery	73 children in 5 groups
Afternoon kindergarten for school children	105 children in 5 groups
Afternoon kindergarten at the tannery	84 children in 4 groups

The kindergartens and nursery schools are for children of three years and above. For children less than three years old, there are day nurseries with facilities to care for up to 100 youngsters. The kindergartens and nurseries are open from 5:30 a.m. to 4 p.m.

The town has two bands, the tannery's and Funkmechanik's. They play at various club festivities.

Four local young people have organized their own pop group, The Elgitas. They play now and then at the Park Restaurant—popularly known as "The Shooting Gallery" —an HO-run facility where dances are held for young people every Sunday afternoon at 3, under the auspices of the Pioneers. There have been dances for young people at The Shooting Gallery every Sunday from 3 to 7 since before the First World War.

---

*Klara Zetkin, a teacher by profession, was a legendary figure in German and international Communism and the German Communist women's movement. She was a member of the Reichstag from 1920–33 and died in the Soviet Union in 1933.

Before the end of World War II, Neustadt's inhabitants were exclusively Protestant in religion, but population movements, principally from Czechoslovakia, have changed this. About 600 people came to Neustadt from Prussia, Pomerania, and Czechoslovakia between 1945 and 1947.

According to the Catholic priest, Father Gehrki, his congregation consists today of 600 people, roughly half of whom are faithful communicants. The Lutheran congregation, according to its minister, Pastor Smidt, has some 6,000 members, of whom about 50, almost all of them elderly, attend services more or less regularly. Thirty to 40 young people are confirmed each year, and 200 school children attend the Christianity class that the Lutheran church conducts for one hour a week. Support of religious instruction is proportionately higher among the Catholics, but Father Gehrki regrets that his bishop has not given him permission to release information or make any statement.

Up until the autumn of 1967, both Protestants and Catholics held their services in the old Protestant church, which, for that matter, is so old that it was originally Catholic.

In 1966 the Catholic parish bought a piece of land— formerly the site of a smokehouse—on Kietz, a side street off Breitscheidstrasse. Their new church was completed in June 1968.

The Catholics used to have their parish house at the corner of Fritz Reuterstrasse* and Ludwigslusterstrasse. The Lutherans have theirs on Petersilienstrasse. Because of the expense of heating the old church, services are held in the parish house during the winter.

A synagogue on Neuhöferstrasse was burned down on

---

*Fritz Reuter (1810–74) was a well-known North German poet and humorist who was also an active revolutionary.

Crystal Night in 1938. The Jewish cemetery was destroyed somewhat later. Today, there is no trace either of the synagogue or of the cemetery.

There are no Jews in Neustadt.

The tannery was Jewish-owned up to 1938, and was called Adler and Oppenheimer. At that time it was one of the major industrial plants in Germany; today it occupies a leading position within the leather industry in the GDR. Weekly production comes to 20,000 dressed pigskin hides, which people in the leather industry in Sweden consider remarkable for two reasons: First, the figure is very high; second, it is unusual to invest so heavily in pigskin.

The leather tanned in Neustadt is used primarily for luggage, shoe uppers, boots, and leather coats.

Many of the workers at the tannery come from neighboring villages such as Wöbbelin, Dreenkrögen, Fahrbinde, Brentz, Blievenstorf, Klein Laasch, and Gross Laasch. Others come from the cities of Parchim and Ludwigslust.

The total value of Neustadt's annual production is about MDN 150 million.*

EXAMPLES OF PRODUCTION IN AGRICULTURE

1968 plan for the Fourth Party Meeting LPG:
   314 tons of milk
   41 tons of pork
   28 tons of beef
   30,000 eggs

Combined plan for the small farms:
   50 tons of milk
   33 tons of pork
   5½ tons of beef
   3,300 pounds of poultry and/or rabbit
   650,000 eggs

*MDN =Mark Deutscher Notenbank, the East German Mark. Official rate of exchange: MDN1=U.S. $0.2387; free market rate: MDN1=U.S. $0.075.

The three largest industrial plants in Neustadt are currently planning for complete change-overs in production.

Until the outbreak of war in 1939 the Hydraulik Nord building on Ludwigslusterstrasse housed Technikum, a technical institute whose students include some from foreign countries. As illustration of Technikum's international renown, the visitor in town is told the following story innumerable times:

> Two people from Neustadt are in Turkey as tourists. As they stand watching the street market in Istanbul, one of them says to the other, "What a strange language they have, these Turks!"
>
> Whereupon a Turk turns to them and says, in Low German, "The language here isn't any stranger than in Klein Laasch."

The town's architectural and historical pride is the fortress, which hasn't yet been dated more closely than to sometime in the 12th century.

The town was devastated by fire in 1694, and again in 1727. Evidence of these fires can still be seen: The houses along some of the streets, Kietz among others, stand in what was once a pile of ashes. After the second fire, conditions required the construction of emergency housing that still stands on Gartenstrasse, Bleicherstrasse, and Grosse Wallstrasse—one-room dwellings without interior ceilings.

Various old buildings remain, since the town was spared the bombing and devastating fires of World War II. The center of town consists in great part of one- and two-story half-timbered houses. The Old World atmosphere is enhanced by the fact that the smaller streets are either unpaved or paved with cobblestones. The town's larger streets, such as Breitscheidstrasse and Ludwigslusterstrasse, have been paved with regular paving stones since the thirties.

Among the oldest neighborhoods is Kietz, in the south-western part of town, where some of the houses still have thatched roofs. The buildings themselves date from the middle of the 18th century, but the plan used for this part of town is thought to date from the 1400's.

The most important additions in the 20th century have been three residential areas, aside from the barracks built just after the war. One barracks area, with 50 dwellings and small gardens, lies along the road down to Neustadt Lake. These were built especially for refugees from the bombing attacks on Hamburg. The units of another bar-racks complex in the southern part of town—on Brauerei-strasse, near the tannery—have by now acquired the char-acter of row houses. These were built in 1948–49 to help relieve the then critical housing shortage. The dwellings that had been vacated because of the war and emigration had proved insufficient for all those who moved in from the former German provinces to the east.

The larger planned residential areas are Liebssiedlung, Fritz Reuterstrasse, and Strasse des Friedens. Liebssied-lung, in the southeast corner of town, consists of duplexes built in the thirties as housing for workers and includes over 70 houses, with gardens. Fritz Reuterstrasse, also built in the thirties, is made up of two- and three-story apart-ment houses. Strasse des Friedens ("Street of Peace") is a vast project begun five years ago. So far, it consists of seven-story apartment complexes with one-, two-, three-, four-, and five-room apartments that include bathrooms, toilets, and refrigerators. The houses in Liebssiedlung have outdoor toilets, as do many of the houses on Fritz Reuter-strasse.

The contributions that Hitler's regime made to the town in the 1930's include, in addition to Liebssiedlung and Fritz Reuterstrasse, the bathing beach on the lake and a rose garden near the old fortress. The airfield was added in the early forties, and toward the end of the war was converted into a concentration camp.

About 600 persons, mostly young, are estimated to have emigrated from Neustadt to West Germany. Some of my interviews were conducted outside the borders of the GDR.

❈ Werner Bahlke, From His Historical Notes

Six hundred thirty-nine estate owners held the lands of Mecklenburg up to the day in November 1917 when the masses in this province too began to move, roused to action by what they had heard of Karl Liebknecht and Rosa Luxemburg. Workers arrived from Magdeburg and Berlin and handed out leaflets. Revolution broke out, even in Mecklenburg. In Neustadt, as in other places, a workers' and soldiers' council was organized. The mayor and town senate were removed from office and imprisoned.

But when the waves subsided after the storm, the bourgeois elements succeeded in re-establishing the old order. Not a single Social Democrat, not a single member of the USPD* made it to the town hall. Dr. Seeler remained the mayor. The revolution trickled out into bourgeois mediocrity here, just as in Berlin. But in Berlin, in the first weeks of December 1918 the Spartacus group was formed, with seven members led by the veteran worker militant Wilhelm Böhm. Not until 1921 did anyone in Neustadt dare to take the decisive step. Only then did Friedrich Schoof, Max Zeise, August Apfelbaum, Adolf Bahr, and Rudolf Schliemann organize a cell of the KPD** in Neustadt. It was these men who in the following years held the flag of

*USPD=Unabhängige Sozialdemokratische Partei Deutschlands—the Independent German Social-Democratic Party, a splinter group under the Weimar Republic.
**KPD=Kommunistische Partei Deutschlands—the German Communist Party.

revolution high, and kept the mass movement from dying. Today they can reap the fruit of their work, and see thereby that their path was right. . . .

✹ Afternoons With Rudolf Schliemann

Rudolf Schliemann lives in Liebssiedlung, several hundred yards from the sail-plane field. He has lived in this same house since the thirties, but during the years when the neighborhood was the site of a concentration camp, he was away in other camps—not concentration camps, but prisons in various parts of Germany. His wife lived here. She saw women in the camp, but knew nothing of what was going on. Rudolf Schliemann had at least an idea—he had friends who disappeared, and friends who came back.

For him it wasn't Hitler who was the great monster. It's too simple to blame everything on Hitler. He was a puppet, Schliemann says. And the people who toyed with the puppet were the big capitalists. The war was the disease of their affluence.

"In the Socialist countries there are only peace-loving people," says Schliemann. "No Socialist country will ever turn its weapons on another."

He is over 70, and lives with his wife on a pension of 150 marks* a month. That doesn't leave very much; but, he says, the state needs its money for other things than old people whose work is already done.

They grow what vegetables they need in the garden beside the house.

They have two rooms in addition to the kitchen, and the house is often crowded. Their daughter and her husband

*See the general price list on pages 126–28 as a basis for comparison.

live with them, and other people often come to visit, from the neighboring houses and from town.

Seven people sit around coffee, among them a farm worker, Fritz Bänsch, who looks in regularly.

"There aren't many who can tell about it any more," says Bänsch.

"You can't tell people how it was," says Schliemann. "You just can't."

Then he tells it. On July 17, 1942, a Gestapo car drove out through the allotment gardens to Liebssiedlung and picked Schliemann up off the street in front of his house. He was charged with violation of Paragraph 138 of the criminal code—high treason—for having sold Communist Party badges, and he was taken to jail in Berlin. At first, the public defender refused to concern himself, and when Schliemann requested another attorney, he was told that, as a Communist, he was not permitted to request anything. Nevertheless, when he stood before the court on September 7, he had counsel.

"A splendid fellow. 'Gentlemen,' he said, 'This cannot possibly be regarded as high treason. At its worst, it is only the preliminary to high treason.' So I was given four years in the penitentiary."

Regensburg was a model prison, Schliemann says.

"I learned to sew there. I sewed all the time, worked hard. There were others who protested by not working. But they just made things harder for themselves. Much harder."

The food:

"We always got good gravy. On Sundays, mashed potatoes and goulash. On the first of September the warden was gone, and each of us got his own pig's foot."

Now and then Fritz Bänsch interrupts.

"Who was the Gestapo man that came to get you?"

Schliemann names him. They had met in later years.

"He used to go riding out here in Liebssiedlung, and we

used to stop and chat. No, he was not an evil man. They weren't all evil."

The further the story goes, the less clear Schliemann's memory becomes.

Zweibrücken: soup you could see the bottom of, bombing raids, disease.

Eberbach: one-eighth of a slice of bread for breakfast.

Schweinfurt: the rock pile, two sausages divided among 140 men.

The way home:

"When we met Russians, they gave us food, cigarettes, and chocolate. The Americans spat on us. We weren't just Germans, after all, we were also Communists. The only ones who behaved well to us were the Negroes. They didn't spit.

"When I got home from Schweinfurt, the first thing I did was take out the Party Badges. I'd hidden them under a board in the kitchen."

The table is cleared.

Schliemann remains sitting. Bänsch reminds him that he (Schliemann) had already been a Communist in the First World War, when he was a driver for an artillery canteen.

"Yes, yes," Schliemann says. "I was always thinking of those who had nothing. I really was. Once in a while I'd butcher a cow on my way up to the front—I'm a butcher by trade. But it was only the foot soldiers who got any, only the common soldiers."

"But it was a different kind of Communism from today," says Bänsch. "It was a spontaneous Communism. You people who held your secret meetings in the thirties weren't the same kind of Communists we are today."

"Oh, no. That's true. Today it's something quite different. What we have today is something we didn't imagine. . . ."

"The old Communists don't understand everything

that's happening in today's society. They don't have the same training as nowadays," the farm worker explains to the foreigner at the table.

"That's true," says Schliemann. "There's a lot we don't understand.

"But remember," he goes on, "there's a lot that's been done. Today the farm workers have automobiles. They couldn't have had them before. And remember, no Socialist country starts a war. War is a disease of surplus—the capitalists don't know what to do with their money."

"Yes," Bänsch agrees. "Socialism will never start a war. That's true. But we also have to remember that capitalism won't give up anything of its own free will."

"That's true," says Schliemann. "But a Socialist country will never start a war with another Socialist country. It's just inconceivable."

"Yes, of course it is," says Bänsch.

✿ The Rathaus

The town hall opens at 8:30 and closes from 12 to 2 for lunch. Mayor Diederich goes out for lunch and usually eats at either the Körner Hotel, directly across the square from the town hall, or the Stadt Hamburg, across from party headquarters. His wife works at VEB Funkmechanik, where she is the party secretary. Deputy Mayor Ernst Thiele goes home for lunch. He lives on Schweriner-strasse, five minutes' walk from the town hall. At 5 p.m. the Rathaus closes; at 6, the shops on Breitscheidstrasse. Both Mayor Diederich and Deputy Mayor Thiele have their doors open to the public—officially, each of them only one morning a week, but in practice, all day every day except Wednesday afternoons, when they are in conference.

✠ Mayor Diederich's Path to the Neustadt Rathaus

Diederich has been a mayor for 20 years now, but not the whole time in Neustadt. He is originally from Bomberg in West Prussia, where his father was a lumberman. In 1920, when the mayor-to-be was ten years old, the family was forced to move from West Prussia to Pomerania. His father got work planting oats to stop sand drift along the Baltic.

"He made 18 marks a week. There were four children. We all had to help try and get a little money into the house. I know what poverty is," he says.

Altogether, Diederich went to school for eight years. After that he became a smith, and worked in his home town. His father had quite early joined the lumberman's union, to which only about 20 percent of forest workers belonged. Diederich joined a union too, and also passed a technical exam, which qualified him to operate industrial machinery. In 1939 he got into a civilian labor battalion stationed at a shipyard on the island of Sylt. They were later transferred to the Luftwaffe shops in Wesendorf, near Braunschweig. "During the war," says the mayor, "I was a civilian."

In 1943 he was taken prisoner by the English and in 1945 was sent to Neumünster, from which he managed to escape. He made his way across the Elbe and hiked to Karstädt, where his parents were living, and where, in 1946, he began to work for the party. He worked on a farm belonging to his brother-in-law, one of whose brothers had been killed in the war, and whose father had died of diphtheria.

In Karstädt, Diederich assisted in carrying out the first land reform, took an active part in the instruction of party cadres in Marxism-Leninism, and helped, through the party, to organize and develop a brick industry. In 1948 the election committee for the Ludwigslust District nominated him for mayor of Karstädt, and he accepted.

After a year as mayor he went for the first time to the party institute in Berlin, and to the administrative school in Weimar. Every year since then he has attended both a party training seminar in Berlin, Weimar, or Ludwigslust and eight weeks of administrative school in Weimar.

In 1950 he became mayor of Mallis, several miles from Dömitz, and certainly a much smaller place than Karstädt, which had a mine, a factory, and a brickyard. But Diederich already knew that he was to be nominated as mayor of Neustadt-Glewe.

On June 9, 1951, he was installed in his post in Neustadt, succeeding the town's first Socialist mayor, Friedrich Schoof, the saddle-maker, who went back to his job at the tannery.

✖ Speech Given by Mayor Diederich, March 1968

The council is the political organ of the citizens. It is responsible for everything that occurs within its jurisdiction. For that reason the daily agenda always includes the question: "How can the standard of living of all citizens be steadily improved?" The standing committees of the Neustadt town council and many of the townspeople have helped with advice on the 1968 production plan. At the same time, a plan has been developed for mass initiative. This plan sets production output to a value of 900,000 marks as the target for the National Front Competition; that is to say, about 200,000 marks more than was achieved in 1967. This goal will be realized by means of housing construction, the building of a freight facility, and other projects.

Relations between the town administration and the factories have also developed nicely, on the basis of cooperative agreements. The tannery placed a classroom at the disposal of the fourth class at the polytechnical high school, and thereby helped to alleviate local school problems. In the course of the year, VEB Funkmechanik increased the number of openings in its kindergarten by 27. During the winter we reached a series of agreements concerning snow removal on the town streets. The Association of Allotment Gardeners and the Small-Animal Breeders have taken over the care of several of the town's parks and greens. The list of examples could go on and on—and yet much remains to be done. For example, there are some difficulties at the moment in transferring all the three-year-olds from the day nursery to the kindergarten. But with the help of our colleagues at VEB Funkmechanik and VEB Hydraulik Nord, we will manage to solve this temporary problem too. . . .

✪ Diederich's Standard of Living

The mayor has had a private house built for himself on Neuhöferstrasse. It is one of the few private dwellings constructed in the town in recent years, and counts among its comforts a glass veranda facing away from the street in toward the garden, which consists primarily of an asparagus patch and a well-tended lawn.

Monthly payment on the house: 175 marks.

Mayor's salary: 1,000 marks a month. Frau Diederich's salary at Funkmechanik: 700 marks a month.

A considerable portion of the mayor's salary is burnt up

in tobacco. He smokes 40 cigarettes a day, at a cost of about 240 marks a month.

Expenditures for meals and snacks during the working day are figured at 90 marks a month for the mayor, and 30 marks for his wife, who eats a subsidized lunch at Funkmechanik.

The mayor's chief hobby is fishing.

✖ From a Conversation on Sports With Mayor Diederich

Now the West Germans have begun provoking our athletes as well. If what happened in Grenoble with our luge team* wasn't political provocation, then what was it? For many years it's been a thorn in the side of the West Germans that our luge team is one of the world's best, and wins medals to prove it.

Most of the people in our republic go to work every day, and at their place of work they know they'll be justly treated. They know they'll be listened to when they offer an opinion. And therefore many of our citizens can't imagine how an outrage as swinish as what happened in Grenoble can be planned and carried out, although the whole world understands how unjust and vulgar such things are, but so it goes, because in capitalism everything can be weighed against money.

Those who have money can always find people who, for a price, will advocate anything or do anything. That's how

*Three women who had represented the GDR at the Olympic Games were disqualified by the judges after placing first, second and fourth in the first day of competition; all were accused of having warmed up their sled-runners just before the start of the race. The leaders of the team from the GDR—as well as spokesmen for the Norwegian, French, Czech, Lichtensteinian and Swedish teams—protested the decision on the grounds that satisfactory proof of the alleged infringement had not been demonstrated.

things are under capitalism, once and for all. Here it shows its true face. In sports it's just the same as it is in politics.

The rulers of West Germany try in every possible way to injure us and discredit us.

✜ Fishing Conversation

The fishermen are sitting on the bridge abutment where Thälmanstrasse crosses the Elde.
—Hello, Peter.
—Hello, Rolf.
—Catch anything?
—Oh . . .
—Big?
—Oh, no.
—Little?
—Nothing.
—No!
—Patience.
—You sit here hour after hour holding your pole while the fish eat the worm off your hook, and you don't even notice. You just doze off. And when you wake up, why, you can still say you've been thinking about food production. You make me think of Tom Sawyer. Remember him?
—Well, you don't get points for being virtuous. To be perfectly honest, I don't care about getting points, anyway.
—Do you get points for patience?
—What was that about Tom Sawyer?
—All I remember is the Mississippi, and there's a tree trunk by the river, and there's little Tom, with a big hat and a pipe in his mouth and a fishing pole in his hand, and he's gotten away from the watchful eyes and constant scolding of the grownups.

—It's recreation.
—Tom Sawyer's recreation?
—We count up points for recreation around here, too.
—It's not either recreation.
—No, I agree. It's not recreation.
—Do you know what it is, then?
—Escape.
—Ha!
—What are you laughing at?
—There were some young men here in the club, right after Brockman went over. . . .
—Went under.
—Yeah, O.K., that depends on how you look at it. Anyway, one evening they were sitting around talking. And of course they all decided they were in the wrong sport. And then there was one of them who said he had an idea. He was going to take a pike and feed it saffron meatballs. A special flavor. He'd get the pike to love saffron meatballs. Fatten it up to 35 pounds on saffron meatballs. Then when the championships started, he'd throw the pike in the water and it would sniff its way up to his saffron-flavored bait, and with his 35-pound saffron-crazy pike he'd qualify for the national team and get to go abroad for international meets.
—Yes, to Lodz and Vladivostok. . . .
—That's about what I told him.

✪ Leather-worker Martin Zeitschel and His Son Dieter, at Home on Bleicherstrasse

I bought some pigeons in Schwerin a while back—the dealer said they were Peruvian. I've read about them in our club magazine. It's a small pigeon, the tail is shorter than the wings, and rounded. It's got iridescent black spots on the wings. It said in the magazine there are 16 varieties in America. Anyway, the spots on the wings are real pretty, shaped like drops of water, you know, triangular, and they're in a pattern. And at the base of the bill they've got a pretty apple-yellow color. And then there's a horizontal dark-purple stripe from the shoulder to the primaries. The man who wrote about them in the club magazine said he suspected there was some confusion about the name. So he wrote a description of the birds and sent it to an expert, with some pictures, to pin down the species. The expert wrote back that a number of birds are mistakenly called Peruvian, but only this one is the true Jacobin or Peruvian pigeon, also known as the Santa Cruz pigeon.

So then I read the description again.

Everything agreed, at first—the whole description of the plumage.

But then it said that the coo was soft, and that sometimes they squeaked. I'd never heard them squeak, so I went out and stood there a whole quarter of an hour and listened. But they didn't squeak. Then I called my wife and she came out, but they wouldn't squeak for her either.

For a long time I wondered what could be wrong with them, but I didn't say anything. You can't go around bragging you've got Peruvian pigeons, and then let on there's something wrong with them. But I was pretty unhappy about it, all the same.

Then one day I went to the health office for a routine physical. I'd asked for a full examination, because I'd been sick. Anyway, you'll never guess what they found—I had a hearing impairment. There were certain sounds I couldn't hear.

I ran all the way home. Everyone in town probably thought I was about to go in my pants. My son wasn't home, so I had to wait for him. You can't imagine how nervous I was.

When he got home, I said, "Come on out to the garden, you musician, you, and tell me what the call of these Peruvian pigeons sounds like."

First he said Benny Goodman. Then he said Dizzy Gillespie. Then I started to get mad, so he said, "Do you mean the squeaking?"

So I went in and told my wife she was hard of hearing. They *were* Peruvian pigeons. Nobody cheats me when it comes to pigeons.

◙ THE CURE

Like I said, I was sick, and anyone who's been sick in this country won't ever complain again. I went to Bad Gadenow for treatment. Let me tell you, anyone who's ever been to Bad Gadenow for treatment won't ever complain again. It was like living in a hotel. It didn't cost me a thing. I've been there twice, and let me tell you, anyone who's ever been to Bad Gadenow for treatment has no right to complain. Anyone who's ever been to Bad Gadenow shouldn't say another word.

And you've got security here.

There was a fellow who let the tanning agent run out in the Elde, 3,000 marks' worth. He was punished—he had to pay for it, not everything, but most of it. But he wasn't fired. You got security in this country.

But I'll tell you. It wouldn't have been that way when the Jews ran things. Adler used to come down before Christmas and say "Merry Christmas," but if you got sick, you couldn't be sure of getting your job back.

◙ WAR REMINISCENCE

I was in Oslo. The Norwegians weren't easy to get to talk to. But one time, one of my buddies and I told two fishermen to send two barrels of herring back to our wives in Germany. "If those barrels don't show up, why then . . ."

That's what we told them. The barrels got there. Honest they were, in any case, the Norwegians. They weren't easy to get along with, but they were honest.

✿ PIGSKIN

The factory's going like never before. We cure 20,000 hides a week, and only pigskins. You see pigskin everywhere. The girls wear pigskin boots. They built huge new vats when we changed over completely to pigskin. The army uses loads and loads of pigskin. Now we're going to change over again. We're going to make artificial leather, only artificial leather. The big vats we built for the pigskins will get ripped out—that's how fast progress goes. Artificial leather is better than real leather. It's been scientifically tested.

"Hogwash," says Dieter, the son.

"It's been scientifically proven," says Martin.

"Hogwash," says Dieter.

✿ THE SON, DIETER ZEITSCHEL,
   LATHE-OPERATOR

I operate a lathe at the tannery. Dad's worked there for 32 years, and he gets 600 marks [a month]. I get 550. You see, it's not seniority that counts, it's production. Our room's in there—my wife and I, and we've got two kids. We've got the pigeons right outside the window. My wife's a kindergarten teacher. It's a popular job—you can take care of your children without being crammed in with Grandma and Grandpa. We've been waiting for an apartment for four years, but we still haven't got anything. But we do have a garden all to ourselves, so we've joined the gardeners club. We had the annual meeting here recently. There's 800 members, and there's been a whole bunch of new, young members in the last few years. I know all about it because Dad's on the board. They ought to choose a new board. I suggested that some of the younger members ought to be chosen—the average age on the board is over 50. The answer I got was that it's not age that counts. The secretary said, "Young," and he pointed to his head, "That means young up here."

✖ FATHER AND SON

I was a member of the labor organization at the tannery. Then I was a member of the party. That's right. It was called the National *Socialist* Party. That was the name.

—Tell him you *had* to be a member.

—Well, yes, we had to belong. At the factory we were required to belong to the party.

—Yes, and that's the way it still is.

—No, it isn't.

—The hell it isn't.

—Well, maybe . . .

✖ PIGEONS

Most of the pigeons here are Saxon pigeons. I don't care for Saxons, but Saxon pigeons are fine. Saxon whitetails, Saxon stork pigeons, Saxon crescent pigeons. I earn quite a bit off of them. On 600 a month I couldn't afford a new electric stove, or a bath in the washhouse. An incubator is no cheap matter either. I sell birds, and mating service. We don't have an indoor toilet yet.

✖ THE ARMY

Dieter: We could just as well do without the Russians. We could have taken care of ourselves better without them.

Martin: It was the French who treated their prisoners worst. The Russians like children. The French didn't. Frenchmen love love, but not children—that's the way it goes. But don't mix pigeons with politics.

Dieter: No, I haven't done my service yet. I'm not exactly longing to go. I registered in '63. My brother did two years. They get a lot of money, but he drank it all up, so he doesn't have anything left after all. Some people break in a plate glass window, so they get punished, and then they don't have to go. . . .

My brother? He's out fishing. Look there on the wall—he got that down here in the lake. It weighed 35 pounds. He made his master's rating on that. Then we sent it out and had it stuffed.

✪ Deputy Mayor Thiele's Account of the Brockman Case

He was 20. Last summer he swam from Boltenhagen to the Bay of Lübeck in one of those skin-diving outfits. We have a diving club that practices down here in the lake. The organization pays for the gear, but Brockman had an outfit he got from his grandmother in Denmark. He'd swim back and forth out here in the lake—under water—he had an oxygen tank and a snorkel, and nobody thought anything of it. Nobody thought there was anything funny about it. Then he went up to Boltenhagen on the Baltic and went into the water there. Apparently no one gave it a second thought up there either. But then he disappeared. In a few days his parents got a telegram from Bremerhaven. It just said he'd arrived safely at his aunt's, and that he was going on to his grandmother's in Denmark, where he wanted to live. We started a big investigation, questioned all of his friends in the diving club. None of them had had any idea of what he was planning. We asked them if he was dissatisfied with anything here. They said he hadn't been unhappy with anything except his parents. He fought with them constantly. He had a good job, and did it well. We knew the family circumstances weren't the best.

✿ Thiele's War Memories

I belonged to an airborne infantry platoon, and in April 1945 I was in Italy.

I intended to leave Italy and go to Switzerland along with two buddies. We went up in the Alps, but we didn't get far before we were stopped by the spring thaws. We were stuck in a little Alpine village for five weeks and couldn't go forward or backward, so we just sat there, scared to death of being discovered or betrayed. After that, we realized we couldn't make it over the Alps, not in that area anyhow, and we didn't have enough provisions for any longer expeditions on our own. We decided to go back down into Italy. But of course, we couldn't possibly go back to our own division. We came down in a valley and landed right in the middle of the Fourth Airborne Division, which at that time, in the middle of May, on orders from Dönitz, Hitler's successor, was getting ready to move on Berlin with American help and recapture the city. As quick as that, it was already not Fascism but Communism that was the enemy. The surrender had been on May 8, and this was the middle of May.

When we found out what was in the works, we deserted again and took a boat over to Tunisia with some Frenchmen.

It wasn't the first time I'd been in Africa. I'd taken part in some jumps in Rommel's campaign. From the air, you know, we could see that those tanks Rommel used to stir up the dust and terrorize the enemy weren't tanks at all. They were just regular little Volkswagens.

✪ Arthur Öhlscheid,
on the Concentration Camp

Yes, of course, we knew about it. We weren't completely blind, after all. They came down the main street on the way to the camp. They came here to Neustadt on foot, women pulling wagons. I saw a convoy on the Parchim road. At the airfield here, it was only women, but at the tannery they had male prisoners, mostly Russians. They were badly treated—beaten and starved. Once I was put in charge of six Russians. They were supposed to work down at the fish ponds, and I was told to beat them if I had to. They should have got that captain at the tannery after the war, but he got away. He was a brutal bastard. Anyway, one of the Russians was sick, he could hardly walk. I told the captain, but it didn't make any difference. The others carried him down to the fish ponds, and I told them they could put him down in the bushes—if they worked hard, nobody would notice. It was hot, I helped them dig. When we went back at the end of the day, I was given strict orders not to help any more. I was only supposed to supervise. Sometimes I tried to give them extra food, but I couldn't just hand it to them. I'd leave it for them in a window, so it wouldn't be discovered.

The whole factory had been Jewish-owned. Most of the Jews got out early, in '34 or '35. Kahn stayed on as plant manager, he was a Jew too. Later they chased him out. I was in the union even then, but only 30 percent of the men belonged. We did piecework. But your wages could only increase by 20 percent. If it went higher than that, they lowered the piece rate. The union's better today. I remember once there was a guy stole some leather. They found out and were going to hold him to account, so we all went on strike, and that wasn't right. The union's better now. But still, things were better with the Jews than they are now. It was more human. One time they let a bunch of us, four families, take one of the factory cars and drive to Eutin, just for the fun of it. They didn't count it as vacation.

Now we've got prosperity, although we only think about our *own* prospern ity. That's stupid. We'll have to pay for it. The world's down and out, people in India are starving, the blacks in Africa are starving, a good part of the people in Latin America are starving. The world is threatened by overpopulation. And here we are, chasing prosperity and having prestige wrangles with West Germany. There are more important problems these days than the partition of Germany. This prosperity just can't go on.

Öhlscheid's monthly salary: 500 marks. Rent: 45 marks a month. Taxes: 16 marks a month. Children: one, now living in West Germany. Wife: housewife, invalid—disability compensation: 117 marks. Apartment: two rooms plus kitchen. Conveniences: electric range, tile stove, outdoor toilet.

✹ First Meeting With Hermann Kuhn, Clerk

All this is only the beginning, you know, but you're wrong if you think it's the *very* beginning. It really began a long time ago. I've read my Marx, but I've also read my Hitler and my Hegel, and I promise you, I know what's in store for us.

I've made my own contribution to it, but at my funeral, no one will say I was a friend to what's taking place.

I was young when I joined up. I was blond and tall and blue-eyed—all signs of merit. I was proud to put on the uniform, proud of the death's-head on the cap, proud when we marched through little towns in France, and villages in Poland. People cleared the streets when we marched through.

In its way, it was a great time. And I advanced very quickly.

It's often said that we didn't know what was happening. But we knew all right. We just kept quiet—a unanimous silence.

My dear foreign friend, everyone condemns us. I was condemned, and I served my sentence at Seven Oaks. But try to understand one thing—it's not I that ought to be condemned, it's men like Brecht, Mann, Becker, Ulbricht, and Brandt who ought to be condemned.

When did it become an honorable thing for all the people who've studied navigation to desert the ship as soon as the navigator gets sunstroke? When did it become an honorable thing to stand and holler from a safe shore, hundreds of miles away?

And the internal émigrés, the ones who sat in their cellars and shivered with fear—what kind of resister can be effective if he's afraid his resistance will be noticed?

There was unanimity, my friend from the Free World, and it was the same unanimity that exists today between the GDR and the Federal Republic.

Nazism is just a link in a chain of fate, where thousand-year-old princes sit like deaf puppeteers in a puppet show, as inaccessible to us as stars that burnt out long ago, but whose light still touches us.

Did Marx really believe you could clip off those beams of light with a scissors?

I assure you, dear guest, German reunification is closer than you dream. And it won't be a Socialist Germany, as they say here.

Vietnam for the Vietnamese. Germany for the Germans.

✖ Open Letter From the German Socialist Unity Party to the Citizens of West Germany*

To the Citizens of the West German Federal Republic!

We in the German Democratic Republic are, at the moment, discussing a new, Socialist constitution. The discussion is quite open. The broadest possible cross section of the population—yes, you could say nearly every member of our society—is taking a lively part.

Since every family has been supplied with an outline of the proposal, it is possible for every citizen to make his criticisms and suggestions known to the commission appointed by the parliament. Therefore, we will be able, in the final text, to say with reason and justice: The people of the German Democratic Republic have granted themselves this constitution.

Many of you will recall that the constitution of the Federal Republic came into existence in quite a different way. No West German citizen was asked for his opinion. The fundamental law of the Bonn government was forced through the parliamentary council of that period by order of the American occupation forces. That will soon be 20 years ago, and that constitution is still in effect.

Naturally, the citizens of the GDR are interested in the way in which political conditions in the Federal Republic develop in the future. The increasing pressures on the West German workers and their labor unions, the reawakening of Nazism, and the entire course of reactionary developments in the Federal Republic—these are things we take very seriously. We therefore appreciate all the more

*From *Schweriner Volkszeitung*, February 29, 1968

strongly the fact that West German workers and intellectuals, large numbers of young people, and many students and even peasants have begun to declare their opposition to the American crime in Vietnam, to discriminatory legislation, and to the lies of the Springer machine.

Our attitude toward West Germany and its citizens can be stated in one sentence: Although nothing binds us to the imperialistic West German social order, we are nevertheless bound by a common Socialist, democratic, and peaceful future to the West German workers, the working farmers, and the progressive intellectuals.

Since the workers in the two German states have not given up hope for a unified, peace-loving, and progressive Germany, it is clear that they are seriously concerned with Germany's future.

An attempt has been made to persuade you that our new, Socialist constitution will put the final seal on German partition. This is not only a lie, but also a piece of consummate stupidity. Germany has been divided for 20 years. And it is not we who are to blame, but rather the West German supercapitalists, the Christian Democrats under the leadership of the separatist Adenauer, and particularly the American imperialists. They divided Germany and bound West Germany to the Paris Treaty, which deprives the citizens of the Federal Republic of their right of national self-determination. They were afraid that the plutocrats and Hitlerite generals would be chased out of West Germany too, and that the workers, salaried artisans, intellectuals, and democratic elements of the bourgeoisie would join us in establishing a democratic and progressive Germany. . . .

Walter Ulbricht

✠ Lily Grützner, 47, Teacher

In every room hung a portrait of Walter Ulbricht. On one occasion she pointed to one of the portraits and said, almost in a whisper, "Did it ever occur to you that he's trying to look like Lenin?" Later she added: "Lenin—now there was a great man."

In the school library she indicated several rows of books: "Here is everything he thought and wrote, including some things he only ought to have thought. And some things he probably shouldn't have thought, either. Have you read him?"

"Some . . ."

"I'd already read most of it nearly 30 years ago," she said. "Yes, he was a great man."

She teaches German and music. She has no problems with the children, thinks they are all very nice.

We went to the school cafeteria, where we were each given a magnificent sausage. The bell rang, the group changed, we stayed where we were.

"You must forgive me," she said. "I'm rather tired today."

Another teacher came and sat down at the table and told us about a splendid new chart he'd gotten for biology instruction. He only had it on approval, but he already thought he could recommend it for use in other schools.

When we were alone again, she said, "You said you wanted me to talk about things, so I will, though I don't know if this is what you want to hear. . . ."

I'm tired today. I'll tell you why. Around here, you know, we all have our own little adventure stories to reel off. I'm going to tell you mine. There are old memories that keep getting mixed up in your dreams, sometimes one thing, sometimes another. But there are memories you can't ever get away from, and can't ever get used to.

When I was in teachers college in Berlin, before the war, I got engaged. My fiancé's father had been a teacher at the Sozialistische Volksschule in Berlin. He was one of the teachers who was arrested in 1933. My fiancé, Reinhardt, had gone to that school as a boy, of course, before it was closed. His father was a wonderful old man, an enthusiastic Socialist, terribly temperamental. No one's been able to discover what happened to him after he was arrested again in 1943. It's quite possible that he wound up in a camp.

My fiancé was also temperamental, and also a politically clear-sighted man. He was the one who woke me up to Socialism, got me to see what Socialism was, and what it could have done in the Germany we had then. He was the one who got me to read Lenin.

But neither he nor I took part in any party activity. We weren't even party members. Perhaps it was I, or my parents, who were the cause of that. As far as I remember, my parents were neither one thing or another. They were just frightened.

Reinhardt was in one of the first units sent to the front in 1939. Once he tried to desert, but he didn't make it. Most of those who tried to desert were shot, but Reinhardt wound up in a punishment company. I'm only telling you this because I want you to understand what kind of a soldier he was, or rather, because I want you to understand that he was more loyal to himself than to his national service.

Myself, I was assigned to a switchboard at the Brandenburg Camp in 1944. There were three of us. There was only one thing that made it bearable, and that was that I knew Reinhardt's interpretation of what was happening.

The three of us who worked there didn't talk much to each other—we got to know each other in other ways.

What separated us, only I knew, and I knew it more painfully with each report that reached us of the Russian advance.

Whenever we asked ourselves who would reach us first, the Russians or the Americans, why, for them the Americans meant mercy, and the Russians meant destruction. But for me it was just the opposite, or at least I wanted it to be just the opposite, even though I too was infected with fear of the Russians. I heard the stories too—about the rampaging Russians.

In the end, it was the Russians who came. We three girls had hidden up in an attic. We lay there and peered out through a little window—it was a ridiculous place to hide. We heard their armor coming up, a hideous growling noise. Have you ever heard tanks coming from a long way away? Now and then we'd hear a shot. We could see that something had started to burn a long way off. Then the attic door was jerked open. It was two other women. We didn't know them. One of them had a small child that was screaming. They came over to us, and were telling us about someone who'd hanged herself. At first, we were absolutely petrified with fear. Then one of the other operators said, "It might be just as well. We'll die anyway, and you can't tell how *they'll* kill us. But first they'll rape us, that's for sure. They always do."

The child was screaming, and we figured we'd all die if the screaming gave us away. We decided we'd better spread out. I ran across the street with one of my friends, and I pulled her into a house. There was an old crippled woman sitting there, she told us to get down in the cellar. There were already five or six people gathered down there, and they told us to get out. I ran out in the street, lost track of my friend. I found a barn to hide in and crawled into the hay. I don't know how many hours I lay there. I heard tanks and shots much closer by. Once I thought they'd gone on, and I went out in the street to see.

Three Russian soldiers came along then and chased me, all three of them, and then raped me, two of them, and then they shot three shots into the hay, and it started to burn. I ran out in the street again and into another house and locked myself in the toilet and watched the barn burn from there. When the roof fell, I saw there was a dead woman hanging from the rafters.

That was the picture that came back to me last night, and it brings back all the others.

I went home over the fields. When I got there, Reinhardt was there already, thank God. He'd escaped from an American prison camp up in Holstein. On the way home he'd met the Russians. They'd wanted to take him, but he told them he hadn't escaped from an American prison camp only to land in one of theirs. So they let him go.

He hadn't changed a bit. It was as if nothing could wound him. We went to look for my parents, but they weren't at home. We heard that a lot of people had gone down and drowned themselves in the lake, but of course we didn't know if my parents were among them. Their house was untouched, and Reinhardt and I stayed there. But they didn't come back.

I was afraid I might be pregnant, so I told Reinhardt about the rape. He said, "War is war. In war everyone acts like a pig."

But the next evening he didn't come home. He'd been down at the canal, helping to fix the bridge. And that was the day the Russians gathered up people and took them off to camp. Reinhardt was one of them.

I don't know how he died, I don't know why—if he, so to speak, let himself die, which isn't the same as letting yourself be killed, or if he passively gave in to a kind of poison he had in him, like perhaps my parents gave in to fear, or if he yielded to some belief he had that he deserved to die like the others, or if he actually had something to expiate with his death, or if he died disillusioned or died from disillusionment, or if my story about the rape and the fire along with what he'd experienced himself was too much for his original idealism, which he'd taken over from his father, and which his father probably died for. . . .

That's also the question I put to myself again and again, when the past starts to haunt me—how many victims, how many innocent victims, is Socialism worth? How much violence and terror?

In itself, I think, it's worth any sacrifice at all. On the 17th of June I was terribly afraid the uprising* would succeed. That time I was happy when I saw the Russian tanks coming. I'd told myself that what I and my people had gone through ought to be the full price for being allowed to live in a Socialist country, and I was afraid I'd paid that price for nothing. I was in Berlin then, finishing my examinations—the old ones weren't valid any more.

The mood among the students filled me with despair. Even some of those who'd been leaders in organizations and in the party were suddenly utterly unreliable. Convictions are so superficial. I know that some of the unreliable ones are still big shots in the party. Maybe they've become more trustworthy since then, but I often wonder.

Sometimes when I see them and listen to them on TV, I want to throw something at them. That's childish—but it's only that I think I have a right to demand high quality. Maybe that's an unjustified demand, even now, this long afterward.

Sometimes I've wished I had become pregnant that time in '45, though it happens just as often that I thank my lucky stars I didn't. It would have created horribly conflicting feelings. But at times I've actually wished it had happened, that I had a child who'd live to experience what I probably never will experience. I'll only be one of those that laid the foundations. . . .

*The revolt against the East German regime in June 1953.

From the Second-Grade Reader

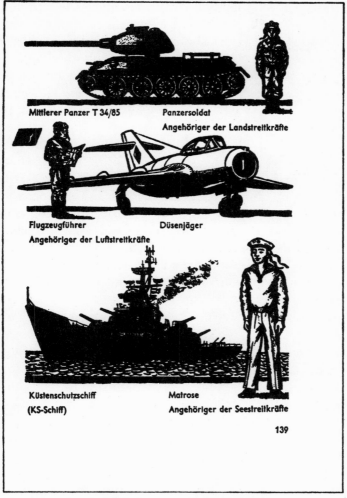

Mittlerer Panzer T 34/85   Panzersoldat
Angehöriger der Landstreitkräfte

Flugzeugführer   Düsenjäger
Angehöriger der Luftstreitkräfte

Küstenschutzschiff   Matrose
(KS-Schiff)   Angehöriger der Seestreitkräfte

139

Medium Tank T 34/85   Tank Soldier
These belong to the army.

Pilot   Jet Fighter
These belong to the air force.

Coast Guard Cutter   Sailor
These belong to the navy.

✿ Third-Grade Lesson, Transcribed Verbatim

The teacher enters the room, then stops and faces the class while the doorkeeper closes the door behind her.
Teacher (to class): Friendship!
Class (in unison): Friendship!
The class leader, a girl, curtsies and reports: Third grade, all present.
Teacher: Let's sing. *The class sings:*

> *Jugend aller Nationen*
> *uns vereint gleicher Sinn, gleicher Mut!*
> *Wo auch immer wir wohnen,*
> *unser Glück auf dem Frieden beruht.*
> *In den düsteren Jahren*
> *haben wir es erfahren:*
> *Arm ward das Leben!*
> *Wir aber geben*
> *Hoffnung der müden Welt!**

Teacher: Be seated.
The class is seated.
Teacher: Is there anyone in the class who knows a song called *Heidenröslein?* "

*First stanza of an international Communist anthem known in English as *Song of the Democratic Youth*. The first stanza of the English version:
> *One great vision unites us*
> *Though remote be the lands of our birth.*
> *Foes may threaten and smite us,*
> *Still we live to bring peace to the earth.*
> *Every country and nation*
> *Stirs with youth's inspiration*
> *Young folks are singing*
> *Happiness bringing*
> *Friendship to all the world.*

*Six students, all girls, raise their hands. One of them is asked
to read the poem aloud:*

> *Sah ein Knab ein Röslein stehn,*
> *Röslein auf der Heiden,*
> *War so jung und morgenschön,*
> *Lief er schnell, es nah zu sehn,*
> *Sah's mit vielen Freuden.*
> *Röslein, Röslein, Röslein rot,*
> *Röslein auf der Heiden.*
>
> *Knabe sprach: Ich breche dich,*
> *Röslein auf der Heiden!*
> *Röslein sprach: Ich steche dich,*
> *Dass du ewig denkst an mich,*
> *Und ich will's nicht leiden.*
> *Röslein, Röslein, Röslein rot,*
> *Röslein auf der Heiden.*
>
> *Und der wilde Knabe brach*
> *'s Röslein auf der Heiden;*
> *Röslein wehrte sich und stach,*
> *Half ihr doch kein Weh und Ach,*
> *Musst' es eben leiden.*
> *Röslein, Röslein, Röslein rot,*
> *Röslein auf der Heiden.*

Literal translation:

A boy saw a small rose growing, a rose on the heath, it was
so young and morning-beautiful, he quickly ran to see it up
close, and gazed at it with great delight. Little rose, little rose,
little red rose, little rose on the heath.

The boy said: I'm going to pick you, little rose on the heath.
The rose said: I'll stick you so you'll always remember me,
and I will not allow it. Little rose, little rose, etc.

And the brutish boy picked the little rose on the heath; the
rose defended itself and stuck him, but weeping and wailing
were no avail, it had to submit after all. Little rose, etc.

*She reads without stumbling, her hands clasped neatly on her
stomach.*

Teacher: That was read nicely, with fine expression. Is
there anyone who can sing *Heidenröslein?*

*Two girls raise their hands. One of them goes to the front
of the room and sings the song. Then—*

Teacher: Does anyone know who wrote the poem?

A boy: Johann Wolfgang von Goethe.

Teacher: Yes, Johann Wolfgang Goethe. Now we'll read
another poem by Goethe:

Ich ging im Walde　　　　　*Ich wollt' es brechen,*
So für mich hin,　　　　　　*Da sagt' es fein:*
Und nichts zu suchen,　　　*Soll ich zum Welken*
Das war mein Sinn.　　　　　*Gebrochen sein?*

Im Schatten sah ich　　　　*Ich grub's mit allen*
Ein Blümchen stehn,　　　　*Den Würzlein aus,*
Wie Sterne leuchtend,　　　*Zum Garten trug' ich's*
Wie Äuglein schön.　　　　　*Am hübschen Haus.*

Und pflanzt' es wieder
Am stillen Ort;
Nun zweigt es immer
Und blüht so fort.

Literal translation:

I went walking in the woods all by myself, not meaning to
look for anything.

I saw a little flower growing in the shade, gleaming like
stars, as pretty as a little pair of eyes.

I was about to pick it when it said gently, Am I to be picked
only to wither?

I dug it up with all its roots and carried it to the garden by
my pretty house.

And replanted it in a quiet place; now it goes on putting out
shoots and continues to blossom.

A boy in the class also reads it aloud. Then—

Teacher: Let's talk a little about the similarities and differences in the two poems. What happens in the two poems?

No hands are raised.

Teacher: Someone is walking out in the world of nature. What happens?

Three girls and a boy raise their hands.

Boy: He sees a flower.

Teacher: In the one poem he goes out on the heath and sees a wild rose. What do you know about roses?

No hands.

—What did the rose look like?

Many hands are raised.

—Red!

—Yes, but answer with a complete sentence. The rose the boy saw on the heath was red.

—The rose the boy saw was pretty.

—Yes.

—It had green leaves.

—Yes, but most flowers have those. And the poet doesn't mention it. The boy on the heath doesn't notice the rose just because it has green leaves.

—It was prickly.

—Yes, but he didn't see that.

—It was young.

—Yes, it was young, red, pretty, and you could see its beauty from a long way off, just the way you do with wild roses. That's why the boy saw it, out there in the middle of the heath. What is a heath?

No answer.

—A heath is a large, flat land area with no trees, no valleys, no streams or rivers or mountains. The soil is sandy. The flowers that grow there are small. And they don't all have the bright, strong, happy colors that a rose

has. The wild rose was the prettiest flower on the heath.
What did the boy do?

A number of hands.

—He picked it.

—Yes, he ran eagerly up to the flower and said, "I'm
going to pick you." Why did he want to pick it?

A few hesitant hands.

—Because it was pretty?

—The poet says why the boy wants to pick the pretty
flower.

No answer.

—It's in the poem.

No answer.

—The poet says, so that you'll always remember me.
The poet doesn't say it was because of the flower's beauty
that the boy wanted to pick it, but so that it would always
remember him. He wanted to own it. He even wanted to
own its thoughts. What might we call his motive, his reason?

No hands.

—We say that he was acting egotistically, because he
didn't think about anyone but himself. What did the rose
do?

—Stuck him.

—Answer with a complete sentence.

—The rose stuck him.

—What does that mean, that the rose defended itself?

No answer.

—It tried to protect itself, but the boy broke off the
flower with violence. Let's read the second poem one
more time.

One of the students reads.

Teacher: "Through the forest . . ." Why was he walking
in the forest?

—For no reason at all.

—What *could* he have done in the forest? It says he

wasn't looking for anything. What might he have been looking for?

Many hands.

—Wood.

—Yes, he could have gone out to look for wood to warm his house with in the winter. What else could he have been looking for?

Many hands.

—Flowers.

—Yes, he might have gone out to pick a bouquet of flowers to brighten his home. What else do people look for in the forest?

—Animals.

—You must answer with a complete sentence. You must have both a subject and a predicate in your sentences. Now, once more.

—He could have gone out to look for animals.

—Yes, if he was a hunter, he might have gone out to look for animals, or if he was especially interested in animals, he might have gone out to study them. But what else?

—Rocks.

—Yes, you might do that if you were interested in rocks, and if the forest ground was rocky.

—Berries.

—Yes, we often look for berries in the forest.

—Mushrooms.

—Yes, mushrooms too. There is so much we can look for in the forest. But the poet hasn't gone out in the forest to look for anything he can profit from, or for anything he can take home, or for anything at all. Then he sees a flower. What kind of flower is it?

No answer.

—We can't answer that. He doesn't care about names. What does it look like?

—It's little.

—It's a small, insignificant flower, growing in the shade.

It hasn't attracted him by its beauty. But when he bends down, he sees what it looks like. What does it look like?

One hand.

—The little flower looks like a pair of eyes.

—Yes, it is as beautiful as a little pair of eyes, and sparkles like a star. He sees the humble little flower's beauty and brightness, and he wants to pick it. But just like the rose in *Heidenröslein,* the flower wants to defend itself. What does the boy do in *Heidenröslein?*

Many hands.

—In *Heidenröslein* he broke off the flower with violence.

—And the poet in the second poem?

—He dug it up together with its roots.

—What did we call what the boy in *Heidenröslein* did?

—Egotism.

—It was an egotistical action. He broke off the rose because he wanted to own it for a short while, even though the rose defended itself, and even though it hurt the rose. It isn't in the poem, but we know what happens very soon to flowers that are picked.

—They wilt.

—They wither and die and bring no more joy to anyone. But a flower that you don't just pick for its own sake, a flower you carefully transplant, will blossom. We said that the boy in *Heidenröslein* was egotistical. If it was a state, a country, then what would we call it?

Many hands.

—Capitalistic.

—We would call it a capitalistic country, and right in the footsteps of capitalism comes imperialism. Can anyone name an imperialistic country?

Many hands.

—America.

—Yes, the United States of America is capitalistic and imperialistic. And one of the roses they are selfishly trying to pick is Vietnam. What do we call a state and a social system that take care of every single unimportant person, that see the beauty of each individual, even of those who stand in the shade, and transplant them into fertile soil so they will always blossom?

Lots of hands.

—Socialistic.

—Name a Socialist country.

All hands.

—Our German Democratic Republic.

—Our liberated German Democratic Republic is a Socialist country. Why do we say "liberated"?

Lots of hands.

—We were liberated from Fascism.

Yes, we were transplanted with great care. Do you know who did it?

Every hand.

—The Soviet Union.

—It was our great friend the Soviet Union, and for that reason we should always be grateful. . . .*

---

*The educational system comprises preschool institutions (nurseries and kindergartens), the ten-grade comprehensive polytechnical school, vocational schools, schools that provide preparation for college entrance examinations, engineering and professional schools, universities and colleges, institutions for the education and higher education of workers, and special schools for physically and psychologically handicapped children. All children are required to attend school for ten years, beginning at age seven. The ten-year comprehensive polytechnical school is the core of the educational system. In grades 7 through 10, students spend one day a week working in industry or agriculture. Basic vocational training is introduced by degrees in grades 9 and 10. At the extended polytechnical school (grades 11 and 12), students receive complete vocational training, which means that they leave school having passed examinations for both college admission and employment. This last program has only recently been introduced in Neustadt.

✪ Fritz Putthammer, 19, Inspecting His Sail-Plane

I get a week off work now, to check out the plane. We're getting ready for the championships—the GDR sail-planing championships.

I get to use the plane free as long as I pay my dues, two marks a month—it's based on your salary. And I get full pay for the time I spend practicing. The people who come here from other places get per diems from their communities. Everyone represents his home town, you know, and if you do well, it's an honor for the town, so the town pays the expenses.

This is a nice installation we've got here, don't you think?

I've been sail-planing for five years. Don't drink or smoke, don't even drink coffee. You have to keep in shape, so there's no point in poisoning yourself.

I'm an electrician, fully trained. I work for an electrical firm, and I've thought about taking a correspondence course—I might get to be an electrical engineer. I'm not dumb. But this week I'm a sail-planer and nothing else, so you'll have to make allowances. It's the GDR championships we're into now.

Have you got a chance?

If I didn't, I wouldn't enter. Or rather, they wouldn't let me enter. There are lots of electrical engineers. But national masters in sail-planing are pretty scarce.

How much time do you spend at it?

I don't keep track.

What do you do in the winters, when you can't go sail-planing?

Read. Partly the theory of sail-planing, partly other things.

How far can a person fly in one of these?
To Berlin.
Have you ever flown to Berlin?
No, *I* haven't.
That means you could also fly over the border.
It would be easier than going under water. If I only knew they'd let me fly back again. I'm sure they don't think as highly of sail-planers over there as they do here.
Is that all you care about?
Obviously not.
What else is important to you?
Having a job, and a girl.
Do you have a girl?
Off and on. Things are a little delicate right now.
What do you read when you're not reading about sail-planing?
Electronics, sometimes.
What does your girl do?
Works in a butcher shop.
Has she ever told you what she wants most of all in the world?
How did you know that?
What does she want?
That's just what it's all about. She wants to have children.
And what do you say to that?
First an apartment. But I don't want to talk about that now.
How do you spend your time together?
Come on, you must have *some* imagination.
Well, what do you do before and after?
Eat.

Putthammer's salary: 650 monthly. Rent: 45 monthly. Residence: room-and-board in a house by the lake. The landlady gives him breakfast in his room and supplies briquettes for heating the stove.

✪ Hermann Kuhn, on Goethe

Did she really fail to say they were love poems?

They're so puritanical nowadays.

Because the fact is, those two poems are about two of Goethe's love affairs, one with Charlotte von Stein, and the other with Christiane Vulpius. Charlotte von Stein, whom he plucked, and then left when he went to Italy, and whose reproaches always plagued him. And Christiane Vulpius, who stood outside his door one day, a woman from another world, whom he transplanted into his own. . . .

And the woods he went walking in are the woods around Weimar.

She really didn't tell about that?

How can you talk about Goethe, and read his poems, without talking about his love affairs?

Didn't she tell about the lovely Charlotte von Stein? The beautiful, fragile Charlotte von Stein?

> *Ach, du warst in abgelegten Zeiten*
> *meine Schwester oder meine Frau . . .* *

That she didn't go into the Christiane Vulpius affair, that I can understand a little better.

✪ Maja Olner, One of the Prisoners

We were all born in Warsaw, and in 1942 we moved to Sosnowiec. After a couple of months my sister was arrested and sent to Auschwitz along with 28 other women. That was the first convoy for us. Then two others, my four-year-old sister and my six-year-old brother, were go-

*Literal translation: *Ah, in times long past you were my sister or my wife.*

ing to be shipped away too. They said there was a school they were being sent to. I went down to the train. There was an SS man standing there—it must have been Eichmann.

"Get aboard, please," he said.

I was supposed to go get a sweater for my little brother. One of the other SS men told Eichmann. He took me under the arms and said, "O.K., run along."

I ran home. Up by the house they asked me about it: "Where have you been?"

"Down at the train," I said.

"And you're coming back?"

"I'm only going to get a sweater," I said.

That's how trusting I was.

Then I went down to the train again, with the sweater. And the three of us went to Auschwitz, a brother and two sisters.

✸ From Ernst Thiele's Memories of His Youth

I remember when they made the Jews march through town with signs around their necks. They got them all together up by The Shooting Gallery, and then they marched them down Ludwigslusterstrasse and what's now Breitscheidstrasse down to the square, which was called Hitler Square in those days. Later it was called Stalin Square. Now it's just called the square. The tannery band marched in front, then came the Brown Shirts and the SS, and then came the Jews. On the placards it said, "I'm a Jewish swine." It wasn't only Jews—their friends too. My family was friends with Hirschfeldt the engineer, a teacher at Technikum, he died quite recently. He was half-Jewish. Some of his friends and ours also had to march along down to the square. "I'm a Jewish swine," that's what it said on their signs too. It was a Sunday afternoon. People stood around on the sidewalks and watched and didn't dare do anything. Some of them spat at the Jews. There were stores here in town that had notices in the windows that Jewish customers weren't wanted. That's the way it was in those days.

✪ Maja Olner Continues Her Story

We were liberated on May 2, by the Russians—not the best liberators.

My sister was in sick bay. I was on the Scheisskommando, the garbage squad—which means I emptied the slops. My sister and I—she was younger—we'd stayed together the whole time, through all the camps. We'd always tried to avoid going to sick bay. At Auschwitz, we knew that anyone that went to sick bay was a candidate. We went to Auschwitz in August 1943—a mother and three children. When we came to the gate, I said to my sister, "If they ask if you want to work, say yes."

They put her in the munitions factory. They always put children there, they thought children couldn't sabotage anything. I worked in the woods in winter, and in the fields. I asked the commandant if I couldn't work in the munitions factory too, since my sister was there.

"You'll get to see her in the crematorium," he said. That was Höss.

He wrote down my number, 52724. My sister was 52725.

I wouldn't have survived if I hadn't had my sister. I wouldn't have cared much, except for her. The way to survive was to look nice, look satisfied, without food, and clean, without soap. That way they didn't hit you. They thought you had privileges, that you were a better sort. And when I got sick, I never went to sick bay.

On the 8th of January the Russians were less than five miles from Auschwitz, and the camp was evacuated. That meant there was a chance to escape. But I knew there were partisans in the woods—they were everywhere—and they'd give us away. I knew the war was nearly over, and I was alive and I wasn't sick. We walked for six weeks, slept in tents. That was January and February. When we got to Ravensbrück, we got a spoonful of bread and a spoonful of snow. Mine were stolen from me. That was the first time I cried since being taken to the concentration camp.

They sent people to Ravensbrück from all the camps. There were 1,500 girls in each barracks. When we got to Ravensbrück, all the trusties were just regular prisoners again, and we old hands, we had possibilities. I could have been block-leader if I'd wanted, but I wouldn't ever want to be block-leader, not even over Germans.

Ravensbrück was worse than Auschwitz. There were some German Jews, holy as Hitler himself. They were still patriots, even in the camp. Everybody was depraved. It was a thousand times worse in Ravensbrück than at Auschwitz, most of the people were non-Jews. My future mother-in-law was there too. She carried ashes out to the fields for fertilizer.

When we started on the convoy to Neustadt, we had to leave without anything to eat. We walked most of the way. First we came to a place called Malchow, where we got a piece of moldy bread. And when we got to Neustadt, we thought it was such a pretty place—every building looked like a doll house. But at Auschwitz you could starve slowly, and in Neustadt you starved fast. The camp was right next to the airfield. I was on the Scheisskommando. I used to pick out the potato peelings from the garbage dump outside the kitchen. We had formation every morning at 5, and you should have seen us run.

One day I decided—I'll steal four sugar beets. I was

terribly scared. When we drove out into the fields, there were some Frenchmen there, picking beets. I had one personal possession left from Auschwitz, a collar. I thought I might trade it for sugar beets, but they didn't want it. On the way back the wagon ran over my leg, and when we got back, we were beaten—25 strokes on the rump. Even if we had gotten food from the Frenchmen, we wouldn't have gotten away with it. The first week we were in Neustadt, three girls were shot dead.

Some of us worked at the aircraft shops. We also had to carry fertilizer for certain people in town. When we asked for food, they gave us two slices of bread for 20 people. They had food, we saw it. At Auschwitz, the ration had been one loaf of bread for 12 people. In Neustadt, it was one slice. We knew the SS themselves had food. Some of the girls went and slept with the Germans to get food. Once is the same as never, you know.

We were about 40 girls in a room this size, about 12 feet by 15. Right next to me and my sister there were some girls who worked in the kitchen, where they stole meat. My sister took a piece of their meat and showed it to me, and I was such an honest little fool I made her put it back. "If you give them a piece of bread," I said, "then they'll give you a piece of meat." And she did.

Later, when I was outside working, some girls told me, "Do you know your sister's about to fall in the latrine?" She'd gotten sick, diarrhea. "I'm so exhausted," she said. "What did you do?" I asked her. She'd gotten hold of something she thought was dried fruit, but it was meat. If she hadn't gotten it, she wouldn't have gotten sick, and they wouldn't have moved her to the sick bay. They wouldn't let me go with her. When I finally did get in, three days later, and asked for her, there wasn't anyone who knew where she was. Finally somebody said, "It must be the one that's dead over there."

I wanted to take her out. She wasn't dead, but when

they'd called her name on the loud-speaker, she hadn't heard it. I took her and started to carry her, and right then all the girls came running up yelling, "We're free! We've been liberated!"

Everyone went to the storehouse where they kept the food, and I carried my sister to the SS cabins. We lived on potatoes and water and margarine.

The Russians told us we could have three days to loot the town, and all the girls went out in the town and looted. Later on I heard them telling about it. They were only interested in destroying homes. I would have been the same way. It wasn't for the sake of food, although there were many who ate too much and died. But I had to stay with my sister.

The Russians were raping—we could hear screams from the rooms around us. So I lay down like I was sick too. Then they came into our cabin.

"We've liberated you," they said, "so now you can give us a lay."

We were scared to death.

"We're sick," we said.

"Bullshit!" they said. They were desperate.

One of the girls told about the looting in town, that she was standing in front of a shop and said to some Russian that she wanted a goose or a duck.

"Go in and look around," he said.

Inside there was nothing but one dress, hanging on a rack.

"Take it," the Russian said. "Take it, or I'll stuff it down your throat."

Another girl told how she was about to go into a house when a Russian came and opened the door. "Get out of here," he said. "This is where I live."

Some disappeared out in the woods. That's where the SS had gone, too. Sixty thousand people died in the woods that night. Apparently there were some SS men who knew what they had to do. You know what Hitler said: "Save the last bullet for yourself."

We stayed in the SS cabins for two days. Then the Russians came and told us we'd have to go home.

"We're Jews," we said. "From Poland. What do we have to go home to?"

"Everyone who isn't sick has to leave," they said. "All the sick are to go to the hospital."

That's what the Russians did instead of setting up a camp.

So I carried my sister to the hospital. I asked if I could stay and help, but they wouldn't let me.

"When can I get a train to Poland?" I asked them.

"You can walk," they said.

Twelve of us set out on foot, but when I was about 30 miles from Neustadt, I went back again. When I got to the hospital, they said, "What do you want? Are you looking for something?"

"My sister," I said.

"Get out of here," they said. "You're a subhuman."

So I left. I slept at the camp. Nobody would help. But there were shops in Neustadt, there was food.

I had to make close to 200 miles on foot. When we came to Stettin, there was a train to take. We had to go in through a window, and some Russians helped us. One of them thought I was pretty.

"What's your name?" he asked me.

"Stockman," I said.

Then he looked at me and uttered the worst insult there is in Russian: "Jewess!" he said.

From there we were deported to Sosnowiec. I decided to go to the Red Cross. I wanted to go back to Neustadt, to my sister.

I got a ride in a car, but we got lost. Somehow I got to Poznan, then to Stettin. Then I started off on foot again. In the ditch by the road there were two men lying, two bodies, and I recognized them, so I knew I was on the right road. They'd been lying there when we came the other way.

Then a car stopped and asked where I was headed. "Neustadt," I said. "Hop in," they said. They were Russians, and they tried to rape me, but I got hold of one of their revolvers. I stood behind them and held it. "Drive," I said, "or I'll shoot you." But we got lost, and after about 30 miles I got out. The Russians didn't want to drive any farther, so there was nothing to do but walk.

On the road I met some girls who'd been in Neustadt, and I asked them about my sister. "The school's still there," they said—the hospital was in a school. When I got to Neustadt, my sister wasn't there any more.

So I went back to Poland, I went back to the farm where we'd lived. The old woman who lived there said, "So you've come back. Well, there's nothing for you here."

We had been seven brothers and sisters.

Then I went around to look at the other farms. There were empty houses everywhere. An awful lot of people had been killed. My father and my brother had been shot in the woods.

Then I went back to Sosnowiec. There we were taken care of, but not by the Poles. The Jewish organization gave us soup and bread. We were taken to Czechoslovakia and put in a camp. In the camp they called me a damned Jewess again. A Russian said to me, "It's too bad Hitler didn't kill all the Jews."

In 1956 we went back to Neustadt to look for some trace of my sister. There are graves in a corner of the churchyard, mostly without names. No papers have been saved. They've destroyed everything. There was one friendly man who showed us around Neustadt.

Somewhere there must be someone who knows. I've told myself sometimes that you have to forget, but we must never forget. No one in my family is still alive. I don't have anything from home. I don't have any photographs. Maybe my sister is dead, but I can't help thinking she's alive. Someone will have to show me that she's dead.

Where are the nurses? They must be somewhere. I was back in Neustadt to search, but I couldn't stay long enough to search properly. I have too many memories from that town.

✸ COMMENT FROM MARK OLNER

We've been back to Poland to look for the family graves. We were in a Jewish cemetery, but it had been destroyed —the stones had been taken away and used for paving stones. I went to a man who represented the town. He said a person can't set himself against the wishes of the populace.

We'll never go back to Germany again.

✸ Willy Köstlin, Doctor

Willy Köstlin thinks of himself as an old Neustädter, although he works at the hospital in Ludwigslust, and was previously stationed in Schwerin, Eisenach, and Greiz. He says he was always homesick for this part of Mecklenburg, where he spent the happiest days of his youth, and where he met his wife, Elfriede, while he was working at the temporary hospital that was set up in the school at the end of the war. In the middle of hell, he says, it was a happy time for him. . . .

While the prisoners from the concentration camp were destroying our homes, we went down to their old camp at the airfield and picked up a lot of things. The flagstones in my in-laws' garden are from the camp. We got fencing, too. And zinc plates from the airfield—we made heating elements out of them down at the factory, like this one.

They're against the law now, use too much current. We found food down at the airfield, too. There were a lot of canned goods. The war could have gone on for a long time as far as supplies were concerned.

There weren't any medical supplies, but it was a very instructive period. You learned what the threshold of death looked like. You think it's odd that I say it was a happy time. I've never seen so many patients die in my hands, but neither have I ever had such a clear picture of my own power over the boundary between life and death. And then too I met Elfriede, and we had Rainer. He's 23 years old now. . . .

Köstlin built his own house when he came back to Neustadt. Elfriede had wanted to move into her parents' house, but it was in terrible condition, Willy says. What's more, there were already people living there, a sick old couple from Czechoslovakia who weren't even married. When they heard the owner was in town, the first thing they did was complain about the roof. "If the city takes over the house, why, then they can take care of it," says Dr. Köstlin. He has a salary of 1,900 marks a month, and they had saved up 45,000 marks. "But there just isn't anything to spend your money *on* in this country," Dr. Köstlin remarks.

If I'd been able to get the family fortune over here from Dortmund, I could have paid for the whole house in cash. That's where my inheritance is. I don't get much joy out of it now. My wife can use it when she goes over to visit her sister. It's nice to have a little something to get around with, you know, we can't take money with us, and it's not especially pleasant to live on other people's handouts. We don't like to do that. Naturally she takes what the West German government gives her—the Federal Republic gives travelers from over here a little pocket money to get around on.

It's no trick for my wife to get a travel permit. I'm a doctor, after all. I don't have to write out a disability certificate for her myself, I ask one of my colleagues to do that. My profession isn't listed on her identity card. Elfriede goes over once a year and visits her brother. And she buys up items that are cheaper over there: nylon stockings, nylon shirts—this is a nylon shirt: costs 90 marks here; over there you can get one for 15.

So we save a little money, and still get some use of the inheritance in Dortmund.

We could have gotten out, before, but money isn't everything. We wanted to come back to dear old Mecklenburg, right here to Neustadt.

And since I'm a doctor, we don't do badly. Of course there aren't a lot of people to mix with here in Neustadt, but we have our friends in Ludwigslust. When you've lived in Schwerin, why, it's no distance to speak of.

✿ Elfriede Köstlin, Nurse

The concentration camp was a shock for us. As soon as I got back to Neustadt, I was ordered to present myself at the hospital for duty as a nurse. The Russians got here the same time I did. They'd turned all the concentration camp prisoners loose, and they came from every direction—there was a big camp in Wöbbelin, and there was one here at the airfield. The Russians gave them permission to loot for three days, and they were a lot worse than the Russians. The Russians were filthy, they used cellar windows for toilets, and they used the toilets for washbowls. They're a primitive people. A Russian once told me that we *Germans* were primitive. In Russia, he said, a place the size of Neustadt would have three delousing stations. In Neustadt there weren't any.

The raping only went on for a few days. Then they got

strict orders, and they were severely punished. But the concentration camp prisoners were worse—they just destroyed. The Russians didn't know any better, but Jews are supposed to be intelligent. They just destroyed things, for no reason. If they'd asked for food, I would have understood. But they just destroyed. One of them came in here. She went straight out in the kitchen and got a knife and started ripping up the furniture and cutting up the beds. We couldn't do a thing.

There wasn't much food. My brother had found some flour, and we had some dried fruit from the warehouse down at the airfield—there were all sorts of provisions at the airfield. Anyway, we'd baked a big fruitcake, and it was standing out on the table. Then this Jewess came in through the door, you know, a regular Jewess with a big nose. I remember exactly how she looked when she bent down over the table. She took the cake, and broke off a little piece of it, and then she threw the rest of it in the toilet. My brother said he could have just killed her, but we couldn't do a thing.

A lot of them died. Some of them were looting a store and found a package of rat poison, and they thought it was crackers. Every one of them died. And many of them just ate too much.

They shouldn't have been turned loose like that. They wandered around the streets in big gangs, a lot of them still in their striped uniforms. They looked frightful.

The ones at the hospital didn't have much life left in them. I can't tell you what things were like at the hospital, it was dreadful. We gave them soup and bread—they had more to eat than we did. But they couldn't eat. I don't think there were many who made it. There were too many, we couldn't take care of them all.

I was sick myself when I got to Neustadt, but I just had to look after myself. There wasn't anyone to take care of *us.*

What happened to the ones that got well?

They were supposed to go home. But for a long time they wandered around on the roads.

Did you know the names of the sick ones?

There were so many. You just couldn't keep track of names. Anyway, they still had their numbers from before.

✪ Transportation Problem

The last train to Neustadt has gone. The station restaurant is about to close. An armed squad of Russian soldiers is patrolling the platform. There is already a long line at the taxi-stand, German and Russian soldiers. Some of the German soldiers are trying to get to Dömitz, the rest to Parchim. Those who've waited longest have been there an hour.

The patrol comes up, and the soldiers speak to their countrymen. They say there's a truck going to Parchim in a little while. They promise to try and get it to stop, so that some of those waiting can ride along. The patrol has hardly gone before the truck rolls up. The Russian soldiers, two German soldiers, and the only civilian in the line are allowed to climb up and sit on some boxes in the back of the truck. The soldiers all say "Friendship!" to each other in Russian and German, and laugh. The Russians correct the Germans' pronunciation of the Russian word, and the Germans correct the Russians' pronunciation of the German word.

One of the German soldiers tries to ask one of the Russians if he has a watch. Halfway to Neustadt the truck stops, and an officer gets out and disappears into the woods.

"They've got an encampment in there," one of the German soldiers says, explaining.

One of the Russians apparently understands some of

what is said, and with his hands, face, and stomach makes it clear that the Germans are mistaken. The officer has a weak stomach.

"Friendship," says the German soldier.

"Friendship," says the Russian.

The Russian soldier who's been asked if he has a watch finally understands the question, and with easily interpreted signs he explains that he does not, but that on the other hand he does have a transistor. The German soldier explains in equally explicit sign language that he isn't interested, since he already has one.

"Friendship," they say.

"Beatles," says the German.

The Russian soldier laughs and starts to sing a song to a melancholy tune.

"Volgograd," he says.

"Is he from Stalingrad?"

"Volgograd."

"Friendship."

"Friendship."

Then he starts to sing again, *The Song of the Volga Boatmen.* One of the other Russians says a long sentence.

"Speak English," says one of the German soldiers, in English.

"Bruder Chinese."

"He says his brother is Chinese," says one of the Germans.

"Friendship," says the other German.

The Soviet soldiers make it clear that this is the wrong place to say "Friendship." The second German soldier says it's impossible for a Russian to have a brother who's Chinese.

"They're different races," he explains.

The first Russian says, "Dömitz."

"Parchim," says one of the Germans. "I don't want to go to Dömitz."

"Bruder Chinese Dömitz," says the Russian.

"Maybe he means his brother is on the Chinese border," one of the Germans guesses.

"Friendship," says one of the Germans, in Russian.

"Ja, ja," says the Russian.

Then the truck is in Neustadt. One of the Russians goes into the Theodor Körner to try and sell an electric razor.

✺ TV Guide in the Schweriner Volkszeitung

Reflections, Remarks, and Rebuttals program on the TV-film
I, Axel Cäsar Springer

"The Wonder That's No Wonder" is the title of a recorded program in the *Reflections, Remarks, and Rebuttals* series to be shown on the German Television Network March 19, at 8 p.m., in connection with the TV-film *I, Axel Cäsar Springer.* Participating in the program will be the men who made last Saturday's film, Karl-Georg Egel and Harri Czepuck, who will discuss the character of the most powerful man in Bonn's ideological poison-kitchen.

✺ First Meeting With Hermann Kuhn, Continued

Dialectical necessity, as presented in the Marxist view of history, is only a description in material terms of an evolutionary process—the process that Hegel says will lead to a stage where the mists will part and true knowledge will appear in the distance like a mountaintop.

But Marx believes he can already see the mountaintop, and describes it as a communistic society.

What arrogance.

For shortsightedness, that dream can be compared with the dream of the Thousand-Year Reich.

Berlin and Bonn bicker, but there is one thing they both want: a unified and powerful Germany. That's the truth of the matter.

Soviet politics alters with the change in party chairman. Here, it makes no difference who the party chairman is, at least not so long as he remains a puppet. That's why Ulbricht is so unpopular—he's a puppet. That's why Kiesinger is so unpopular, not because he was a Nazi, but because he's an errand-boy. No one cares whether he was a Nazi.

For most people, the years of the Second World War are not primarily the Nazi Years, but the Years of Defeat.

I came to Hamburg in the winter of 1945 to look for my young wife and my child.

✪ Ernst Thiele, on Egypt and the Six-Day War

We were sent to a POW camp in Egypt. The officers and men of the Fourth Division were already there when we arrived. We weren't treated with any benevolence—we were swine. We had to fill out a form with 98 questions. One of the questions was about profession, and there was only one profession for us. The only thing we were allowed to put down was "Murderer." I said we weren't murderers any more than anyone else in the war. So they took out a map—they had it all drawn up as early as that. Every German concentration camp was marked. They asked me where I was from. I said Neustadt-Glewe. We looked for it. Here, they said, here in Wöbbelin was a concentration camp. "That's wrong," I said. "That's only three miles from home. I was there seven months ago. It's a lie." And so I thought the whole map was a lie. Later, when I got permission to write home, I wrote that there in Egypt they were insisting that there was a concentration camp in Wöbbelin, and I asked if it was true. The answer I got back was that it *was* true, and that not only was there a concentration camp in Wöbbelin, but that there had been concentration camp prisoners in Neustadt too.

It was in Egypt that I heard about the Nazi mass murders for the first time, or at least that I first understood that the reports of them were true. In the camp there was a young man from Lithuania. He'd lived in a little Lithuanian town. One day the SS came to his house and took him away. They made him put on a black uniform. At first, he refused. But they put a pistol to the back of his neck, and so he put on the uniform, and they took him out to a forest and gave him a pistol, and then took him deeper into the forest until they came to a wooden fence, and in front of the fence they put 20 prisoners with their faces to the railing, and they ordered him to shoot them one after the other in the back of the neck, while the SS officers stood behind him with their weapons drawn. That was his daily work for a month, from dawn to dusk, but after a month of it he couldn't take it any more. He decided to refuse. But it seems they thought he had fulfilled his duties quite adequately. They accepted his refusal, gave him a commendation, and shipped him off to the Eastern Front, which at that time was equivalent to sending him to his execution.

Later on, he deserted, and got himself some different identity papers. In the prison in Egypt he wasn't living under his real name. He told me what his real name was, but it would never occur to me to betray him. I got to know him very well during the years we were together.

I got to know the kind of anxiety he suffered, and I think I can judge men well enough to say that that man would never have done what he did of his own free will or desire, and that the fact that after a month he'd had the courage to refuse, and had his refusal accepted, didn't make it any easier for him. Before a court of law he'd never be able to evade the responsibility for all those murders he'd committed. I don't know what happened to him afterwards. But I imagine they caught him. Men like that are always caught. Maybe he stayed in Egypt—there were a great many Nazi officers who did.

When the Egyptians first got us, they called us swine and murderers. When I was released, on September 13, 1948, the mood was different. They bowed to us and called us "Sir" and "Honored German Officers."

Obviously, today, the GDR stands alongside Egypt in the quarrel with Israel, and in the war last year. No other course is possible. But in the same way that we ourselves have no terribly honorable history—we're Germans, after all—we must clearly understand that Egypt, immediately after the war, was a haven for Nazis.

✪ Thiele the Shoemaker—on Grosse Wallstrasse, Where He's Lived for Over 60 Years

It was the Communists' fault that we had Nazism. That's why I'll never be a Communist. My son's a trade expert. He's a Communist, of course, but we never talk politics.

But he smokes West German cigarettes—they mix paper in the East Zone cigarettes.

We call it the East Zone. You can't call this creation a country. They don't realize themselves how insolent they are. They call Berlin their capital, and they yell at the West Germans because they hold some government meeting in West Berlin once in a while. They can't have read the Potsdam Agreements. Berlin is supposed to be under the supervision of the victors, so how can they make it the capital of the GDR? And the East Zone TV is just like the cigarettes—crap, just like everything they produce. I heard, for example, that Zeiss buys the springs for its cameras from West Germany—they can't make them here. Or leather. I'm a shoemaker, and I know what I'm talking about. For years and years they've been dressing pigskin. I can't really imagine there's another place in the whole world where they do that—dress pigskin. Every place else, the pig still has its skin on when it leaves the slaughterhouse.

They don't cure them like they used to, either. In the old days they had vegetable tanning acids, from trees. Nowadays they use all sorts of chemicals. The shoes are way too hard—the leather doesn't bend around the foot, around that little bump by the big toe. Your feet get hard. That's why everybody walks so funny around here. You can see the difference when West Germans come to visit in the summer.

It's all because all the intelligent Germans went west. There wasn't any talent left over here. If my son had gone over, he could really have made it. Over there a businessman owns his own house.

That border is a curse. Eight years ago my wife and I went to Sweden. My son-in-law works in a shipyard in Gothenburg. We could have stayed there, but we didn't want to. We wouldn't have gotten any pension there. Here I get 178 marks a month, and my wife gets 129. Now is that any kind of pension to speak of? It's shameless. But we couldn't do without it—we couldn't make it on the pension alone, either. It's just not enough.

When we left Sweden, there were 13 people on the platform in Gothenburg to say goodbye to us. Every one of them had a can of coffee as a going-away present. When we got to the border, the German customs men asked us what we had in our bags. "Thirteen kilos of coffee," I said.* That was in Sassnitz, in the middle of the night. So they made me climb off the train. I told them I couldn't carry the suitcases, but they said I had to. "No," I said. "You're crueler than the Nazis were," I said. Then they told me I'd have to go up for questioning. I said I couldn't say a word until they gave me some water. "I'm a sick old man," I said. "I've got rheumatism." They said they didn't have any water. So I said, "You can't treat an old party veteran this way." That set them back on their heels. They carried the bags.

Then this major asked me all sorts of questions. I said I'd gotten all the coffee as presents. He said I couldn't take in more than one kilo. It's absolutely insane. He seemed to think I should have just stood there on the platform in Gothenburg and said "No, thank you" to all that coffee. Why, you can't do that. You can't be that impolite.

Believe it or not, I never even mentioned it to my son. Although he found out about it anyway. And he didn't mention it to me. He didn't even talk about it to his own father.

I had some stamps in my suitcase too, for my son—he's a stamp collector. But they confiscated them. They said they were currency—canceled stamps, a box of canceled stamps. So I protested again. "I myself, I'm an old party veteran," I said. "And my son is a deputy mayor. What do you think we're up to? Do you think we're currency smugglers?"

The customs men in Ludwigslust checked to see if I was telling the truth. But it's all down in black and white. It tells when I joined the Social Democratic Party, and I

*One "kilo" (kilogram)=2.24 pounds.

can't help it the Social Democrats were finally absorbed into the Communists. There isn't anything any Social Democrat can do about that. But I can insist they recognize who I am, that's the least I can do.

I had to go to Ludwigslust three times before I got the stamps back.

In 1945, when the Russians came, they took me to a camp in Neubrandenburg. It didn't make any difference *then* if you were a Social Democrat. So I sat there in the midst of a bunch of Nazis—well, not only Nazis. Everybody got sucked in that time, I wasn't the only Social Democrat. Later on, when they had to strengthen the Communist Party, then the Social Democrats were good enough to join forces with, 14 years too late. And why did they suddenly decide we were good enough? Why, it was simply a question of eliminating the Social Democrats, that's all. Where's the Social Democratic influence nowadays?

✖ Robert Schröder, Party Veteran, Tells Why He Left the Social Democrats

When Kapp and his men tried to overthrow the Weimar Republic in March 1920,* we were ready to fight too. At that time I was a farm worker and lived with my family in Granzin. The tenant was a Herr Peters, and the leaseholder a man named Ditzmann. In their eyes I was "that Red," a troublemaker. Feudalism was over, of course, but our standard of living hadn't changed. We were day-labor just as before, and we worked like dogs for a starvation wage, and we had to obey our masters. I was allowed to have a cow, and during the summer I was given free pas-

*Wolfgang Kapp and his followers seized Berlin at this time and attempted to set up a right-wing dictatorship with Kapp as chancellor. Their revolt was suppressed.

ture. On top of that I had a little garden with potatoes and fodder beets. The wages were 60 pfennigs a day, and they didn't change in the inflation. During the inflation we had to deliver a pound of butter to the farm every other week. They claimed that was so the tenant could pay our health insurance.

It's no wonder we wanted the revolution to spread, it's no wonder we were ready to fight. All my co-workers stood right behind me on the Kapp thing. I myself was on the so-called "blacklist." One morning I found a threat pinned to my door—"If the Reds come," it said, "you'll be the first one shot." But that wasn't the way it happened. The general strike failed. The delegates from the Farm Workers Union and our comrades in the SPD—none of them had enough gumption to change anything. They compromised with the class enemies at every turn. So in 1924 I came to the conclusion that I had to leave the Social Democrats and join the Communist Party.

When they set up a new town council in 1945, the Russians offered me the job of mayor, but I said, "No, I can't. I only went to school for four years, I can't be mayor." So they asked me for suggestions, and I gave them three names. One of them was Schoof, and they took him. He was a saddle-maker at the tannery.

■ EVALD SCHRÖDER, 39, ROBERT'S NEPHEW

Yes, Schoof was a fine mayor. He tried to do a lot for Neustadt. He was the one who fixed up the cemetery—the only pretty place we have left. But then he bought the town some machines from West Berlin. They didn't like that in Ludwigslust. So then we got Diederich.

Zollverwaltung
der
Deutschen Demokratischen Republik

Bezirksverwaltung

Postzollamt

den ████ 68

G

Diese Nummer ist im Schriftverkehr stets anzugeben.

Beschlagnahme-/Einziehungs-Protokoll (P)

Die ~~Aus~~ der Postsendung Pkt. Pn. Nr. ████ ohne Aufgabepostamt unlesert.

Absender: _____ (Vorname) ____ (Wohnort)

(Kreis, Straße, Hausnummer) — Schweden (Land)

Empfänger: _____ (Vorname) ____ (Wohnort)

(Kreis, Straße, Hausnummer) — DDR (Land)

Lfd. Nr.	Genaue Bezeichnung der Waren, Gegenstände oder Zahlungsmittel	Gebrauchs- wert in %	Mengen- einheit	Anzahl	Ge- wicht in kg	Be- merkungen
1	Zeitung "Expressen"		St.	1	Nr. 33	
2	Zeitschrift "Mytek."		St.	1	Nr. 5	
3	Zeitschrift "Svensk Finla"		St.	1	Nr. 12/66	
	Eintragung beendet.					

Periodisch auftretende Zeitungen u. Zeitschriften, die nicht in der Postzeitungsliste enthalten sind, sind zur Einfuhr nicht zugelassen.

Gesetz, Best. § 1 der 5. DB vom 30.11.1961 zur GVO vom 5.8.1954

Grund der Beschlagnahme / Einziehung:
Vorstehend aufgeführte Waren, Gegenstände oder Zahlungsmittel werden wegen Verstoß gegen die Verordnung über den Geschenkpaket- und -packetverkehr auf dem Postwege mit Westdeutschland, Westberlin und dem Ausland vom 5. 8. 1954 (GBl. S. 727), den dazu erlassenen Durchführungsbestimmungen bzw. anderer im Postverkehr geltender gesetzlicher Bestimmungen beschlagnahmt / eingezogen.

STEMPEL

Die Sendung war postwidrig, eine Ersatzleistung durch die Deutsche Post ist ausgeschlossen.

_____ Unterschrift ____ Grad

Blatt 4 für den Betroffenen

ZV 172

DDR 14232/172 1. Aufl. 66 1,1 Bl.

Customs Office of the German Democratic Republic
District Office
Postal Customs

Always refer to this number in correspondence.

Record of Confiscation/Impoundage   (P)

Postal item number: none   Post office of origin: unreadable
Sender: _____

Addressee: _____

Item No.	Precise description of goods, objects, or media of exchange	Depre-ciation in %	Unit	Quant.	Wt. in kg.	Remarks
1	Newspaper "Expressen"		copy	1	Nr. 33	
2	Magazine "Nytek"		copy	1	Nr. 5	
3	Magazine "Svenskt Fiske"		copy	1	Nr. 12/66	
	End of list.					

Periodical newspapers and magazines not mentioned in the postal list may not be imported. Leg. art. par. 1 etc.

Reason for confiscation/impoundage:

The goods, objects, or media of exchange listed above are hereby confiscated/impounded due to violation of the regulation of 5 August 1954 on gift packages and postal material to West Germany, West Berlin, and abroad, violation of the provisions for execution of this law, or violation of other laws applying to postal traffic.

STAMP

The contents were contrary to postal regulations.
The German Post Office will pay no compensation.

German Democratic Republic
Customs Office
Postal customs
_____   _____
Signature   Signature/Service grade

Copy 4, for the affected person.

✵ Some Data on the Schröders

Robert Schröder lives on Grosse Wallstrasse and is a neighbor of his son, Manfred, and his family. Robert Schröder is 76, Manfred 38.

Manfred is on sick leave at the moment—the result of a back injury—and is away at a health resort.

The older couple help the young Schröders take care of the children, particularly in the mornings. Manfred works at the tannery, and his wife, Inge, has a job in a bakery, where she starts work every morning at 5. The oldest boy's school day doesn't start until 8. Manfred takes the youngest child with him to the factory nursery, and his wife picks the child up there around 12, when she's through at the bakery.

The two families help each other out in the afternoons as well.

Robert spends his days working in their garden, about five minutes' walk from home. It's a kitchen garden, with both early and late potatoes, several kinds of peas, white beans, beets, and, first and foremost, an extensive asparagus patch. The garden provides both families with a large share of their annual vegetable supply.

At home, in the backyard, Robert has a chicken coop with 20 white Italian hens. Once in a while he borrows a rooster from his brother Otto, who lives across the street, or from Otto's son, Evald, who has a large poultry farm in Kronskamp, a half-hour's walk from town.

Robert also does some carpentry. Inge is making a few improvements at home while Manfred is off at the health resort, and Robert is helping out with new doorways while Inge paints.

The whole family gets together for coffee most Saturday and Sunday afternoons, and occasionally on other days as well. The elder Frau Schröder does the baking—two voluminous coffee cakes, which are set out freshly baked on Saturday and finished up on Sunday.

Robert and his wife have three rooms, Manfred and his family the same.

Robert has a pension of 178 marks a month, plus an honorary pension from the party of 100 marks a month. His wife gets 123 marks monthly.

Manfred and Inge Schröder earn, together, about 900 marks a month.

"If we didn't both work," they say, "we simply couldn't make it."

✿ Robert Schröder Begins at the Beginning

I grew up in a poor family, and as a child I had to work hard. I've had to suffer a lot of injustice, the sort of injustice that doesn't exist today. Today the worker has rights, he's protected. You can get sick and you don't lose your job or your income. Without the Russians' help we wouldn't have Socialism here. But of course we had to pay for it.

But it isn't democracy we have—there are still too many spineless people in this country. That's the way it's always been, and still is.

I was the oldest of eight children. My father was a farm hand for a rich farmer in Klein Laasch, one of four farm hands. But when the family got too big, we had to leave. We had to pack our things on a wagon and go off to look for work someplace else. We pulled ourselves along from one farm to another. Father would go on ahead, but when they'd hear how many of us there were, the answer was always no. I went to school for four years. But my mother couldn't help with the farm work very much as long as my brothers and sisters were little, so I had to quit school so we could offer my labor too. We got temporary work at one farm after the other. I always offered myself as a goatherd. That way I could stay out with the goats overnight, or stay in the pens with them, so it wouldn't be so crowded for the others. Mother used to help with the washing and cooking and cleaning, but they didn't count that as work.

For two years we went around from farm to farm and worked as long as they could use us. We wandered around like a band of gypsies. But we didn't even have a horse to pull our wagon. That first winter we got to stay in a farmhand cottage on a farm in Matzlow, but in the spring the farmer couldn't let us stay on. At the end of the second fall we didn't know what was going to become of us. So my father went to his brother in Neustadt, and then we came and lived with him. There wasn't really any shortage of jobs in those days. My father got a job at the factory, and I took up smithing.

I was in the army in 1911 and '12, and then again from 1914 to '18, during the war. An imperialist war. Even that war was a great mistake. And it could have been avoided—we weren't fighting for anything real. But German history is too full of treachery for any one man to have been straightforward and honest, and then too, there was the question of whether you thought your life was worth it. But in spite of everything, I still believed that one day there'd be a different Germany. We didn't know what was going to happen before the new Germany came about—you couldn't have known that, not then. All I knew was that the Social Democrats had betrayed us, that the war was a mistake, and that all the same I had to go along with it.

It was the Social Democrats who betrayed Germany, by making themselves the tools of the petty bourgeoisie. If they'd handled things better then, Germany would look a lot different today.

There were a lot of Communists here in Neustadt. We

held our meetings at the Korup* once a month. See, here's my party book. It says here that I joined in 1919. That's wrong, it ought to be 1909, but there's nobody left to confirm it. If it said 1909, I'd get a bigger pension. I'm the only one here in Neustadt that still has his party book—these stamps, they're for monthly dues, five pfennigs a month.

We held our last official meeting in August 1932. Then we were outlawed. I went home and bricked up my book in the wall here. The only one who knew about it was my brother Otto. Didn't even tell my wife. Women have a hard time keeping quiet, at least if they're tortured. Yes, we saw that coming. She *wasn't* tortured, as it turned out, but we knew the possibility existed. We wouldn't have been surprised. They were always running around making investigations, even as early as that. They asked me where I'd put my party book. They knew I had one, of course.

"They already took it," I said.

"Who did?" they said.

"I don't know," I said. "I don't know all of them."

There were all sorts of people running around asking questions. They didn't all know each other themselves. Well, I knew them all pretty well anyway, by the time it was over.

So then we had our meetings underground, sometimes here in town, but usually out in the villages around here, in Wöbbelin, in Blievenstorf, Klein Laasch, Gross Laasch. Apfelbaum was from Gross Laasch. There weren't so many police and informers in the villages. Well, of course there were risks there too. In Wöbbelin, once, we were surrounded by a bunch of farmers with sticks and clubs who wanted to beat us up. And we had quite a fight.

Frau Schröder: I was always afraid when my husband was

---

*"Korup" is the former name of the Theodor Körner Hotel, and the name of the family that once owned it.

away at the meetings. I was afraid someone would come here and ask for him.

Robert Schröder: No, they didn't shoot at us, not then. But it was worse later. I had two men stationed in front of my house every night, so I couldn't go to any meetings. Couldn't get out.

Yes, they were from Neustadt—we knew each other. Why, my neighbor here, Stampeck, he was a great Nazi. He had a six-foot swastika hanging outside his door. It hung there for years. It was the first thing we saw when we looked out in the mornings. He was a night watchman in town. We knew each other.

Sure they had weapons. They shot at us too, they did indeed. But I don't think Stampeck ever shot anybody. They didn't generally shoot people down in the street. But they shot all right, to scare us, if nothing else.

Frau Schröder: One day when my husband wasn't home, some men came from the Security Police and knocked at the door. They asked for Robert. I said I didn't know where he was, but I thought he was at work. Then they told me to come up to the Rathaus.

"But don't go yelling 'Hunger,' " they said.

"All right," I said, "I won't yell 'Hunger.' "

So I went over to the Rathaus. It was completely full of people, and people were standing out in the street. They were having a big hearing on the Communists. The whole council room was jammed, mostly with women, and they were all yelling "Hunger, hunger, hunger . . ."

So naturally I joined in, started yelling "Hunger." I couldn't not.

They were going at it with Apfelbaum. He was splendid. He could really talk, and he wouldn't give up. It took a long time, that was Apfelbaum's tactics. He knew he was the one of us who talked best. They could pound on the table as much as they wanted, but Apfelbaum kept right on talking. And we kept right on yelling "Hunger, hunger, hunger." And then it was really true, of course, that the longer the hearing went on, the hungrier we got. And then right in the middle of it I had to go to the toilet. An SS officer went out with me. At the door to the toilet he took out a big bologna sandwich and gave it to me and said, "You know," he said, "I'm just as Red as you are." I think you should tell that too.

Manfred: I remember when the Communists used to stand in the square and yell "Hunger, hunger, hunger," my friend Alfred's mama used to be one of them, although God knows she didn't look hungry.

Anyway, one day there was a pause in the chanting, and just then Alfred came running up and screamed out clear across the square, "Mama, mama, you have to come home now. Grandma has dinner ready."

Robert: No, they weren't all bad. They were bought, even if some of them were bought pretty cheap—like, for a drink. But they weren't all bad people—there can't have been as many evil people as there were SA and SS* men. There were plenty of them here—it was probably worse in the small towns than it was in the cities. It's true. He may have *been* just as Red as we were. Who knows why he joined the SS? You can't judge people out of hand.

For that matter, not all the Communists were real Reds. In 1932, when we were outlawed, we had 80 members here in Neustadt, but of those 80 at least 20 were spies. None of them are left now. They were informers. They were Social Democrats. But as I said, they're all dead now. That sort of thing catches up with you. They didn't gain anything by betraying us.

Just after the war, one of them fell down a flight of steps,

*SA=Sturm-Abteilung—the Nazi storm troopers; SS=Schutz-Staffel—the special Nazi "security" forces.

drunk, out in front of the café on Breitscheidstrasse, the Einheit Café. Broke his neck. He was a traitor, but he passed himself off as an old Communist. He got one of those magnificent funerals, honored as an old hero of the working class. I objected to it. "Don't you know what you're doing?" I said. "He was a traitor." But right then they needed old heroes to bury, for God's sake. If the war had ended the other way, he would have gotten just as grand a funeral, I'm sure of that.

No, you couldn't count on everybody, not even everybody you *thought* you could count on. And they weren't all as bad as the organizations they joined.

But there are still things it's hard to understand.

Like right here, across the street from us and the Stampecks, there was this gypsy family, six people.

One day, 20 SS and SA men drove up in two buses and took their guns and surrounded the house. Blocked off the whole street.

So here sit the Stampecks, and they can see through their windows how the gypsies are being taken away. The Stampecks aren't bad people, but they must have known what was going to happen to those gypsies. We all knew. It was no secret they weren't coming back. They auctioned off all their possessions up at the Korup. It wasn't very hard to figure out.

Actually, one of them survived. He usually comes here in the summers and sets up an amusement park down by the lake.

We didn't go to the auction. If we had, they would have grabbed us too. They watched everything we did, took down the time when we went out and when we came in. If we'd gone to the auction, who knows what they might have thought we were up to. They knew what we thought, of course. We never just stood by silently and let things happen. We couldn't have done that anyway, not as Communists. But Stampeck, now, he sat there and watched them being taken away. But then . . . he was in the Stahl-helm.*

I don't understand it. They aren't bad people. A couple of years ago I asked Stampeck what he ever did with that big swastika flag of his, if he'd buried it in hopes of better times to come. He said he'd burned it. I believe he did, too. I was only kidding with him, we weren't enemies. But just think if he walled it up in the house just like I did with my party book in 1932.

We weren't exactly friends, either. But when the Russians came in 1945, then the Stampecks thought we were fine neighbors. It's true, the Russians weren't exactly gentle when they got here. They'd come a long way, and they'd seen a lot. The Germans weren't exactly gentle when they pushed through Russia, either. You can't blame the Russians. The awful part was that business with the women. That was terrible. No woman could be sure she wouldn't be raped.

They put a guard around our house. Two Russians stood outside to protect us from the other Russians and the looting and the concentration camp prisoners they'd set loose. I had my party book to show, after all. They weren't exactly tenderhearted, believe me. But they weren't all anti-Fascists either. There were bad elements among them too.

So then Frau Stampeck came and asked for help. We hid her up in the attic—she wasn't the only one up there. One day the Russians came and knocked on the door and asked about the Stampecks.

"Ampe," they said. They couldn't pronounce it.

"Ampe?" I said, as if I didn't understand. "Ampe? Ampe?"

I wasn't actually lying.

---

*The Stahlhelm (literal meaning, "steel helmet")—a veterans' group formed after World War I, strongly nationalistic and, later, pro-Nazi.

But then my wife came to the door and said, "They've disappeared."

That was really about the truth. So they left. No, I couldn't have handed them over to be shot. You just can't do things like that, no matter what.

Evald Schröder: Sometimes I tell my father, Otto, that he was as much a Nazi as a Communist. He can't understand that. But if he'd been a real Communist, he would have done something against the Nazis, instead of treating them like old neighbors.

Robert: We had a whole lot of people hiding up in the attic. Earlier, we'd had a Russian up there. He was there for several weeks. He was sick, and every day I'd run to the drugstore for medicine. The druggist was in the SS, and he knew perfectly well who I was getting the medicine for, but he didn't concern himself. . . .

✪ Kurt Stampeck, Still Next Door

He has a pension of 125 marks a month, his wife says she gets nothing. On a bureau in the living room there is a portrait of one of their sons, who fell on the Eastern Front in 1945. He's wearing the SA uniform. In addition to the bureau, there's a sofa, a coffee table, a larger table with three chairs—none of it newer than 1945. On the wall is a landscape of the kind you keep finding in Neustadt's older homes. In the thirties, one summer, a man came around selling landscapes. The room also has a tile stove. There is no central heating. Just off the living room is the bedroom. Kurt Stampeck stays in bed all morning in the winter— a leg injury he suffered in the thirties has been getting worse in the last few years.

—But the disability compensation stays right at 50 marks

[a month]. If I had anyplace to go, I'd get a discount on travel. But where would I go?

In the mornings he drinks a cup of ersatz coffee and eats barley bread with margarine. Other items in the daily menu; barley pudding, bologna from Schumacher's butcher shop, and in the evenings, brockwurst with white bread and margarine. Frau Stampeck spends most of her day taking care of her husband. She does the shopping, cleaning, and the like before he gets up. In the afternoons, sometimes with his wife, he goes to visit his daughter, who's married and lives on the same street. The daughter works half-days at Schumacher's, and the son-in-law works at the clog factory.

During the thirties, Kurt Stampeck worked for the town, as a policeman and night watchman. In 1939, partly because of his disability, he was given a sit-down job at the Rathaus.

His happiest memories are from the thirties. He tells laughingly of the pranks of the foreign students in town, of the carnivals the Technikum students held every spring. He laughs with real amusement at the story of how the students once shut him up in a closet with Korup the innkeeper in what is now the Theodor Körner Hotel, and he has happy memories of police hunting trips with horses and wagons, which ended with a dip in the River Elde.

"Things like that don't happen now. Now everything is gray and boring," he says.

"These are bad times indeed," says his wife.

He sighs.

Ernst Theile: No, he wasn't one of the big ones. Just another one of the petty informers.

Robert Schröder: I had a nephew that tried to flee to the West, but they found out and stopped him. No one outside the family knew about it. You can't even trust everyone in your own family.

✖ Robert Schröder Continues

Then my son came home, from Russia. He'd been in the war right up to the finish.

First he was in prison in Hamburg for four years. He was in the party too, the Communist Party. But he was young then, and he wasn't as careful as we older people.

Well, so he was in prison for four years. He was sentenced to seven, but when things started going badly for Germany, they sent him to the Eastern Front to fight the Russians. That was the punishment. I don't know how they could be so dumb—sending a Communist to fight the Russians.

While he was in Hamburg, we corresponded the whole time. We had two correspondences going.

First, we had the kind of letters that started "Heil Hitler!" But we also wrote letters where we said what we thought. But they didn't go by the official channels. I sent them to an address I'd been given, and he put his under his dish, which is where he got mine. He didn't know who it was that took care of it, who the postman was. Later, when we looked for the address I wrote to, it turned out there wasn't any such address.

They sent him to Russia in the winter of '43, straight to Stalingrad. In the spring we got a letter from him. Just five words: "Hold out, we shall win."

He came back in June 1945. When he came back, in his uniform, the Russians were looking for all the men who were coming back from the war. Manfred had barely come in and taken off his uniform before there was a knock on the door—a Russian. My wife quickly pushed Manfred up the chimney in the kitchen. We were scared to death. He asked if there was a German soldier in the house—he'd probably seen him come, or heard about it. "No," we said.

And so he went all around the house, and didn't notice anything. Then I took Manfred's papers and fixed them up to show he'd been in the party. There were a lot of people who tried to show, afterward, that they'd been party members. My brother-in-law stole my party book and used it as identification. Imagine what that was like, reporting your brother-in-law. . . .

There wasn't anybody you could trust. And the Russians didn't just trust anybody, either. It was a question of knowing who the Russians trusted, and who'd already tricked them. . . .

✿ Hermann Kuhn, on Defeat

I deserted and buried my uniform and my papers in the woods in Poland. I took some clothes off a corpse on the road. The big refugee movements had already started.

My father was an engineer at a shipyard in Hamburg, and he was as proud of me as I was myself. I was planning to study engineering too. In 1939 I got engaged, much too young. I got married on my first leave, and on my second leave I had a child. She was the daughter of a wholesaler —a pretty woman, blond, like me, and well-built. I wrote to her twice a week. The postal services were pretty bad that last year.

I did my service in the belief that what I was doing was right, and I was proud to be able to serve my country.

I was there when Königsberg fell.

Afterward, Hitler spoke to us.

I'll never forget the effect that speech had on me. It was like an injection of strength and self-confidence. But he'd been speaking to us like that the whole time. He gave us a belief in our own worth, and in the end, when we started to doubt, he united us again. Through his words, everything we did became heroic. His words gave us the power to believe we were human beings, no matter what we did.

And toward the end, when we were in despair, he gave us comfort.

I longed to get away from that hell.

I had my pretty young wife, and I had my child. When I realized that not even the strength we got from Hitler was enough, I deserted. I wanted to go home, I wanted to protect my family. Hamburg had been bombed, and I wasn't getting any more letters. We were losing. Let me tell you what it means to lose.

I deserted. It's not easy to desert, but it was easier in a black uniform than in a green one.* There were green ones that deserted too. It was a question of choosing how you wanted to die.

The first sentries weren't any trouble. There was some milksop from Swabia who was obviously surprised and scared when he saw me. First he said "Halt!", so I put my finger to my lips and showed him he had to keep quiet. Then I stood and talked soothingly to him, and then he didn't notice which way I went. I would have had to be a civilian to get through the enemy lines—as it was, I had to crawl through. I knew what they looked like. In the daytime I'd lie low and make observations and dig in and try to sleep. I lost all track of days and weeks. I didn't have any provisions—I had weapons, but I didn't dare get close to any buildings. I was hoping I'd meet somebody who could help me, but I didn't want to kill again, ever. So I was glad when I found a corpse—he was already dead and I couldn't change that. I can remember exactly how the clothes smelled—it was a ghastly stink—but it was my salvation. I took his identity papers too.

That's the beginning of degradation. Not the running away, but the willingness to change identities.

It was spring when I got to Hamburg—a pile of rubble

*The SS wore black uniforms; the regular army, green.

where I was supposed to look for my pretty little wife and my child.

I searched in the ruins. There were a lot of us digging in the rubble, afraid we were going to find someone we loved underneath. I looked in the streets. I looked everywhere. Then somebody told me they'd gone east when the bombers came.

So I started wandering east, back again, back over the same fields I'd already tramped across, got captured by the Russians when I tried to get something to eat on a farm outside Hagenow, taken to a camp, brought to court, where false identity papers weren't any help, where I was so tired I figured they could do whatever they wanted to me.

At the camp I met a young fellow who said he'd been picked up by the Russians in Neustadt-Glewe, where he'd gone with his family to get away from the bombing in Hamburg.

He told me about his family.

It was my family he was talking about. It was my wife and my boy.

I thought I'd gone crazy.

One day I went to the Russians and told them they didn't have the whole truth about that fellow, and he was taken away from the camp.

I was set free in 1953.

Then I came here to Neustadt to look for my wife and my son, and I found them here in the barracks they'd built for the Hamburg refugees. She was living with a railroad man.

He was a good man. He'd been married before too, but his family was under the rubble in Hamburg. When I came, he moved out in the kitchen.

But I'd changed a lot in all those years. I found out I wasn't a man any more. And I had a 13-year-old son to whom I was a total stranger.

I let the railroad man move back in with my wife.

From out there in the kitchen I could hear them making love. One day my wife got a letter from Omsk. About half a year later, she and my son disappeared. I think they moved to West Germany, but I don't know for sure. All I know is, they didn't go to Omsk. For a long time the letters from Omsk kept coming. One of our neighbors said there'd been a man there one day asking for his wife. Only it was my wife. He said he had come from Siberia. The railroad man and I sat up nights watching the barracks.

That was when we started talking to each other about her. We discovered, or at least I discovered, that we weren't talking about the same person.

For him, she was just a woman, who did the things a woman does around a house. For me, she was the only human being I could talk to, the only person I ever had the courage to talk to honestly. I think the railroad man was jealous of me, although, to make any sense, it should have been the other way around. . . .

Germans don't care about the defeat of Nazism. What matters to us is that it was our own personal defeat. At one time we believed that we, as human beings, were worth more than other human beings. I believed it because I'd been taught that so many of the world's great minds were Germans, and because the Neanderthal man was found in Neanderthal. We had the oldest culture—we were the chosen people. By virtue of my superior genetic qualities, I had a duty to survive—it was my duty to mankind. The Jews thought they had a duty to survive, too, but theirs was egoistic. They also thought they were a chosen people, but they thought they had to survive so that the Scriptures would be fulfilled, and for the sake of their own salvation. We believed it was for mankind's salvation, and so that gave us certain rights.

But in the course of a few months, the duty to survive was transformed into pure animal instinct. That's what it means to lose.

❈ ERNST THIELE, ON DEFEAT

A lot of what happened to people was unjust.

My father thought it was unjust that he had to sit in the camp at Neubrandenburg. I found it unjust to be called a murderer. When I wrote my father, later, and asked him to get me an affidavit that I'd been a member of the German Worker Youth, and my father did it and sent it to me, and the only answer I got was: "You can buy a paper like that for some cigarettes in Germany these days"—well, I thought that was unjust too.

❈ Documentation of Lübke's* Guilt

Essen (ADN/SVZ),** March 14, 1968—Documents proving Lübke's participation in the construction of concentration camps were examined by Dr. Kaul and submitted to the court in Essen on Tuesday. A petition has been pending before the court since March 8 for the examination of Lübke as a witness to crimes of violence committed by the Nazis at Concentration Camp Dora.

The documents establish what has long been known to the general public: that Lübke's firm, the Schlempp Architects Bureau, was active in the so-called Mittelbau Penal District, to which Camp Dora belonged. It is apparent from other records that Lübke was a Gestapo agent.

---

*West German President Heinrich Lübke. Lübke had already defended himself against the East German charges in a nationwide television address (see pages 170–72), and had received the support of all the major West German parties. He resigned his post early in 1969.
**ADN =Allgemeiner Deutscher Nachrichtendienst—the East German news service; SVZ =Schweriner Volkszeitung.

✖ From Werner Bahlke's Notes

When the thunder of cannon was heard from Blievenstorf, where hysterical SS men had at the last minute decided to win the war, Friedrich Schoof, Kurt Speckmann, and Johann Kröger made the only reasonable decision—namely, to raise the white flag and surrender the town of Neustadt without resistance. But it was more easily decided than accomplished, for a demolition team, led by three officers who had barricaded themselves in the Rathaus, had set charges on the bridge on the Parchim road and on the bridge to the tannery.All that was lacking was the order to detonate. Hermann Buschmann went out to disarm the charges—it cost him his life. Schoof spoke in the square, while Speckmann clambered up to the roof of the Rathaus to raise the flag. Meanwhile, the three officers had disappeared. On the 4th of May the Red Army arrived. . . .

✖ Liselotte Gericke, 33,
   ## Elfriede Köstlin's Niece

The streets were empty and silent the day we expected the Russians. The previous few days and nights, a column of refugees had streamed by from east to west—farmers with their families and belongings on horse-drawn wagons, soldiers who were tired of the war. One day they met American jeeps on Main Street, which is now Breitscheidstrasse —that's where we lived. They greeted each other like old friends.

But then we heard shooting from far away. We heard that in Blievenstorf, a few miles from Neustadt, the people were opposing the Russian advance. How can people in a tiny village go on fighting and sacrificing human lives when the war was already over, when we'd already lost?

About noon I ran into a girl friend from next door.

"Go stand in the middle of the street," she said, "and you can see a Russian tank."

There was a Russian tank just at the end of the bridge, not far from us. The bridge was mined, so it was dangerous for large vehicles to drive across. Some American jeeps drove down to the bridge—to negotiate, we decided. We'd been told the Russians were wild, and cruel to women and children. But the Americans were friendly—they gave us chocolate and cigarettes.

We were told that the Russians were going to set up camp for the night and leave town the next morning. My mother and several neighbors decided to move down to Grandmother's house on Wasserstrasse. Our bags had stood packed and ready for a long time, and we put them in the baby carriage with my little sister. Another family of relatives came to Grandmother's the next day. Their daughter, who was 16, was dressed in a dark, ragged dress and had an old shawl over her head. My mother and the other women put shawls over their heads too, and made themselves look like old women.

When there was a knock on the door, they all ran down in the cellar before the door was opened. But it was only the neighbors.

The rumor about the Russians only staying overnight proved to be false. They were going to stay until further notice, and the populace was instructed to stay indoors.

The town was going to be looted.

Several months before the end of the war, 2,000 concentration camp women were moved to Neustadt, and now they were going to let them take whatever they wanted from the townspeople. Anyone who resisted would be punished.

I heard the adults talking a lot about Communism. Once

when we were at my grandmother's in Matzlow, I heard my mother whisper to someone about a neighbor that he was the biggest Communist in the village. The neighbor had a small, muddy farm and a lot of filthy children he was always screaming at. That was my first conception of what Communism was.

At Grandmother's we were four children, four women, and two men. The girl who was 16 had an older brother who'd just come home from the war—he'd lost an arm. Their father was the manager of the Neustadt dairy.

Once in a while a couple of Russian soldiers would knock on the door and ask if we had any soldiers or ammunition in the house, which we could always deny with a clear conscience.

Once a couple of women came from the camp. One of them looked at my little sister and said, "I had a daughter too. But not any more."

Mother and Grandmother very quickly said how sorry they were, and how the common people had never wanted to do each other any harm. So then the women left without taking anything.

The Russians were out after radios, wrist watches, and gold. They wanted anything that "went by itself," anything they called a "machine." The adults said the Russians must be underdeveloped.

We heard how bad the looting had been on Main Street. All the food had been taken from the shops, by the towns-people too—it seemed like a good idea to have it on the shelf in the pantry in case rationing started. We had some butter from the dairy hidden at Grandmother's, but otherwise we couldn't shop for food while the looting was going on.

Several people had killed themselves. A good friend of my parents had drowned himself in the river when his wife was raped by the Russians.

One time we met two women out in front of Grandmother's house. "You've got pretty shoes on," one of them said to my mother. "I want them."

Mother took off the shoes, and the woman tried them on. They didn't fit.

"It doesn't matter," she said. "The stockings are pretty too. Take them off."

Mother objected. "Do you want me to go barefoot?" she asked.

"I've suffered too," the woman answered.

So Mother took off the stockings.

When they'd gone, Mother told me she still had a pair in the cellar.

When things were calmer, Mother decided to go see how matters stood at home. When she came back, she was practically crying.

"Everything we've worked for, saved up for, all these years," she said, "it's all been destroyed in a few days."

The Russians had fouled the beds, emptied the closets, broken up the furniture with axes. Mother had made a mistake—she'd locked the cupboards and taken the keys with her when she left, and thought it would be safe. We children were very unhappy because all our dolls and doll carriages had been taken away from us.

✵ Hermann Puttain, 90 Years Old, Laughing and Singing (Saturday Night at the Theodor Körner)

Yes, I was at Blievenstorf when the Russians came. Yes indeed, we defended Blievenstorf. I fought in the *First* War. I was in France that time. There were 14 of us from Blievenstorf, and I was the only one that came back. The Russians came with tanks, horses, and cannons. We went out in the fields, finally, and hid. I was 67 then. I crawled across the fields to Neustadt. Now I live here with my daughter and son-in-law. I have a fine life with them. I get porridge and bread and real coffee, and I get to sleep as late as I want to in the mornings. But on Saturday evenings I leave them alone.

> *Kuku, Kuku, ruft in dem Walde*
> *Kuku, Kuku.* *

On Saturdays I come here and have a cognac, or two, or three. Now I've got it made. In my youth I sang in the Blievenstorf church choir.

> *Ein Vogel wollte Hochzeit feiern*
> *in dem grünen Wa-a-lde . . .* **

✖ Frau Evald Schröder, on Collective Friendship

I lived in Frankfurt-an-der-Oder. For three months the front went right through the town. They burned our houses, shot at us on the streets, raped the women.

There were women who didn't disguise themselves, and I don't condemn them. You can't judge people for what they do when everything around them is falling apart, when all around them there's nothing but atrocities and the smell of corpses. When the Russians drove the Germans back, we were ordered out to collect the bodies. There wasn't a place in town where there weren't bodies. They lay in heaps in the streets, and we piled them on trucks, and they carted them off.

**Cuckoo, cuckoo, calls out in the forest,*
  Cuckoo, cuckoo.
***A bird was to be wedded,*
  In the woodland gree-een . . .

The stench was appalling. Last summer when we were at Buchenwald to look at the camp, I recognized that smell —it was still there in the walls. Well, I can't say the Russians had anything to be compared with those camps, but when everyone at the post office was going to join the German-Soviet Friendship Society, well, I said I didn't want to. I said that after the way I'd gotten to know the Russians, I couldn't join a friendship club. They can talk as much as they want to about what the Soviet Union has done for the GDR, but I won't choose them as friends of my own free will, not after living with them all those months in Frankfurt.

Now we're all members anyway—voluntarily.

✸ Köstlin's and Gericke's Punishment

It was toward the end of May 1945. I was on my way home from the hospital when a Russian came up on a motorcycle and told me to follow him to the town hall—he wanted me to help him with something. I said I was on my way home to dinner, and asked him if it couldn't wait till later. He said it wouldn't take very long, I probably wouldn't even be late for dinner. He took me down in the Rathaus cellar and then closed the door behind me. The next time it opened, five more men were locked in. Then we started to understand what it was all about. The cellar kept filling up all afternoon. There were finally over a hundred men down there.

Kurt Gericke: I was in my shop, making a sign for the Russians, when this Russian came and said I had to go with him to the Rathaus. I said I'd promised to have the sign ready that afternoon. He said I'd be right back.

Willy Köstlin: Along toward five o'clock they opened a back door to the cellar, so we wouldn't come up on the square. They put us in a line and counted us, but apparently it didn't come out right. Then old Thiele came along. He'd been in his garden. He had his bicycle and his slippers on. They took his bike away from him and pushed him into line, and so that was all of us.

Then we started to march out toward the Parchim road. We hadn't had anything to eat the whole day. When we passed the city limits, we began to realize we weren't ever coming back. There were armed Russians in front of us and behind us and alongside us. When we were right outside Brentz, there was one man who jumped over a fence at a curve in the road and ran into a garden. There was a dog in the garden that started to bark, and a woman who started to scream, out of sheer terror. They caught him and shot him, on the spot.

Then the Russians went into a house and got another man and shoved him into the line where the man who was shot had been.

It was already dark when we got to Spornitz, and they loaded us into freight cars and shut the doors behind us, and there we sat all night. In the morning, when we got out, we were right outside of Parchim. Then we walked again, straight through Parchim. They'd collected a bunch of men there, and they joined the line. The line got longer at every place we came to. As we were going through Lübz, there was a man in front of me, and when we came to a corner where the line turned, he just kept going straight ahead. He took some woman by the arm and they just strolled along together.

Sometimes we spent the nights in barns. After they'd counted us in the mornings, they'd search all through the barn. The ones that tried to hide in the hay never got away with it.

One time they lined us up in front of a barn, facing it. Then they threw their rifles down into the hay like spears. And after we saw them drag out a man with a bayonet right through him, why, there wasn't anyone who tried to hide in the hay again. They didn't make any distinctions that time. Most of us had been Nazis, but there were others too. Thiele was no Nazi—he grumbled in the Kaiser's time, and he grumbled under the Nazis, and he grumbles now.

Kurt Gericke: There's a camp in Malchow where we were questioned, in two groups, with the political prisoners in the group that was going to Seven Oaks. We were taken to Neubrandenburg in freight cars. There'd been 5,000 women there in a concentration camp, and the camp had been cleaned up and enlarged, and now there were 25,000 of us. At night we were locked in the barracks and not allowed to go out. We tried to keep one corner of the barracks free for excrement, but it was impossible. It was too crowded. If somebody died during the night, he just had to lie there till morning. We spent the mornings carrying out the dead and burying them. We put them in holes, one in each, but there wasn't always someone who could say who we were burying. We'd been gathered up from different places. There were several of us from Neustadt in the same barracks. Thiele, among others. He'd sit up whole nights and talk to a schoolteacher and get madder and madder at him.

The mood in the barracks wasn't good. There were Communists there who'd turned out in the questioning to be Nazi informers. Their lives weren't worth much.

No one could betray anyone, and no one could white-wash anyone. Not any more. Everyone knew the Russians already knew as much as they wanted to know, and it wasn't such a lot they wanted to know at that point.

For breakfast we got a loaf of bread to divide among 17 men. How do you divide a loaf of bread into 17 pieces if you haven't got a knife? They'd taken our knives from us in Malchow. All we had were the clothes we'd had on when they picked us up.

And we didn't have any water. What water we had was needed in the kitchen for the water soup. Every day we made water soup. At first, we were busy emptying the kitchen that had belonged to the concentration camp. We spent half the day passing food supplies from hand to hand from the kitchen down to the railroad—the provisions were being shipped to Russia. Then we'd go home and eat our water soup, and after the water soup, straight to the barracks and be locked in. In the middle of the night the Russians would come and call us out to formation. They just wanted to count us. They did that a couple of times every night. There were always some who died between formations, and others who didn't have the strength to get up. In the beginning we only carried out the dead in the mornings, but later on we used to carry out a few who weren't quite dead yet, too. There weren't enough doctors around to say if someone was dead or not.

A couple of years ago I was in Neubrandenburg and I went out to look at the place where the camp had been. There are big apartment houses there now, right where the dead were buried. There must be thousands of dead there—first the ones from the concentration camp, and then all those that died when we were there.

✹ Fascist Excesses

Warsaw (ADN), February 19, 1968—With "great agitation" the newspaper *Trybuna Ludu* on Wednesday accused West German seamen of repeated fascistic excesses in the ports of Gdansk and Gdynia. The newspaper characterized their actions as expressions of the Bonn regime's revanchist and anti-Polish policy.

"Polish bandits"; "Too few of you Poles died at Auschwitz"; "Watch out, old man, we're coming back"—these are only a few of the outrageous remarks made by West

German seamen on Polish territory. During the last two
years alone, 15 seamen have been convicted of such acts by
the court in Gdansk.

✺ Kurt Gericke Continues

My brother, Erwin, did the right thing when he went over
while there was still time. Since they left, we don't have
anyone to talk to any more.We don't dare. Köstlins—
they're from a different class. Since Erwin moved, it's just
not the same. If it'd been up to me, we would have gone
too, but my wife didn't want to, she had her parents here.
Grandpa's 98 years old, and Grandma's 95. But now we
can't go anywhere. We just have to be satisfied with the
TV.

The TV is our window to the Free World. We can get
Hamburg. Have you heard what they call the Hamburg
channel? They call it the "Hagenow channel"—Hagenow's in the same direction, but on this side. Or sometimes they call it the "Thälmann transmitter,"* because
Ernst Thälmann was born in Hamburg. Everything over
here is propaganda. Information, now, that you have to
get from the other side. But we're used to it, it was exactly the same way before. We've learned not to speak too
loud.

You go to the polls, and you get a paper and you give
it right back to them. Twice I just didn't bother to go—
so they came and got me. There are a few people who stay
home, and then when they come from the party to get
them, they say, "Get me an apartment first" or "Put a new
roof on the house first. Then I'll vote." They mostly go and
vote anyway, in the end, and they don't get an apartment
any quicker because of it. But there was a retired woman

*Thälmann was a leader of the Communist Party under the Weimar Republic.

here—her son was a police detective and so she wasn't allowed to travel to West Germany like other people get to, so she didn't go to vote. She made them confirm her travel permit before she'd go off and put her paper in the box.

You can cross names off, of course, but nobody does. They'd find out. You can't trust anybody: That's what the whole system depends on. And then it's also true that the Germans are an authoritarian people. There wasn't any uprising against Hitler, and there won't be any against Ulbricht. You learn to put up with it.

My brother, Erwin, was in the SA. But he joined it for the same reason people join the party these days: because you have to. He was working at the tannery, that was why. Otherwise they would have called him a "Jew-lover." But he wasn't an activist. I was free—I mean, they didn't make me join: not then, and not now. If Erwin had known what it was, he probably wouldn't have joined either.

Hasn't anyone tried to get you to join a collective?

My father was a carpenter, and I took over the business after him. At first, I was determined not to give up, but in the end I couldn't make it. It's not easy to keep a private business going. If I take on an apprentice, I also have to take on all his social insurance. If he has an accident, I have to give him disability for the rest of his life. If he goes into the service, I have to agree to give him his job back afterward. During the time he's away, of course, I have to have someone else to help, but I can't fire him when the first one comes back. Firing people is against the law, and I just can't keep two apprentices. If an apprentice has to get off for some sports event, I have to pay him his salary anyway. If he gets sick, I have to give him sick pay. I have to take on practically all of society's obligations to him, and I just can't afford to live in that kind of insecurity. And if I get sick myself, no one takes care of the business for me. And I did get sick. Now I'm helping a good friend of mine. I have a little savings. I just refuse to involve myself in their system.

The hell of it is that you're forced to do such a poor job in the painting business too. There aren't any materials. A lot of the work is like what I did before when I was a carpenter. Last fall I was supposed to do some restoration work at the castle—you know, the school on the square. There's some plaster stucco work on the ceilings. But in order to make stucco, you've got to have wax that's put into the mortar, and the only wax you can get here isn't any good. Another hard thing is that they only sell ready-mixed paints, no powders, so you can only use the colors they already have, even if they happen to be completely wrong. You can change a color by changing the surface—you know, changing the surface material. But there isn't any choice of surface materials either, you have to take what they've got. It's like nobody understood how much a thing like that can mean for the environment as a whole. Everywhere you look there's the same materials, the same colors. But surely that isn't necessary, even according to Socialist ideas. They make huge investments in environmental design, but have you ever noticed how monotonous and dull the painting work always is?

When Erwin left, he signed over his land to my wife's parents, so they could do what they wanted with it. But one day the LPG confiscated half the land—without asking or anything. They just came driving up with a tractor and plow. I told him he'd better watch out for the clay in the corner, and so he drove straight out in the clay and sat there a whole day before they could pull it out with the help of two other tractors.

My in-laws weren't exactly despondent about it—they couldn't work that much land anyway. But they still have to pay taxes on it! Well, it's not very much, 4.60 a year. But the principle of the thing seems damned odd.

Salary: 450 marks a month. Housing: private house, two rooms, kitchen with pump, bathtub in the washhouse, outdoor toilet, a stove for heating. Outside: 15 white hens, potatoes, asparagus, three cats in the woodshed. The old workshop has been sold to a bicycle repairman.

✖ TV Programs, March 4

9:45 Program Guide
9:50 Medicine to Music (repeat)
10:00 News Camera (repeat)
10:35 *A Very Special Girl:*
  TV-film by Achim and Wolfgang Hübner (repeat)
12:00 Musica Viva:
  Music, folk-song, and dance program from Dresden (repeat)
  INTERMISSION
3:20 Program Guide
3:25 Medicine to Music
3:35 TV School—English for You,
  Lesson 17 (seventh grade): "At the Garage"
4:00 *The Known and Unknown CSSR:*
  A cinematic ramble through Czechoslovakia
4:30 Children's Program, for ages 5 and over:
  Rolf and Reni, "The Birds' Wedding"
5:00 News
5:05 *The Lady with the Little Dog:*
  A love story, filmed from Anton Chekhov's story of the same name;
  directed by Jossif Cheyfiz
6:30 Guest on German TV: The German Communist Party
6:45 Program Guide
6:50 Our Little Sandman: Good night to the children

7:00 A Look Around: at science and technology
7:25 Weather
7:30 News Camera
8:00 Chosen for the Film-Lover—*An Actor's Love Story:*
An Egyptian feature film with Fatan Hamama,
Emad Hamdi, Sahret Al-Ula,
and others; produced by Barakat
9:10 The Black Channel:
A program by Karl-Eduard von Schnitzler, our political commentator.
9:35 *What Do You Tell the Children?* Popular science film
10:00 News Camera and Commentary

✖ Hans Pallin, Manager of the HO Furniture Store

It was 700 years ago that Germans first settled in Zipser,
which is one of the German language-islands in Czechoslovakia. German language, but our dialect is a little unusual.
We were under the Czech government, in Slovakia. Slovaks are simple, good-natured people. Anyway, it's a
mountainous place and hard to farm, and we had to work
hard. There were about 500 people in our village.

Then they started a German Party in Czechoslovakia.
For us it wasn't called the Hitler Youth, but the German
Youth. We'd get together and sing the old songs, and have
dances five or six times a month, and put on plays—we had
a German teacher who was a good actor. That's the sort
of thing we did. Nowadays the young people don't do
anything—they've changed, all they do is listen to their
transistor radios.

My father never went to school, and we all had to help
on the farm. Necessity knows no law. We had horses and
oxen and cows, but we didn't have much land, and what

there was was in different places, some of them pretty hard to get to. That land was so hard to work, I can't say I long to go back.

In 1942 they asked for volunteers for the SS. I didn't even know what the SS was—I was 16. Forty-four of us applied, but only eight were accepted, and I was one of them. When my mother found out, she was furious, and she managed to get me out. She saved my life—I was only 16.

In 1944, when the Russians started getting closer, they organized the German Home Guard, which was also under the SS. I went to a regiment in Bratislava. In January 1945 there were 200 of us who were supposed to hold off the Red Army with a tank and 30 rounds of ammunition. We spread out in the woods, and three Czechs and I just took off. I wanted to go home. Each of us had his own horse to ride, and we slept in barns, and worked on farms. It wasn't so bad for the three Czechs, they were at home, but I didn't speak any Czech at all.

When I finally did get home, I hid. The Slovak police would come by regularly and search the house, and they finally found me and sent me to Košice on the Hungarian border. It was all Germans there—we were building a railroad bridge, and when that was done, we were supposed to cut timber. But one day I just took the train home. I arrived at an opportune moment, it turned out, because the police had just arrested the mayor, who'd been the thresher operator, and so I got to operate the thresher for nine weeks, and things went fine.

During the winter I built a spinning-wheel. And then later, the new mayor—he'd been a partisan—he took me on as the carpenter on a tunneling job. In April my mother and the others came back—and then they came and told us we had to leave.

My mother took two suitcases, and I took two suitcases, and they took us to a camp, a barracks. The Slovaks didn't treat us badly. We had Czech dance music, and they let us have church services The first convoy left on June 24, 1946, St. John's Day. We climbed into a cattle car full of lice and fleas and they gave us dehydrated food, and the Slovaks said they were sorry we had to leave. We went to a quarantine camp near Berlin—clean, but otherwise pretty bad. Stayed there for two weeks. They they divided us up among different villages, and we were sent to Rottstock-bei-Brück, where we men worked at a vulcanizing plant. Then we went on to a village where we worked for an old Prussian, who wasn't satisfied with my work, but my father got to stay.

Later, my father moved on to a head gardener's job in Ludwigslust, and the rest of us went to visit him. The trains were so full there wasn't any point in standing in line for a ticket, but when the train left Berlin, we were on it. And they didn't check tickets until Ludwigslust, so we just got off on the other side. We others got jobs at the place Father worked, so for several months we lived on fodder-beets and carrots. Then I went and applied for a job at People's Solidarity, a cabinet-maker's shop, where they made beds for refugees. I got to go to vocational school at the same time and learn cabinet-making. I worked there for six months and finished my apprenticeship.

At night we used to go out in the fields and steal grain. We'd ride our bicycles—sometimes as far as Lübz. People who were stealing from one field would be afraid of people stealing from another. There were lots of guards, and sometimes the farmers would beat the thieves so badly they died. One time an inspector rode by just 20 yards from where we were hiding in a grainfield. The people who worked at the tannery used to steal leather and take it to Lübz and trade it for sugar.

I had a girl in a village on the other side of Boizenburg. I remember once she traded some potatoes for a violin, and I was carrying it when I took her home. At the border they asked her where she'd gotten the violin, and I said it was my violin. So when I was going back, they asked me what I'd done with the violin. They gave you a hard time about everything. After that we used to meet in a cellar in Boizenburg, where we could lock ourselves in.

I got a job at Funkmechanik. They only had 37 workers then. I made radio cabinets. I did private carpentry too, of course, I was already a go-getter. I was there for 11 years. I didn't join the party—you know, if you've been involved once, you don't want to get involved again.

I could do carpentry and cabinet-making that they used to have to order from a factory in Leipzig.

I became a furniture salesman in 1957. Went through a course in selling, and they made me manager of the HO shop here in Neustadt. Also, I bought the old house up by the Park Restaurant—it was standing empty after some people had gone to the West. It looked terrible, but since I'm a carpenter myself, I've been able to fix it up fine, and since it was so dilapidated, I got it for next to nothing.

In the beginning we sold curtains and rugs too. The cooperative used to have a furniture store here too, but later on, they stopped selling furniture and we stopped selling curtains and rugs.

I still do cabinet work on the side. I'm the only cabinet-maker that does repairs in the districts of Ludwigslust, Parchim, Lübz, and Perleberg. HO have their furniture warehouse in Parchim, and they send their repairs here to me. The fact is that since furniture isn't solid wood any more, but only veneered fiberboard, you have to be an expert to repair it, at least if it's damaged on the surface. Just the finishing alone is a complicated business. I get paid extra for the repair work, of course, and then I do some private carpentry too. I couldn't make it just on a shop manager's salary—440 marks a month, not counting bonuses.

I do my purchasing from Parchim once a week, buy

everything I'll need for the week. Every January you buy for half a year ahead—kitchen layouts, bedroom sets—we mostly sell whole rooms at a time, everything in standard sizes. The trouble is, the standard sizes often don't fit the old houses people have around here. That's the problem. They ask, but we don't have what they want.

We have a sales quota we're supposed to meet. It's supposed to increase by four percent a year. Three years ago we had a big turnover, but they still wanted it to go up four percent again the next year. We just couldn't do it. So they refigured the quota and took a percentage from the difference in inventory, and that year we didn't get any bonus. It was only that one year, though. The next year we got our bonus again.

Every month, on the 22nd, I send the books to Grabow to be checked.

I'm not allowed to build a warehouse here. What I can't sell, I have to sell back again. Or sometimes I sell it to another HO shop somewhere else, where there's a demand. You don't run any great risks, but you can't make any great profits, either.

Ten percent of my salary goes for social security. And I pay 16.50 a month in taxes. That's not much. I've got two children, and so the taxes are low—though my net income is low, too.

But then I also make some money with my beekeeping. My father and I both keep bees, we own a bee truck together. We kept bees even back in Hohe Tatra. When you get into it, beekeeping is a whole science. There are a lot of people who keep bees around here—it's encouraged. You make an agreement with an LPG or a farmer, and then when the time comes, you drive the truck out to the field. We have a contract with the LPG in Lübz.

So there isn't much time left over.

Now in the spring here, pretty soon it'll be time to let the bees out for the first time. When the willows bloom, then the bees get their first natural food for their colony, which is in the process of developing. The beekeepers plant new willows every year to make food for their bees, but a lot of people haven't learned to appreciate that—you still see people going out and cutting willow branches to take home and put in a vase. There's a law protecting willows. Beekeeping gives quite a boost to the economy, so the willows have to be protected.

✖ Saturday Evening With the Aulbachs

Heinz is 19, and in the middle of his 18 months in military service. He's come home on a pass, which he does faithfully every three weeks, or whenever he can. His mother, Frau Aulbach, lives alone in one room, overloaded with old furniture. The big cabinet is Biedermeier. There are copper engravings on the walls—a baroque castle, a landscape —maybe the Alps. The windows are covered by heavy drapes, made for other windows somewhere else. Frau Aulbach brings out crystal brandy snifters and lets them ring against each other so that you will hear and ask, and she is happy to tell you about them. Heinz has brought home a bottle of Rumanian cognac.

It's almost evening.

Heinz makes tea. His mother turns on the TV, in a corner by the bookcase. She's saying she bought venison for Sunday dinner—it was very cheap. She gets Hamburg, but the picture is streaked. "In Hamburg it snows almost all the time," she says. "But anyway it's Hamburg."

Heinz comes in with the tea. In Hamburg some girls are dancing with enormous feathers on their behinds.

"In the East they talk as if we'd never gotten out of school," says Heinz, "and on the programs from the West they act as if we'd never started." He turns off the TV.

With the voice of a schoolteacher, his mother asks him —it's as if a play were beginning—

—Well, Heinz, what have you learned since I saw you last?

—To shoot, Mama.

—Who are you going to shoot?

—Our deadly enemy, German imperialism. I told you that a long time ago.

—That's nonsense.

—Well, that isn't the way it goes, either. It's "Our deadly enemy, German imperialism, if it should attack us."

Nothing more on that subject.

Frau Aulbach tells how she went to the cemetery that afternoon. She had met Frau Schneider there, and Frau Schneider had said she'd gotten a letter from her son in Braunschweig (West Germany). He wrote that he still hadn't decided about coming to Neustadt for a summer visit—now that all those who'd gone west were being counted as citizens of the GDR, he didn't want to take the chance of being detained and then drafted.

"Do you think," Frau Aulbach asks, "we should write to Helmut and tell him not to come till later?"

"They don't dare hold anyone right now," is Heinz's view.

His brother Helmut usually comes with his family for a visit of several weeks in the summer. He lives in Wiesbaden, where he works as an electrical engineer. He moved to the West after finishing his education, as did his school friend Klaus Schneider.

Heinz himself is planning to study law. His father was a lawyer. Frau Aulbach has tried to keep Heinz from going into the same field, but Heinz has made up his mind. The father died three years ago.

"It took him ten years to die," says Frau Aulbach.

He had just embarked on his legal career when the war began. At that time they were living out on her parents' estate. Her mother had moved in to this apartment in town —it originally had three additional rooms, but they've since been divided off.

Heinz's father had risen quickly in his field. In 1943, at only 30 years of age, he became a judge.

When the war ended, however, he was immediately dismissed.

Together they had tried to get her parents' estate into shape, but found it would be more profitable to sell it, although there was no one right then who could afford to buy.

He worked as a farm hand, then as a house painter. Most of his colleagues had fled to the West. He was tried and sentenced for the trials he'd conducted according to Hitler's law.

When his colleagues fled, the Aulbachs talked of leaving too.

—But my husband said that the law must run its course. He said no one escapes anyway—but he was wrong there. Our friends and my husband's colleagues never went to trial. They sit there in West Germany conducting trials themselves again.

He lived in a three-man cell in Brandenburg Prison until 1950, when he was moved to Bautzen I, which had been used as a concentration camp during the Hitler period. He contracted a lung ailment that he carried with him to his death.

The first year he was in prison his wife sold the estate. Her mother was ill, and the whole family—in addition to Frau Aulbach there were Heinz and Helmut—moved into town.

For the whole estate, Frau Aulbach got 15,000 marks.

—That was a good price. There were other properties that were just confiscated.

One night after my husband came back, we were sitting here in front of the TV, and he started talking about his law career. He'd take up different cases he'd had but he would always make himself the defendant, and when I tried to comfort him, all he said was, "Haven't you gotten over that yet?"

When Helmut told him that he and Klaus were thinking of moving over to the West, he didn't react at all.

—Then it was I that cried, because it seemed to me that I'd lost two men at the same time, and I only had Heinz left.

Heinz says he once thought about going over too.

—My plan wasn't nearly as sophisticated as Brockman's. I practiced under-water swimming, and I could finally do about 50 yards—I was going to cross the Spree, or so I imagined. I didn't tell Mother anything. She never would have made it. But Peter and I, we went down to the lake and practiced three times a week, and when school was out, we went to Berlin—feeling very cocky.

The first thing we did was buy a map, to see where the best place would be. We figured we'd better wait for a rainy night. So we picked a building that was being torn down, where we could lie and watch how the guards went. As it happened, it rained hard that first night.

We were both of us so scared we were shaking. We sat crouching in that old building, and we were on the verge of falling asleep when we heard this machine gun sputtering outside. We looked out, and there were two guards drawing lines on the river with machine-gun bullets. We were so scared we could hardly breathe. We just sat there and shook for about 18 hours, I think, before we could get up the nerve to leave the building, and we went straight to the station to see when the next train left for home. That was only two years ago.

Heinz says he's now given up all plans of disappearing.

—You have to try and accept it. Freedom is insight into necessity. Other things aside, I'm a well-schooled Marxist, and as a matter of fact I believe that Socialism is the only political system that's worthy of mankind. If only it weren't served up to us in such a vulgar way. I can hardly eat a piece of pastry without thinking the whole time how I'm supporting our republic's baking industry. It sticks in your throat. Our newspapers are written as if they suspected every reader of being an unbeliever. In the military we're taught that West Germany is our deadly enemy, and that "shoulder to shoulder with our Soviet friends we'll crush West German imperialism, as soon as it raises its head." That reservation, I think, is important to keep in mind. In every village and twist in the road, not to mention the cities, there's a sign about how we have to defend the peace. There are almost as many signs as there are soldiers —and that's quite a few. But it's only because everyone is afraid. The ones who are loyal are afraid that Communism will be threatened, and the ones who aren't loyal are always whispering because they're afraid what they're saying will be taken as the threat. . . .

✪ Erwin Gericke Tells Why He Left

I'd been a member of the Nazi Party, I was even in the SA. I'd gotten back my job at the bank, and everybody there was very helpful. See, first I'd been punished by being fired from the bank—I'd had to work as a night watchman at the tannery, along with Robert Schröder, my old neighbor. Then when I was back at the bank, in my old job, they asked me if I didn't want to join the party. I couldn't do that—I'd been in one party, and that had been wrong, so I couldn't just right away join the next party that happened along.

Then they came to me one day and told me that the farm collectivization was going to be extended, and so I should be a little stingy about giving loans to farmers. I didn't like that.

Then one day a man came from the police and asked me if I wouldn't like to have a job with them.

"I'm in such bad shape I'd never make it," I said. "Besides, I've got heart trouble."

And the policeman said, "That isn't what I mean. I mean, you sit here at the counter all day and talk to the farmers and hear them talk about one thing and another. Don't you think you could give us a few reports?"

So then I decided it was time for me to get over the border.

Have you been back to Neustadt?

No, I don't want to take the risk.

One weekend in May, every year, everyone from old Mecklenburg meets in Ratzeburg. We all go to church together, and eat together, and drink and talk—we all speak Plattdeutsch.* A relative of the old duke of Ludwigslust usually comes, but he hasn't been there the last couple of times, he's been sick. This year it wasn't like it usually is, either. The minister that usually preaches couldn't come, so another man came instead, and he didn't preach in Plattdeutsch. It wasn't at all like it used to be.

---

*The Low German dialect.

✪ Kurt Gericke, on Longing

There's only one thing I really long for. There's just one thing I want to get in on before I die.

I had a very good business. But we won't talk about that. Things were going well, and then later they didn't go so well any more—let's not talk about it. It's all a question of politics, and let's not talk about it. Anyway, I'm about due for my pension. I'm sick too. The doctor says I shouldn't smoke cigars—but now? when we've got Havanas? The doctor says I shouldn't drink cognac, and I don't either, not every day.

No, there's just one thing I long for, but I'll never get to do it. I'd like to go to the Mecklenburg Reunion in Ratzeburg. That's the only thing I really long for, the Ratzeburg Reunion.

✪ Inge Schröder, at Afternoon Coffee
With Her Father-in-law, Robert

My parents had a big farm in Czechoslovakia. We had heard that all the Germans were going to have to leave the country, and then one day the Czech police came and told us to gather up 25 kilograms* of goods out of everything we had, and take it with us, the train was leaving in 24 hours. That is, 25 kilograms per person. Communists were allowed to take more—they got to load up a whole cart. We only lived a few miles from the border.

*About 55 pounds.

In the evening they came back and took us down to the railroad and stuffed us into cattle cars that were overloaded already. We got nothing for the farm, and nothing for all the stuff we left behind. The Czechs took it. Not the Russians—the Russians didn't do anything to us there, down there they were very decent. So then we sat in the cattle cars, and we had no idea where they were taking us, except that it was into Germany. It didn't seem to us that it had to be such a long way, since we lived near the border. I can't remember any more how long we sat there. They didn't feed us on the way.

Finally we came to Ludwigslust, where they made us get out. We found out there that we were headed for a place called Neustadt-Glewe. And so here we came. They gave us a place to live right away, and they gave me a job at the tannery. You have to admit it was well organized. But imagine, down there the Russians treated us so well, and then here—the first thing I saw when I got off the train in Ludwigslust was two old women who'd struggled along with their 25 kilograms all the way from Czechoslovakia, and so they were climbing off the train, and along came two Russians and took their sacks . . . and so they just stood there, with nothing. . . .

I've never been back again. We always thought we'd go there on our vacation sometime, but we never did. Now we probably never will—I heard the border's closed. Well, maybe it doesn't matter. I don't really wish I was back there again. We're well off here. Lots of things are wrong, but we live well. In Czechoslovakia the Germans were never well liked, at least not where we were. At first it was hard here too, very hard, but I don't think it would have been any easier there at home.

And now, when I say we couldn't make it if we didn't both work, I don't mean I want to be a housewife. Why shouldn't we both work? My mother worked on the farm.

My great-grandmother worked on the farm. Manfred's mother has always worked. All his grandparents worked. I can't see what's so special about that.

In the beginning I worked at the tannery. I operated a stamping press. It was essential work then, at the beginning, when there weren't so many men—they'd all been killed. But it got to be too hard for me, so I went to the bakery. Nowadays they don't have to put women in such heavy jobs any more. Now they try to place them in jobs that don't require so much physical strength. You see, the system is, every worker gets paid according to his output, so there's no distinction made between a man and a woman. And to that extent, that's the way it should be— there should be equal wages. But then it's still true that some jobs pay better than others, and often as not those jobs are held by men. I think that's undemocratic.

We won't even talk about the kind of money doctors get. It just can't be compared with what we get. Intellectuals in general are better paid than us common workers. Teachers, for example, get a much higher salary than leather-workers, and then their pensions are *ten* times as high, since pensions are figured on salaries.

And the doctors! They write out invalid passes for a lot of fine ladies so they can travel to the West—pensioners and invalids are allowed to travel. People sit here with children or parents in the West, but they don't get to go visit them, and then there are these fine ladies who go to the doctor whenever they want to travel, and buy an invalid pass, whether they have relatives or not.

I don't call that democracy.

It's true, there are things here I don't understand. I have a sister in West Germany, but my family's here, I'm a party member, and I haven't ever even thought of leaving the country, especially not of leaving my family—and yet I'm not allowed to travel. Anyway, Frau Thiele was

over there, and when she came back, she said she wouldn't
live in West Germany for anything. . . .
Robert Schröder: No, you can't call that democratic.
Inge Schröder: That's the sort of thing we'd like to change.
Mayor Diederich: Well, obviously you have to pay intellectuals more. Otherwise no one would go to college.
Willy Köstlin: We're well paid here. Otherwise even more
of us would have gone over. They have to do something,
after all, to hold on to at least *some* of the elite.

✺ Willy Köstlin, on People and Health

People live too well here, that's their trouble. I was here
in '45—I told you about that. People were dying of diphtheria and typhus, epidemics and malnutrition. A lot of
things have changed in the past few years, not least of all
in medicine. The diseases we have to fight now are all
diseases of prosperity, like cancer and diabetes. We can't
tell you what causes any of them, but they're not deficiency diseases, not in the accepted sense of the word.
Anyway, we *can* say, of cancer, that tobacco has a definitely conducive effect.

People eat too much carbohydrates. Maybe you've been
to an LPG. They're very particular about hygiene and diet
for the animals. The livestock is completely free of tuberculosis. You can't go into a pigsty without washing your
shoes first to remove any particle that might be injurious
to the animals.

Well, people in this country aren't one-tenth as hygienic
as the pigs. There's a whole lot of them who don't have
access to a bathtub or shower. What they *do* have access
to is rich food. Our diet is long since outmoded. To a large
extent, our housing standards are, too. They're starting to

come up with a new diet here in this country, but it should have been done a long time ago. They should have worked it out the same time they worked it out for the cows. But that's the way human beings are—the last thing they want to change is themselves.

People smoke and drink and eat brockwurst and pig's feet seven days a week. And in the summer they take their baths in the lake.

People get TV sets—and they ought to, by all means. They ought to have a little look at the world. But there are so many meaningless things they buy themselves—like these damned transistor radios the young people run around with, because they can't sing and make their own music any more.

They lay out good money for all sorts of medicines, which they prescribe for themselves, against overweight and headaches and muscle pain and bad digestion and hemorrhoids and heartburn and pimples—and then finally they come to a doctor and think we ought to straighten out the whole tangle for them.

They come and wait in long lines with their idiotic complaints.

Remember now, health care in this country is *free.* That's a magnificent thing. But remember, too, that means long lines of people waiting to see us. You can't make people wait in line, not for health care. People say we get big salaries, but by God, we work for them.

In the cow barns they've eliminated tuberculosis. *We* haven't been able to do that. But we've put a stop to poliomyelitis. And a lot's been done against TB. A lot's been done for diabetes, and a lot's been done in treating cancer.

A couple of years ago, here, they slaughtered all the hogs at an LPG near Ludwigslust, because field mice had gotten in with them. You don't as a rule slaughter human beings, but this blind prosperity can be like mice, and right now

Rudolf Schliemann, one of the men who raised the Red Flag on the tower of the old Neustadt fortress on May 1, 1932.

"Socialism needs healthy, happy people!
Participate in sports regularly!"
Sign on Brauereistrasse.

The H.O. station restaurant in Ludwigslust—9 o'clock on a
March morning.

Trucks of the National People's Army headed north on Breitscheidstrasse.

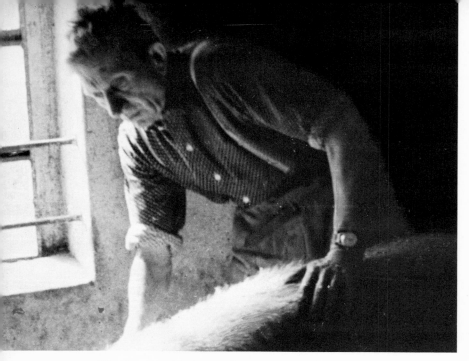

The foreman in the hog barn on the Theodor Körner collective farm in Wöbbelin.

Birthday party on a collective farm founded on the combined holdings of three brothers.

Collecting firewood.

Graffiti in an alleyway
between Grosse Wallstrasse
and Kleine Wallstrasse.

Soviet soldiers on the
station platform in
Ludwigslust.

Brick transport,
Bleicherstrasse.

*Roller skating
on Thälmannstrasse.*

*Kindergarten children
on their daily walk*

*On the way home from
the allotment garden.*

People's Owned Schwerin Gravel and Concrete Works
—Neustadt-Glewe Factory
In Honor of the 7th Congress of the German Socialist Unity Party
The Naujok Brigade (Concrete Finishing) Pledges Itself
To Advance the Plan by One Day with Extra Production
To a Value of 6,088 Marks.
The Böttcher Brigade Pledges Itself
To Produce 500 Extra Reinforcing Steel Cages
And to Donate Wages of 137.40 Marks
To the Solidarity Fund for the
Fighting Vietnamese.
(Sign at the corner of Brauereistrasse and Strasse des Friedens.)

Outside the August Apfelbaum tannery.

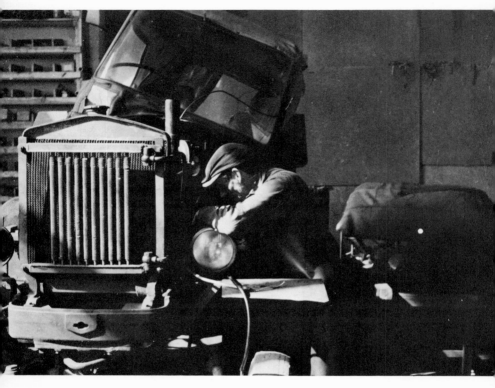

In the machine shop at the Theodor Körner collective farm.

it's a question of stopping them—in any case, of stopping the kind of mice that are causing all the trouble.*

⌘ Willy Köstlin, on Democratic Behavior

The plant manager lives up here on Fritz Reuterstrasse. Otto Bentin lives on the corner of Ludwigslusterstrasse. He's a cripple. In the mornings, when I ride my bicycle past the plant, I see the manager come by in his Tatra. Once last February, when there was ice on the street, I saw him drive past Bentin. Bentin works in the warehouse. He was walking along with his two canes, and he couldn't go very fast. But the manager didn't stop. It would have been a simple thing to stop. He could give Bentin a ride every morning—but he never does. Many years ago he got himself a Trabant. After a few years he traded it in on a Wartburg, which is a little more expensive. Then, a few years later, he bought a Volga. Now he has a Tatra. It's one

---

*Social security, with a pension plan and sickness and accident insurance, is in the hands of the Free German Trade Union (FDGB). All laborers and civil servants are automatically insured. They pay ten percent of their gross income up to 60 marks a month, and another ten percent is contributed by the employer. Students at universities and technical schools are insured free of charge, as are retired people.

Social benefits include free medical treatment as well as free preventive and protective measures. All medicines and services, such as hospital care, are free. Visits to spas and sanitoriums are also free. The sick person receives sick pay for 26 weeks, from the first day of sickness. For the first six weeks he also receives wage equalization from his employer. The sick pay and wage equalization amount to 90 percent of his net income. In the case of an accident on the job, this 90 percent is paid until the injured person can return to work. Other financial benefits given by social security are family support, maternity allowances, and funeral expenses. The state pays a baby bonus that comes to 500 marks for the first child, 600 for the second, 700 for the third, 850 for the fourth, and 1,000 marks for each additional child. The dependent's allowance is 20 marks a month each for the first three children, 40 marks a month for the fourth child, and 45 marks for each additional child. Since October 1963 there is a paid vacation of 14 weeks for pregnancy and confinement.

of those black ones that the diplomats have in Berlin. But
Otto Bentin has to walk with his two canes. Is that the sort
of thing you call equality? Things wouldn't have worked
that way before. There you see the way the comrades
think.

✻ Price List

1 kg. coffee (2.24 lb.)	MDN 80.00
100 g. tea (3½ oz.)	2.00
125 g. cocoa (4 oz.)	4.00
1 liter milk (slightly under 1 qt.)	0.72
1 kg. butter	10.00
1 kg. margarine	4.00
1 kg. cheese	8.00
1 kg. wheat flour	1.40
1 kg. sugar	1.75
Mixed root crops, canned, 1 liter	1.75
Canned peas, 1 liter	3.75
Canned beans, 1 liter	1.50
1 kg. onions	0.72
1 kg. grapes	3.20
1 kg. apples	1.50
1 kg. lemons	5.00
1 kg. oranges	5.00
1 head of celery	0.35
1 head of lettuce	0.35
1 kg. beef	5.80–13.20
1 kg. pork	4.60–10.00
1 kg. veal	4.00–13.00
1 kg. sausage	10.80
Men's shoes	45.00–60.00
Men's socks	3.00
Man's pull-over	40.00–120.00
Man's suit	300.00–500.00

Strawberries (in March), 1 liter   2.20
Apricots, 1 liter   2.07
Cherries, 1 liter   1.09
Peas, 100 g.   1.45
Spinach, 100 g.   1.31
Cucumber salad, 100 g.   0.82
Herring salad in mayonnaise, 100 g. 0.54
Herring salad with beets, 100 g.   0.44
Salted herring fillets, 100 g.   0.62
Potato salad with mayonnaise,
100 g.   0.19
Radio, "Carino"   180.00
Radio, "UKW Super-Traveler"   515.00
Record player, "Duett"   258.00
Record player, "Duo"   120.00
Tape recorder, "Bändi"   245.00
Tape recorder, "Uran"   600.00
Vacuum cleaner   129.00–239.00
Electric heater   136.00
Camera, "Pouva Start"   16.30
Camera, "Exa 1a"   238.00
Washing machine   420.00
Waffle iron   35.00
Hot plate   36.00
Electric iron   23.00–35.50
Saucepan   6.30–7.50
Pressure cooker   59.00–63.50
Hot-water bottle   6.00
Jena fire-resistant glass pot   7.70–8.05
Women's leather boots   62.00
Men's rubber boots   18.80
Lady's handbag   4.00–29.00
Steel-blue men's long underwear 12.15
Gold-and-black men's long
underwear   12.45

White cotton shirt, permanent press	45.00
TV set	1,700.00–2,810.00
Lady's wrist watch	39.00–135.00
Deluxe doll carriage	93.00
Electric alarm clock	75.00
Roller skates	35.00
Table tennis set for children	4.85
Toy airplane, light metal	5.80
Brassiere	8.25–25.90
Lady's underpants	2.45
Men's overalls	11.25
Women's overalls	21.80
Doctor's coat	10.00
Colored shirt	10.25
Supervisor's coat	12.80
Sewing machine	632.00
Complete bedroom set of birch veneer, including 2 beds, 4-compartment wardrobe, 2 bedside tables, dressing table with mirror and stool	1,321.00
Sofa	638.00
Living-room wall set, containing 4-drawer cabinet, writing table, 2 open bookcases, 2 glass-front bookcases—total width 11′10″, depth 16″, height 5′9″	1,636.00
Easy chair	220.00
Crib	89.00
Hassock	14.80

✿ Berthold and Ursula Dunkelbeck
on the Family Homestead

They live in three rooms, and they have three children. He works at VEG* Lewitz, as does she periodically. He is 32, she 29.

Their home consists of part of the half-timbered farmhouse that belonged to his father. There is a large kitchen with a wood stove and a pump for water (cold only). On the wall, a sampler with the adage: "God is the friend of the poor."

Heavy beams—red, freshly painted—support the inner walls.

Directly off the kitchen is the room that serves both as woodshed and laundry room. The washtub is built in.

"We generally use it for a bathtub too," says Frau Dunkelbeck.

They have a root cellar directly across the yard.

"My father built it as an air-raid shelter during the war, but we never used it," comments Herr Dunkelbeck. "When the Russians came, they didn't see it and drove right through the roof with a truck. That was the end of *that* shelter."

The toilets are in the other corner of the yard.

"We fertilize with shit. It's no worse than cow manure, and a lot better than powder. Out to the fields with it!"

They have their own chickens, their own pig, their own kitchen garden. The chickens run loose, occasionally coming into the kitchen. Frau Dunkelbeck has a name for every hen. They call the pig Frederick the Great.

"But it's a she, isn't it?"

*VEG=Volkseigenes Gut—State Farm

"We're not so particular about details around here," says Dunkelbeck.

The old stable stands untouched and uncleaned. Dunkelbeck and one of his neighbors have turned the old barn into a table tennis room. They have polished the floor and painted the walls red and white.

"We almost never play. Sometimes we get up a dance in here, but it sounds better to call it a table tennis room."

Frau Dunkelbeck's mother, Frau Steppel, lives in the former farm-hand's cottage. She's 69 years old, an invalid. She mostly stays in her cottage, which is half-filled with immense leafy plants.

During the cold half of the year, her daughter or her son-in-law comes over in the morning and lights a fire in her stove. She takes care of everything else herself, and she usually helps out by taking care of the children when her daughter is out in the fields.

Once in a while she comes over to her daughter's home in the evening to watch television. The TV set stands in the largest room, which otherwise contains only a well-stuffed sofa, a table several square yards in area, and a grandfather clock marked 1836.

"It was my grandfather's grandfather who made that clock," says Berthold Dunkelbeck. "He could do all those sorts of things. It still runs. It's been running continuously since 1836."

"But if it stops," his wife adds, "it stops for good. There isn't anybody who could fix a clock like that."

*   *   *   *   *

Frau Steppel has come over to watch a music program on TV. She doesn't care for any other programs.

The program is called *Gallery Music* and this week features a tape of a concert at the National Art Gallery in

Dresden. Frank Martin from Switzerland stands on the podium. The performance is of his Tristan Oratorio, *The Magic Potion.*

"*Schön,*" says Frau Steppel. "Music is a magic potion for me. All music is a magic potion. They have the Gallery Concerts every Monday—they make up for a lot of things I miss."

She says this after the concert is over—during the concert, she sat absolutely quiet.

"I don't care for the rest of it," she says again. "I don't understand things any more. I can't keep up with it any more. For me, 69 is old."

Frau Dunkelbeck takes out a bottle of cognac and pours it out in small glasses. Everyone has a swallow.

"Well, that's not so bad, either," says Frau Steppel.

✖ Frau Veronika Steppel's Story

When I was young, I lived in the Sudetenland. My papa was the village merchant. There were vineyards on the hills, and on Saturdays we dressed in lace collars and ruffles, and the boys played concertinas, and we sang and danced to the music.

On Sundays, Father Bernhard absolved us of our sins. Father Bernhard had a good heart. My worry was always which kisses I should confess. For some kisses he gave absolution at once. But I had to carry three buckets of water to his house as a penance for having danced past midnight with the *Patron*'s* son, and for having given him three kisses—one pail of water for each kiss.

What a disgrace it was for a girl to have to carry water to Father Bernhard's house, what a disgrace for the merchant's daughter!

---

* *Patron*—the local squire, or landowner.

After that I never confessed my kisses with the *Patron's* son, which means I didn't count them either, and when I was 18, I was a bride, one late summer's day just before the grape harvest, and the *Patron's* son, my husband, said, "Now, now, my bride, you shall carry a pail of water for each kiss you deny me."

And such was life, when we were young in the Sudeten.

My husband became the *Patron*. His papa died; his mama died; my mama and papa died. We took over my papa's store. I bore three children.

One day a man came to our village from Munich. He came to my husband. "*Herr Patron*," he said, "you are German, and you live here, and I assume you know your duty. We must establish a German Party."

My husband went to Father Bernhard, who was an old man then, and asked him for advice, and Father Bernhard said to him, "You are the richest man in our village, and you know the proverb about the eye of the needle. Choose, then, between your earthly and your heavenly Lord. If you choose the heavenly Lord, you will share your wealth, and if you choose your earthly Lord, you will increase it."

My husband came home, and we talked about what Father Bernhard had said, and we asked ourselves, "With whom are we to share our wealth?" There were no poor in our village. And so my husband asked Father Bernhard again, "With whom are we supposed to share our wealth?"

And Father Bernhard said, "Go to Max Fischer and talk to him."

Max Fischer was the smith in our village, and the smith told my husband about what was happening in Germany, and he told my husband what kind of man it was that had come from Munich, and he told him that the man had gone on to the next village and to the next and the next, and that the Seligmanns in the next village had had their windows broken the night after the man's visit.

And then he said, "You yourself are a rich man, you have property and possessions. You may find it hard to understand, but a man who has very little asks himself why another man has so much. And in Germany today there are many who have little and few who have much. Dear *Patron*, I'm glad you came to me, and I don't accuse you of evil. You are a good man, and your father was a good man. You shall not share your property with others, because in our village there are none who complain and none who begrudge you your wealth. But you shall not defend your property either, for outside our village there are those who need your help—the Seligmanns are not rich. But they have crooked noses."

My husband told me all this when he came home, and we went to Father Bernhard and told him what the smith had said and asked for advice, and Father Bernhard laughed.

Before the man from Munich came back a second time, we had agreed to establish a German Party, and we brought the Seligmanns to our village, and we brought Jews from other neighboring villages to our village, and we decided to use cunning.

But one day a large black truck came to the village. It took away Father Bernhard and the smith, and then they came to our house and took away the Seligmanns, and to our neighbors and took away the Jews who were living there, and none of them ever came back. A new priest came, but no new smith, and we no longer dared confess to the new priest, because we no longer knew what was good and what was evil.

And the schoolteacher in the village was taken away, and a new teacher came, and no one tried to be cunning any more.

"What we've always been taught was wrong," our children said.

And we didn't answer them.

And so faith and joy and truth were gone from our village.

Our eldest son was called into military service, and never came back.

Our next-eldest son was called into military service, and *he* never came back.

My husband—who for some reason I never understood was not taken away by the black truck when it drove off with Father Bernhard and the Seligmanns—my husband went to the party leaders and said, "I want to leave the party."

And they said, "No. There's no such thing. You don't leave the party, you disappear."

When my husband wasn't taken away in the black truck at the same time as Father Bernhard and the Seligmanns, other people in the village began to wonder who he really was. Why not him? And there were those who thought he was the informer. Why should he, who had everything to gain, be against the party? And our friends began to turn away from us.

But my husband went to the party leaders and said, "I want to leave the party."

And they said to him, "There's no such thing. You don't leave the party, you disappear."

They shaved his head, and they stood him up by the church, with two guards. Around his neck they put a sign that said, "I am a traitor." It didn't say he was a "Jewish swine," because then his friends and enemies would have known what he was. It said, "I am a traitor."

And no one knew, any more, what he had betrayed.

He was thrown into a truck and taken away to a camp for Jews.

But when the Americans came, they picked out him and the other Germans, and they asked them, "Were you party members?" And he answered, Yes, he was a party member. And no one believed his story of *why*, any more, and they took him to another camp.

The Red Army came to where we were.

I thanked God when they came, when I saw clouds of smoke beyond the mountains. The Brown Shirts in the village went out in the woods to fight them, but I never noticed any fighting, so perhaps they went out in the woods to hide. The Reds marched into the village in ranks, on horses. They carried a flag in front, and they had drums and trumpets—it was as if they belonged to another time. They gave out chocolate to the village children.

And so the day came when we had to pack our things. It's difficult to leave your land and your home and everything you own, forever, in order to travel into an uncertain future. The only thing I had left was my daughter, and the vague hope of someday seeing my husband again.

We came to this North German village, where everything was so different from what we knew, and our only goal each day was to survive.

It was an uncertain time, when every man who wanted to go on living was turned into a criminal, and when a bit of food could be worth another man's life.

One night I went out in the fields to gather grain, and that night I was struck across the back and made an invalid.

When I came back from the hospital, my husband returned.

I was living with my daughter in the farm-hand's cottage, where I still live. He'd heard about our relocation while he was still in the camp, and he'd been looking for us for three months.

He came in the evening, when we'd gone to bed. We talked the whole night.

A week later he was dead.

My job on the farm was to feed the hens. Now I can't manage that either, but then, hens are cared for in a different way now anyway.

I've got my pension, my invalid's pension. During the days I read in the Scriptures, and every Sunday I go to Mass. Father Gehrki is a wise man. He has a good heart.

Every Monday I listen to the concerts on TV.

Once a day I go to my husband's grave. And the flowers in my cottage, they take time too.

✹ Martha Gottlieb, Who Has Served the Church for 50 Years

Frau Martha Gottlieb lives in a half-timbered house on Breitscheidstrasse. She is 83 years old and a widow. She came to Neustadt as a schoolteacher in 1908, and pursued that profession until 1936, after which she continued to work as a private tutor.

Now she fills her days with work for the Lutheran parish. Her job consists of going through the old church registers, taking down the names of those in the congregation who were confirmed 50 years ago, and trying to find their present addresses. Golden-anniversary confirmation classes are invited to a jubilee every other year. The first was held two years ago.

Frau Gottlieb also keeps track of all the birthdays in the parish. Retired members of the congregation get a little card, written by Frau Gottlieb and signed by her and Pastor Smidt. Sometimes they also make birthday visits together, sometimes Frau Gottlieb pays these calls alone.

"Pastor Smidt has only been in town ten years," says Frau Gottlieb. "Naturally, he's not well acquainted with everyone."

She has served the church for 50 years now, she says— 50 years here in Neustadt. Frau Gottlieb has also lived in the same house for almost 50 years, from the year she married. The house has been owned by four generations of Gottliebs. Now she lives in two rooms on the second floor, and the ground floor has been divided into two apartments that are rented out, one for 25 marks a month, the other for 30.

The upper floor is also divided into two apartments, each with two rooms. For the half she doesn't occupy herself, she gets another 25 marks a month in rent. Her pension is 182 marks a month, and you can't live on that, she says. For those rents, she can't afford to make repairs, and she complains that the tenants do nothing themselves. The old Gottlieb house is deteriorating, and this grieves her.

She's had a little kitchen built in the space between her two rooms. It has an electric hot plate and a water tap and sink, as well as an old sideboard of richly carved oak, where she keeps the family porcelain and some large wineglasses. One room is a bedroom only, holding two enormous beds with tall canopies. Her daughter, Elizabeth, sleeps in one of them when she comes to visit her mother, once a month for three days. Elizabeth is a nurse in Schwerin. The beds have belonged to the Gottlieb family for three generations.

The second room is where Frau Gottlieb spends her days. There stands the big glass-doored cupboard, and next to it a TV set and a radio. On one wall are a photograph of a crucifix and an old portrait of a young man: her husband in his youth. They had two children—there was a son who died in the war. Her brother-in-law's son and his family live two houses away. The sister lives in West Berlin and sends Frau Gottlieb packages of coffee and of HB cigarettes, which she offers to guests.

The room has double carpets—underneath, one that covers the whole floor, and on top of it another, with an oriental design.

Frau Gottlieb also has a brand-new green tile stove that cost her 600 marks. She burns briquettes and takes care of the fire herself.

Once a week she goes down to eat at the Theodor

Körner. If the menu has mixed salad, she asks for red cabbage instead.

At the hotel she meets another woman, who also helps with the parish work. This woman takes care of all the church vestments—the altar cloth and chasubles.

For a long time, Frau Gottlieb also served as catechist, at least to the extent that she led the confirmation classes and assisted at or conducted the Sunday school.

—It hasn't always been easy. This is a Godless time we live in. The teachers in school revile God. One really ought to report it, but if it is reported, what happens? Nothing happens, even though it's now against the law to vilify religion. The children would come and say that at school Miss So-and-so says such-and-such. "Yes, yes," I'd say. "She can believe what she likes. But now you're here, and now you must believe in God." No, it's not an easy time we live in. They say we have religious freedom, but what does that mean? Christ bade us proselytize. But try to do mission work around here—no, no, it's not allowed. There's a great deal that's not allowed.

But it won't last forever. Alexander's empire fell, the Roman Empire fell, Napoleon's empire fell, and the system that rules today will also fall.

No, before 1945 it wasn't like now. It can't be compared. It was wonderful then. Well, there were difficulties then, too. At first, all the SA men were ordered to go to church. Then they were ordered to stop going to church. But when I think about 1945, everything whirls around in my head. It was terrifying. My husband worked at the Rathaus, and they wouldn't let him leave. We had to abandon our home. No, I don't want to talk about it. Almost all of our furniture went to the Stift Bethlehem Hospital in Ludwigslust. What could *we* do with it?

It's a time of evil we live in, and have lived in—and not only here. I was reading in one of our newspapers about

South Africa, about apartheid. It's shocking. They can't help it that they're black. They're human beings too, obviously. But then I don't think it's advisable for black and white people to marry one another—that's a different matter. They shouldn't do that. But apartheid is terrible. People shall turn against each other, and the earth shall quake, and in this earthquake . . . well, what it says in the Bible, that shall be fulfilled. You know, I've had to give up a great deal, and I can give up everything. But I cannot give up my God.

✸ "My Name Is Jack"
(From the Second-grade Reader)

I am an American Negro boy, and I have seven brothers and sisters. Our father is a poor farmer. In the stable behind our house there is an old horse and a scrawny cow.

My mother has to work on the land we own. She plows and plants the corn by herself. She even has to bring in the harvest all alone.

We children would be happy to help our mother. But when we are six years old, we have to start getting up at four o'clock in the morning to go with our father to the cotton fields. They belong to the white master. My brothers and sisters pick almost as much cotton as the grown men, but they get very little pay for their work. We come home, very tired, at nine o'clock at night.

We are very happy when we can sometimes go to school. But our government builds no schools for the poor Negro children.

So our parents collected money for a school. It is a simple little wooden house. Each Negro child can go to school only for a short time. My sister and I take turns. One of us always has to pick cotton.

The rich children have a much better life. They ride in buses to their large, pretty schools. They often make fun of us, and no one tells them not to.

A white worker once told us about the Soviet Union. There the children have bright, pretty schools. In the summer they go to the seashore or to the mountains. They can wander about and play happily. I would like to live in that country. But my father says that some day American children will also live happily, and learn many things.

✺ Elfriede Köstlin, on Negroes

Just imagine—Rainer, who's studying in Leipzig, says the Negroes aren't happy here. There are a whole lot of foreign students in Leipzig. There are students there from almost all over the world, a great many from Vietnam and a great many Negroes also. The Vietnamese are so grateful and so happy to be able to study here. But there's trouble with the Negroes almost all the time. They don't even like to be called Negroes. They don't show the least gratitude or politeness toward the German students. Why shouldn't they be called Negroes? They *are* Negroes. They want to be called Africans. But they're still Negroes.

✺ Berthold Dunkelbeck on the Way Up

When the new mayor came in after the collapse in '45, he decided he was going to root out the capitalists. The large farmers were capitalists. There were people coming into town from all over, and places had to be found for them to live. My mother-in-law and my wife were among them, and they got to live in our farm-hand's cottage. The mayor decided.

The mayor couldn't just simply divide up land that

didn't belong either to the town or to the state, so he tried to chase away the big farmers, the ones that hadn't already been expropriated, so in that way he could get rid of the capitalists painlessly, and acquire land at the same time. But the state was in a dilemma, because they were forced to encourage big farms in their price policies, because the country needed food. The situation was really crazy for a country that's trying to push through Socialism.

We provided housing cheerfully enough, because that way we got labor. But at the same time, they hit us with a systematic administrative squeeze.

For example, a big farmer didn't have to render an account just to himself any more. He had to sign a contract for his production, and they assigned him quotas, which weren't always suited to his particular conditions.

And then in regard to the people who worked for him, they imposed all sorts of responsibilities we hadn't had before. People who work for a state-owned company have certain kinds of insurance, So the private employer had to take on all that insurance. He had to function like an insurance company all by himself.

It amounted to a huge risk, as if it were deliberately designed to scare you away from hiring people. At the same time, there wasn't much choice. The prices for land weren't such that anyone was tempted to sell. And it wasn't very tempting, either, to just let the land and the whole farm go into a collective. My father would be too proud to take orders from someone who'd been his hand, or in any case from someone he knew had less knowledge than he did about how to run a farm. And it was out of the question, of course, to make one of the big farmers the leader of the collective. That would just be preserving the old system.

The mayor was tough. He exercised a kind of authority and control that finally got to be too much for my father. It wasn't like that in other places, but this fellow had made up his mind that he was going to drive off the big farmers with every available means. And by a few other means as well. We felt like we were being kicked off our own houses and lands.

Finally we gave up. We moved to West Germany.

We didn't sell the farm—that wouldn't have paid. That would have meant that we'd have a pile of money sitting in a bank over here, since we weren't allowed to take money with us. And there wasn't any point in smuggling money out. Nobody will pay anything for an East mark, and it'll be a long time before they do.

Father went on ahead. The labor market in West Germany was already crowded then, but he got a job as an agronomist. Then the rest of us followed, with our suitcases jammed. We lived just outside Hamburg.

There were a lot of people here that gave up. And that was the dumbest thing the GDR could have done. The old big farmers could have shown the new collectives how to avoid a lot of the mistakes they made in the beginning. There was a tremendous amount of waste, just out of sheer ignorance.

They didn't know what different soils were good for and what they weren't good for. Today it's a different story. The young LPG managers are extremely competent. They've made colossal increases in production since collectivization was pushed through all the way. But the figures they put out are still misleading, at least when it comes to proving that agriculture has improved by being made more and more scientific. Because they made so many mistakes when collectivization first started that the results were downright catastrophic, and compared to a catastrophe, almost anything at all looks good. Still, you've got to be impressed anyhow these days.

When I finished school, I went on and studied agronomy. After my exams, I decided to come back here and look at the farm. It still belonged to my father, after all.

It was just a whim.

Everything was changed, even then. The collective had taken over the land, and the fields were full of rye and rape. It was the time of year when the rape looks its best.

The people who lived here in the house paid a little rent to the town, which had taken over the care of the building, and from that rent I was allowed to draw out a little money from the bank in Ludwigslust. It was still our house, after all. And my father had been clever enough to write me out a certificate of part-ownership before I left—not for the land, but for the house. We also had money on deposit for the animals we'd sold. That was all we sold when we left.

And here in the farm-hand's cottage there were Frau Steppel and her daughter, who'd grown up to be a very pretty girl in the meantime. She worked at the farm machine shop, at the smithy, and that impressed me. A few years earlier, we'd played together. We'd been real good playmates. Now she was a smith and I was an agronomist, and she was a young woman and I was a young man, and, well, the result was, I decided to come back and visit.

When I went back to West Germany after the vacation, I got a good job as an agronomist, well paid. After three months I got on my bicycle and rode back here for a week —the ride only takes one day. And when spring came, I cycled over here again. At that time you could still do that.

And then we decided to get married.

I spoke to the mayor here—the new mayor. He said, of course I could live in my own house. And if I was going to come back, I also wanted to have a promise that I could go back to West Germany now and then to visit my parents. I got that promise, from the highest authorities in Berlin. I already knew quite a bit about how the collective functioned, and I talked to the manager. I was to get a job that corresponded to my education, although the salary was somewhat less, of course. But you can't compare salaries unless you compare a whole lot of other things at the same time, and anyway, the salary didn't matter as far as my decision was concerned. We could have gone to West Germany, but my mother-in-law was sick and didn't really want to leave, and we didn't want to leave her alone. Now, of course, we can't go over to visit, after all. I've written to Ulbricht about it, but he says no. It's a broken promise.

You could say it's unfair. After all, I chose to come here, and I've become a party member. If I were a grumbler, I'd figure they didn't trust me. But on the other hand, you can't take a regulation like that as if it were a personal reprimand. There are people in similar situations who say, "But I've got my family here. Certainly I wouldn't abandon my family." But there are people who would look at it as a perfect opportunity to do just that—get away from their families and their family responsibilities. There are plenty of examples. And the GDR doesn't just lose a worker, it also has to support his family.

How would it be if party members got to travel, but nobody else? Well, no doubt we'd have more party members, but think how corrupt the party would be. You have to understand what's necessary, even if it means limiting your own personal freedom of movement.

But let me tell you about it. I came over. I loaded a few things on a freight car and left—I didn't have much. In every sense, I guess, I was more at home over here than over there. We had our wedding, set up our house, we even had a honeymoon in Dresden. We came back, and my wife was expecting a baby, and working as a smith was too heavy for her. I started working, and after only two weeks they promised me that if I took correspondence courses I could take the place of the accountant and assistant manager of the collective, who was leaving to go back to school in order to be manager for an LPG.

So I started the correspondence courses. It was fascinating—not just how much there was to learn about the job, but also the way the perspectives opened up.

I'd always liked my work. I have to admit to a certain romantic strain in me—I liked the smell of grain, and the stable smell, and the smell of warm milk. I got a sensual pleasure out of farming.

When I'd studied those correspondence courses for a while, though, I understood that that wasn't enough. A person has to know *why* he's working, he has to be able to motivate it from outside himself and his own immediate interests. In the old days it used to happen that a big farm would just fall apart, because the farmer's wife had been unfaithful, say, and the farmer had started to drink. We can hold on to private motivation by means of bonuses. But there are levels where bonuses are no attraction, simply because it isn't money the person lacks, but rather some reason for existing in the first place.

In the old days there was religion. But what's religion? Marx called it opium, but that's too simple.

My wife is Catholic. And I can't tell her not to be, we have freedom of religion. She's a party member too. She knows what she's doing.

A Communist never has to doubt the meaning of his work. I know, there are people who imagine that you can't become a supervisor unless you're a member of the party. But that's a simplification. It's just that you make a better supervisor if you can explain to the workers why they're working—it's not that you get to be supervisor just because you're a party member.

I studied by correspondence for two years, and then I applied for party membership. Now I'm assistant manager of the collective, and I'm still going on with the correspondence courses. In five years I ought to be able to make manager, probably not here, but some other place. When you get right down to it, there's not such a big difference between the old-fashioned big farmer and the collective manager nowadays.

The old big farmer wouldn't get very far these days either, without a proper education and extensive automation and increased efficiency. But he'd have a tough time getting it.

I know that farmers have gotten together and formed cooperatives, with machine pools, in a few capitalist countries. But what do they actually do when the weather looks ugly and there's a rush to get in the crops? Whose crops get sacrificed? Those of the guy with the fewest shares— that is, the guy with the least land? That's how social inequality gets started. Or do those with less land pay just as big a share for the machines as those with a lot of land? In that case, they get, percentagewise, a smaller return on their investment than the big farmers do. In any case, the risk that a part of the total crop will be ruined gets greater. We don't take those risks here.

✿ Some Statistics From the LPG Theodor Körner, Wöbbelin

Three thousand acres, 137 members. Its lands originally comprised 17 large farms, 25 poultry farms, 50 small farms.* Employees of the LPG: 148.

Livestock: 1,200 cattle, 310 dairy cows, 1,100 sows, 100 boars, and poultry. In the fields: rye, mixed grain, sugar beets, potatoes, corn.

Milk production per cow: 3,000 liters** per year (average butterfat content: 3.5%).

---

*In the land reform program, large landowners—those with over 100 hectares (247 acres)—had their holdings expropriated without compensation. By this means, 514,730 farm workers, peasants, settlers, and refugees were provided with 7,776,000 acres of land at no expense.
**Equal to 3,170 quarts.

The membership includes 50 people who do not work because of age or disability.

The LPG has two day nurseries, a doctor, and a common dining room.

A veterinarian is called in from the district government in Ludwigslust.

Of the five members of the Wöbbelin town council, three represent the Theodor Körner LPG.

AGE DISTRIBUTION AMONG THE EMPLOYEES:

Under 25 years	5,	of whom	2	are	women
25 – 30 "	10,	" "	4	"	"
31 – 40 "	35,	" "	15	"	"
41 – 50 "	25,	" "	14	"	"
51 – 60 "	33,	" "	16	"	"
61 – 76 "	15,	" "	6	"	"
76 and over	25,	" "	10	"	"

❁ LPG Farmer Rudi Hoffs on Chickens

No, no, no, you have to watch out for these huge poultry farms. They don't get any good eggs. I went and looked at one of them. The hens live in little compartments from the time they're born until they die, and they get artificial food. It can't be any good. The meat won't be the same, either. It's all fake, the eggs and the hens, and the fertilized eggs that come out of hens like that will hatch into fake chickens. And when those fake chickens grow up and lay eggs, why, they'll be even more worthless. Eggs like that just can't be worth a damn. And they'll get worse with each generation of chickens. Oh, it'll catch up with them all right. Hens have to be let out. We've always had the hens running around loose. They push through some of those reforms without thinking things out. Like, they think they can transport milk cheaper by building pipelines. But did they ever stop to think who's going to clean out their pipelines, from the inside? They never thought of that, by God.

✵ Notes on
Joachim and Wolfgang

Joachim was born just outside Königsberg. His father was actually a carpenter by trade, but Joachim only remembers him from the war years. Joachim is a Catholic but doesn't go to Mass. Still, it would never occur to him to leave the Church. His five children go to Sunday school, and he says he never could have married someone of a different faith.

"Religion doesn't mean anything to me," he says. "When I was in the Foreign Legion, it meant something. We started praying as soon as we stopped killing."

He remembers that as a child he used to go with his father to a park on Sundays and sit and listen to a band. Joachim was the only child. When he was four years old, they moved into town, to a three-room apartment on Oreler Ring. In 1945 they moved by a roundabout and circuitous route to Hasselförde, where one of Joachim's aunts had a farmhouse and 40 acres of land. Joachim lived there until, at 19, he crossed the border to West Germany and set out to join the French Foreign Legion.

—Then came five years in the Legion. I've been all over the world, almost, but I finally came back. They needed people in agriculture, and I had a little experience. But I didn't go back to Hasselförde, I went to an LPG—the Einheit—in Spornitz.

I never even thought of staying in West Germany. I had my mother here, you know, and I was born in Königsberg —I just wanted to get as far east as I could. I felt more at home here. And everything I owned was here. It wasn't much, but it was here. Then too, I might have had trouble getting a job in the West, but over here they needed people. I started off in the cow barns. The pay wasn't particularly good in those days.

Then I met my wife. She was working with the hogs—she's from Pomerania. Anyway, we had twins, and then all the trouble started. They wanted her back with the hogs afterward. They said the children would be just as well off at the day nursery, but we didn't think so. We thought a mother should be with her family, so we said the hogs would just have to get along without her. So they said we couldn't make demands on the whole commune if we didn't both of us work. That was the LPG chairman who said that, and it sort of burned me up. Anyway, they said my wife was trained to take care of hogs and at the nursery they were trained to take care of children, and so we didn't make any more trouble. But then we had our third baby. It's not easy for Catholics to stop.

Then they decided at a meeting that everybody in the LPG should each do an extra 2½ acres of beets. But I didn't want to, and neither did my wife. We wanted to be with the kids. So we didn't do any beets—and they sent us a bill for damages! We just didn't pay it. Then we had our fourth child, and we told them again that my wife wanted to take care of the children instead of the hogs. They said it would be less work for her to take care of the hogs. So she just didn't go any more. And so they told us we'd have to leave.

The worker is protected here, you know. You can't be fired, they just transfer you, and that's exactly what we wanted. Now we live here outside Neustadt. We've got three rooms for 35 marks. Yes, my wife works, otherwise we couldn't make ends meet. I make 450 marks [a month], and she works half-time and makes about 200. She's in the kitchen at the nursery. My mother works in Hasselförde. I haven't seen her for five years.

▣ WOLFGANG, 21 YEARS OLD

Born in Rom, on the railway line between Parchim and
Lübz. Left school in 1960, the same year his parents moved
to West Germany: "I don't know why, and I don't care."
Where do they live? "I don't know. I'm not interested. No,
I don't have any brothers or sisters. . . . What do I do with
my spare time? I read. . . . No, we never had any books
at home."

▣ JOACHIM ON WOLFGANG

We've been working together for two years. He told me
once about his father—he worked for the railroad—that he
spent all his free time on streetcars. I mean, there weren't
any streetcars in Rom, and for that matter he'd probably
never seen a streetcar in his whole life, but he read everything he could get about streetcars. At work it was all
trains and timetables, but off work it was all streetcars.
Once he went to Rostock to see some real streetcars. The
whole time he just rode streetcars, just sat there in the cars
and took down every little detail he could see. Finally the
Secret Police came, wondering what the hell he was doing
—they thought he was some kind of spy. They let him go,
of course, but he got so mad at the secret police that he
emigrated. That's what Wolfgang told me. He's never said
anything else about his parents.

▣ Joachim and Wolfgang
—A Free Afternoon

They were supposed to have spent the afternoon putting
in a drainage pipe at Lewitz. The trench was finished, and
the pipe was supposed to have come during the morning,
but when it didn't show up, they put down their spades

and went to call the supervisor to find out what had happened.

"It's on its way," he answered.

"*Where* on its way?" Wolfgang asked into the phone.

The pipe was due in from Kleinlübz. The first shipment was supposed to have been loaded and sent off that morning, but the truck driver had stayed home with the flu and there was no available replacement. Or so Wolfgang was told when he called a second time, after the supervisor had had a chance to look into it.

"So what'll we do now?" Wolfgang asked him.

"Is the trench done?"

"Yes."

"Then you can wait."

"How long should we wait? Do you want us to wait till the driver gets over the flu?"

The supervisor promised to get a driver.

"Well, we don't mind waiting," Wolfgang answered. "We've got plenty of time."

"That pipe has to be in the ground this week," the supervisor said.

"That depends on when it gets here."

Wolfgang and Joachim sat down in the Stadt Hamburg to wait. According to Wolfgang, there was nothing else to be done.

Wolfgang is 21 years old, Joachim 36.

Wolfgang (loudly): Well, this is the Socialist Planned Economy for you. If somebody gets the flu, it all falls apart. The pipe has to be in the ground this week, hah! What was it we were supposed to do next week, Joachim? The pipe won't get put in, and there won't be any drainage. It's going to be a wet summer, the water won't run off, and the grain'll be ruined, all because some truck driver who was supposed to drive from Kleinlübz to Neustadt one Monday morning in March came down with the flu. That's called a Planned Economy.

Joachim: Take it easy, and don't talk so loud. We'll get the pipe this afternoon.

—Well, it hasn't come yet. The boys at the LPG will get extra work and even less pay—and no bonus—because they haven't managed to increase production. And the truck driver who got the flu, which is really a hangover for all I know, he doesn't lose a penny. That's the Planned Economy for you!

—Come on, Wolfgang, quiet down. You're not losing a penny, either. After all, *we're* sitting here getting paid, and *we're* not working. Besides, you're just assuming that guy in Kleinlübz has a hangover—that's not fair. If you're going to talk like that, I think I'll sit at another table. If you have to criticize, then don't just make guesses.

—Afraid, Joachim?

—No, I'm not afraid.

—You know what *I* think.

—I don't think you should talk about it here.

—If we'd won the war with England, things wouldn't be the way they are today.

—Bullshit.

—It's not worthy of the German people to live like we live.

—Bullshit.

—We're not going to go on living like this, either.

—Come on, what's that got to do with drainpipes? Some guy gets sick and we wait a few hours, that's all. That kind of thing can happen anywhere. You're 21 years old. You're sharper than I am, you've read more, but you ought to be more careful about what you say.

—Hah! Listen to that! Exactly! Do you know what happened to me in school? I was expelled. I didn't get to go on as far as I wanted to, or even as far as they said I could. You say yourself that I'm sharper than you are. Do you know why I had to leave?

—You told me, and I don't doubt it.

—An "inadvisable remark," that's why.

—Yeah, so you said, and that's just what I'm telling you: You should watch out you don't talk too much.

—Why? Why do I have to watch what I say? You don't change society by keeping quiet. . . . Do you agree that we live under a dictatorship?

—I don't want to answer that.

—You have to answer that. Have you ever read *Neues Deutschland?* *

—Of course.

—What is it it says right up under the name? Doesn't it say "Workers of the World, Unite!"?

—I guess so.

—No guessing about it. That's what it says. And what does it say in all the books that Communism is?

—I won't answer. I don't want to talk about it. Look, I'm not a Communist, anyway. I'm not a political person. And I don't want you to trap me.

—You *are* afraid. You're a member of the proletariat, and what it says is that Communism is the dictatorship of the proletariat. So who can deny that we live under a dictatorship?

—We have the same job, Wolfgang—we're both workers, members of the proletariat. It seems to me you could use your intelligence to see the consequences of that—I mean, if you say that we live under the dictatorship of the proletariat.

—Well, listen to that! Don't underestimate yourself, you can think too, you know. But do you really mean that my intelligence should make me keep my mouth shut? In that case, you just don't understand. We've worked together for two years, and you say you know my views on things. Well, have you ever noticed that I'm against Socialism?

—I wouldn't say that.

*"New Germany"—the official East German party newspaper.

   —And I'm not. If I were, then I'd really say to hell with the damned drainpipe.

   —But isn't that what you *do* say? I mean, I'd really like to know. Are you mad because production is being slowed down, or do you really enjoy it?

   ——Joachim, you know this business with the drainpipe isn't just something that's happening to us, here, this afternoon. You know it's not just an accident, that's never happened before and won't ever happen again. You know there are other workers, and not only workers, who are sitting around this afternoon with nothing to do and still drawing their pay, just because of some stupid accident. You know damned well, Joachim, that there's nothing in this country they talk about as much as production, and the necessity of increasing production, and that even so we don't produce enough—and that it isn't our fault. Everybody knows that. Germans know how to work. Germans aren't lazy. If we'd been able to choose our own form of Socialism, things would look different around here. We're just a part of Russia, for God's sake. That old fart in Berlin doesn't do anything without asking the Russians first, you know that. The kind of Socialism we have here was designed for the Russians, for a primitive people. The Germans are a people of culture, and they ought to be allowed to choose their own Socialism. . . .

   —You mean we should do what they've done in Prague* and Warsaw. . . .

   —No, that won't work here.

   —No, I don't think so either.

   —There are too many weapons here. They've got a carbine for every ten workers.

   —Oh, you mean because of that. There isn't enough opposition.

---

*This conversation takes place in the early part of 1968, while the liberal Dubček regime was in power in Czechoslovakia.

—Everyone isn't as sluggish as you are.

—Weapons won't make the difference either way.

—That's what you think. I know. I've been in plant security. One shot in the air, one in the ground, and the third shot to kill. . . .

—Would you shoot, Wolfgang?

—Of course. It's an order.

—But after what you just said . . .

—Absolutely. If I've got a carbine in my hands, it's because they gave it to me to shoot with. After that, it doesn't have anything to do with what I believe. It's orders.

—Wolfgang, I'll say it again: You're 21 years old and you don't know what you're talking about. You may read more and spend more time thinking than I do, but you still don't know what the hell you're talking about.

—You just keep bringing up my age—that's not much of an argument.

—O.K., then, have you ever killed anyone?

—No.

—So you don't know what it's like. All right. You can kill once without knowing what you're doing. But you can't stop a real revolution with one shot, and the second shot you aim right at somebody isn't as easy to squeeze off as the first one was. *I* wouldn't shoot.

—You can't refuse to carry out an order!

—Doesn't it make any difference to you who you're shooting?

—You can't take it personally. When I'm ordered to open fire, then I'm no longer Wolfgang Rentz. In principle I'm just a part of the rifle, or a part of the trigger, just like the lieutenant who orders me to shoot. The man who pulls the trigger is just a part of the law, that's all.

—And it doesn't make any difference to you who the bullet hits.

—No, it's not *me* shooting him.

—It doesn't make any difference to you who you point the sights at.

—Yes, that's what I'm saying.

—If you miss, is it the law that misses?

—No, in that case I'd be a bad shot. But I'm not a bad shot.

—O.K., youre not a bad shot. But what if your hand shakes?

—My hand wouldn't shake. If my hand shook, I'd be a bad shot.

—All right, your hand wouldn't shake. But let's say a fly lands on your eye just at the instant you fire.

—Then it's possible I'd miss.

—So it's possible you'd miss. So you miss . . .

—And?

—Who is it that misses?

—I do.

—If you make the shot, who is it that makes it?

—The law.

—And when you carry away the body, who are you then?

—I'm not involved in it. It's not my doing.

—And when you wake up at night in a cold sweat and your heart pounding because you've just seen it all over again in your sleep? I can promise you, Wolfgang, you don't ever get free of the people you kill. It's not that simple.

—If I didn't know you, Joachim, I'd say you were soft.

—You're the one that's soft—in the head. First you say that the Socialism we have is bad, and then you say that you wouldn't hesitate to shoot anyone who wanted to change it, that is, if they ordered you to shoot them. I don't understand that. Listen, when de-Nazification was going on, all the war criminals said they'd just been acting on orders, and there were other people who said we shouldn't judge them too harshly, because if they hadn't committed

those crimes, why then they'd have been punished themselves. But do you know who it was who said that? It was
the ones who hadn't been involved in it, or else the ones
who had something to hide. The ones that weren't involved in it themselves were suckers for that romantic crap
about command.

—But, Joachim, *you* weren't involved.

—Right, and *I* believed all that crap too. I admit that.
But you can't deny that I did what I could to find out what
really goes on in a war. Why do you think I joined the
Legion?

—You wanted adventure.

—Right, I wanted adventure, that's right. But why do
you suppose I wanted adventure? I mean, I'd grown up
during the war. I wasn't a soldier or anything, but I grew
up during the war. You didn't, but you can figure out that
if you lived in Könisberg, there wasn't exactly any shortage of adventure.

—Joachim, I'm tired of war stories. You can't meet anyone in this country who was born before 1945 who doesn't
start telling you all about what happened to him during the
war. Since 1945 there hasn't been a novel written in this
country that isn't all about somebody's experiences during
the war.

—All right, I'm not going to talk about the war. I only
want you to know that it's possible to refuse to obey an
order.

—Not without getting shot yourself, it isn't. Maybe *you*
can let yourself get shot, but not me. It's not me that's
going to get shot. First somebody would have to convince
me that the guy I was going to shoot was superior to me
as a human being. Even then I'd shoot. If I didn't, somebody else would.

—My father was in the SS, Wolfgang. What did your
father do?

—Who cares? I don't care what your father did, or what

my father did. I'm like Goethe. He didn't care about his
children, and he didn't care about his parents. I don't have
any children, and I don't care about my parents. I'm
beyond that.

—Right, Wolfgang, I know you're superior to most of
us. But listen to me: My father was in the SS.

—You said that.

—Forgive me for saying so, but I think you would have
been too.

—I'll admit I don't see what's so awful about it.

—Do you think I'm just sitting here insulting my father? What was your father? Was he in the SS too? Or
don't you know?

—He wasn't in the SS, but that doesn't have anything
to do with it. He was a railway clerk. He still is, for all I
care. He was born a railway clerk and he'll die a railway
clerk.

—I'm not trying to give you a hard time, Wolfgang. But
listen: My father was in the SS. I was his child, and during
the whole war I didn't doubt for a single moment that what
he was doing was right. You know how that goes—that's
just the way it was. But no matter what you think, you'll
never get me to believe that what the SS did really *was*
right. Nobody will ever make me believe that. But we
believed it then. My father believed it, my mother believed
it—everybody believed it. For two years he was stationed
in Königsberg, and he used to come home in the evenings
once in a while. He didn't talk about what he did, or at least
not so I could hear it, but I don't think he talked about it
to Mother either. I never saw him rub his hands about
having had a good day down at the SS, but then, on the
other hand, I don't remember him ever complaining about
what a stinking job he had. And it was a stinking job, I
know that now. When we fled from Königsberg, he meant
to go to France, but as you know, it wasn't so easy to get
all the way across Europe. Anyway, the Russians got us

and took him away. He was executed. They got him to confess that he'd killed 12 Jews, and that in 1942 he'd hit a Russian woman in the mouth. That was enough. He wasn't one of the big war criminals, you couldn't call him that, but even so, just think how carefully they kept track of everything he did. Do you remember if maybe you slapped some woman on the mouth three years ago?

—I said I was tired of war stories.

—This isn't a war story. This is an after-the-war story. Anyway, my father was going to join the Foreign Legion. He and one of his friends were going to meet each other there. That's what belief in the Fatherland had come to: He was a deserter, and his friend was a deserter. Anybody that found him out in some field could kill him. Defending Germany just didn't matter to him any more. The only thing that did matter to him any more was to be able to go on practicing his profession, which was killing people.

—You're condemning him too easily, Joachim. That's not you talking, it's all the postwar propaganda that's gotten to you.

—Who was it that lay out in the hay fields with him? Who was it that joined the Foreign Legion for him? I can say for sure that I didn't know my father, since I'd never really talked to him before we were out crawling around in the fields. But I know one thing, and that's that he gave me a very simple idea of what it means to kill.

—You don't expect me to believe that that's why you joined the Legion!

—You know, deep down I don't really believe for a moment that he liked killing. But what was he supposed to do? There was only one safe place he could go, or pretty much safe. He couldn't just lie there and say the job he'd had for ten years—and the only job he could still live on —was a stinking job. He couldn't very well say that to his wife and his son the first time he talked to them about it. The only thing that was important for him was to escape, and the only way he could escape was to go on with the same work, which was killing—and killing anyone, killing with all the idealism peeled off, all the racism, all the nationalism, all the National Socialism. There were a lot of old Nazi officers in the Legion, let me tell you.

—I don't doubt it. But *you* weren't one of them.

—No, but even so I went there in order to live up to my father, somehow.

—Bullshit.

—Maybe, maybe not. I still think that's about what it was. You know, you can say "Bullshit" because you don't know what that black uniform stood for, and the death's-head. But when you talk about shooting to kill—"third shot to kill" and that stuff—and when you talk about having to obey orders, then I can see that it would be just as easy for you to get trapped by the system as it was for me. You shouldn't make yourself out better than you are.

—Listen, I'll say what I said before. That death's-head insignia was pretty naive, O.K., but otherwise I don't understand what was so terrible about being in the SS.

—You don't understand. . . . One day in Morocco I was ordered to shoot down an Arab woman and her children. I refused. "I won't do it," I said.

—That's idiotic.

—No, believe me, I've done a lot of killing. And I've seen the people I've killed, I've seen them crumple up and double up and lie all stretched out crooked. . . . I looked a Frenchman right in the eyes before I put a bullet in his stomach. I'm not bragging about it. It's nothing to brag about. But I wasn't afraid of doing my job in the Legion. A year ago I put in my name as a volunteer for Vietnam, and I would have been accepted—I know I would, even though there aren't very many who are—but my wife didn't want me to go. I've got five kids. So I dropped the idea. The point is, I'm not afraid to fight, but I won't shoot a woman and her children.

—You're a sentimentalist.

—I don't care. It doesn't make any difference at all *why* I said I wouldn't shoot. The main thing is that I said it. The main thing is that anyone can say it. I don't think the discipline in the Legion is any less strict than it was in the SS. It just never occurred to anyone that they could refuse.

—But the Arab woman did get shot, and her children too.

—Yes, but somebody else did the shooting.

—Well, does that make you any happier?

—He could have refused too.

—In that case, the third guy would have shot.

—And he could have refused.

—Then the fourth guy.

—We *all* could have refused.

—Then *you* would have been shot.

—Well, you have to take that risk. Anyway, I wasn't shot. And the others wouldn't have been either. You don't really think they would have executed a whole company for the sake of one Arab woman.

—Joachim, you know, we actually started out talking about a revolt here in Germany. You can't answer that with a story about your father or some Arab woman.

—I don't believe in a revolt in this country. I said that.

—I don't care what you believe. If I say a revolt is possible . . . For that matter, how do we know there hasn't already been a revolt? They'd never tell us about it anyway.

—We'd know about it. Things like that always get out. There hasn't been any revolt, and there isn't going to be.

—But if I say a revolt is possible, then all this talk about how you can refuse to shoot is still beside the point. The only weapons around are Russian.

—No, German.

—They were Russian in 1953.

—Now they'd be German. The Germans want Socialism.

—The Russians would help out, that's for sure. You

certainly don't think they'd just let it happen here too? All right, in Poland they can let the students revolt, and in Czechoslovakia they can let them do anything they want. But not in Germany. Do you know why?

—Well . . .

—Quite simply because they're afraid. Pure fear of the Germans. And they have reason to be, after everything the Russians have done to Germany.

—Or after everything the Germans have done to Russia.

—Why did Germany lose the war?

—Don't get into that.

—Did they lose because their soldiers weren't as good?

—I don't think so.

—You know so. You know the German soldier was superior to the Russian, the English, the French, and the American. Everybody knows that. Everybody knows the German soldier had the best morale and the German army had the best discipline of any army ever. Everyone knows the Germans had the best weapons. Everybody knows Wernher von Braun was German, and that he gave us weapons that no other country in the world had anything to compare with. But we lost, and do you know why?

—We're not going to talk about it. You just can't say things like that about Wernher von Braun, and about how the German soldier was superior. That kind of crap just won't stand up any more.

—You've seen the Russians, they're primitive people. Have you ever met a Russian that can speak German? And you were here, you know what it was like when the Red Army came to Germany—they behaved like animals. But what soldiers do you think it is the Russians send here? Don't you really think it's their best troops? Do you think they'd dare send anyone else? But if the best are like the ones we have around here, then what do you think the rest of the Russians are like? . . . But O.K., for the time being these primitive people are our friends, and we've made our

form of Socialism to suit them, although the only thing
they know how to do is smuggle watches. In spite of all
that, it's East Germany out of all the Socialist countries in
Eastern Europe that's developed the furthest. What does
that tell you? Have we had any help? Our factories were
all shipped to Russia after the war, and God knows what
all we've had to pay in reparations. And what does that tell
you? Doesn't it tell you that the German people were
meant to rule? Doesn't it tell you that the Germans are a
superior people? You say we shouldn't talk about Wernher
von Braun, but why shouldn't we? Because he was one of
those overly gifted men the German people give birth to,
and because he happened to work for a government that
suffered military defeat, that's why. But let's take Goethe.
Is there another poet like Goethe? Is there any other poem
like *Faust*, Part Two? The first part is good too, but it's
narrative. It's in the second part that he's a genius. No
regime can keep Goethe quiet. . . . So which people do you
think is the rabble? And which one is going to be the
aristocracy? Why do you think Germany is divided? Because they're afraid of us, they're afraid that the strongest
will win out in the end, after all. You can't turn a master
race into slaves.

  —Shut up, Wolfgang! That's all bullshit! The German
people have already shown the world what they're like.
You just can't talk like that any more.

  —In the world of the future there's only going to be
room for intelligent people. That's what it's all coming to.
Right here we're doing all sorts of work in order to produce high-class livestock. On all the LPG's they feed the
cows scientifically so that they'll give the highest possible
production. And look at hog breeding—the worst animals
certainly aren't allowed to breed new ones. They're going
to come to realize that the same thing has to be done with
human beings, and there isn't much time left. It's no
longer a question of being a humanitarian in general and

soft-hearted to some Arab woman now and then. The inferior specimens should be sterilized.

—Shut up!

—That's typical. People don't dare listen to it. You don't dare listen to it. You've bred five children yourself without knowing what you're doing.

—Of course you know that Hitler tried breeding stations.

—Hitler made a mistake: He shouldn't have let himself be defeated. And it wasn't necessary, either. He was surrounded by cowards and traitors.

—Damn it, Wolfgang, you're only 21 years old.

—That has nothing to do with it. You admit that I'm one of the overly gifted, and they're afraid of me. They won't give me the education my ability deserves.

—That's your own fault. Anyway, I can't say you're very gifted when you can't see the consequences of what you're saying.

—You think only the cowards are gifted.

—Well, actually, I don't see what was so smart about what you were expelled for.

—Well, that was the day Kennedy was assassinated, and I said it would have been better if it had been Khrushchev. Would the world look like it does today if Kennedy was alive? And what happened to Khrushchev afterward? They got rid of him. Why shouldn't I tell the truth about it? Today most people agree with me: It would have been better if Khrushchev had been murdered instead of Kennedy. Kennedy was gifted. Khrushchev was a peasant, who had to bang on the table with his shoe in order to sound convincing. That's primitive.

—It's just a custom. I've been all over the world, in Africa and Asia, and people don't all do things the same way. I've been clear around the Mediterranean.

—Well, then, it's a primitive custom. Have you ever seen a German bang his shoe on the table?

—I've seen Germans do other things that are what you might call "primitive."

—Yeah, those people you hang around with. I'm talking about people who are supposed to be educated. In the world of the future, primitive people just won't have the right to exist. The rabble can be exterminated—they're worthless.

—Things aren't going to work out for you, Wolfgang. You're really going from bad to worse. If you were 80, I wouldn't say anything, but you're 21. You were a Pioneer. You've been in the FDJ. You said you call yourself a Socialist. Now, I don't know anything about politics, and I don't belong to any party. I was never in the FDJ or the Pioneers and I don't even go to militia meetings. And I don't call myself a Socialist, because I don't know what Socialism is. But there's one thing I do know. You're no Socialist—you're a Nazi! I'm not saying I'm morally perfect, I've done lots of terrible things in my life. I've killed people, for example, and you haven't. But I know one thing, Wolfgang: Of the two of us, you're the one that's a criminal, not me. . . . You see that man over there—that's Karl—I know him. You see how he walks—O.K., you laugh at him. You say you're superior to him because he can't control his arms and legs and because he has trouble talking. You'd be able to shoot him. Absolutely. That's the way you talk.

—Yes, I could shoot him.

—For you he just doesn't have any value as a human being. Let's take the Arabs, what do you say about them? And the Jews, what about them? And what about the Negroes and the Chinese and the Indians and everybody else that doesn't look like you, tall and blond, the perfect SS type. What *about* them, Wolfgang? You don't even have to say it. I know exactly what you think. They should be exterminated.

—Yes, they should. They should be exterminated.

—Who's going to do it?

—The German people.

—What German people?

—The unified German people.

—There's no such thing, Wolfgang. You forget that. I live 25 miles from my brother, but I can't go see him. And your parents live in Germany too, but you can't go visiting. The weapons the "unified German people" *do* have are aimed at each other. Aren't you forgetting that, Wolfgang?

—You just don't have any perspective, you're too shortsighted. You're talking about today. I'm talking about tomorrow.

—It won't be any different tomorrow, Wolfgang. You've got to look at things the way they are. When you *do* take up weapons, you'll be pointing them at your parents, Wolfgang. Are you going to shoot?

—No question about it, yes.

—But you won't be shooting in the name of Nazism, Wolfgang. You'll be shooting in the name of Socialism. And I know good Socialists who'd hesitate.

—You just don't understand, Joachim.

✹ Declaration of Solidarity in Warsaw*

Warsaw (ADN/SVZ), March 20, 1968—Throughout Poland, meetings are being held in which the people continue to express their enthusiastic confidence in the Polish United Workers' Party and its Central Committee. Fifty thousand party members in Dolny Slask and 10,000 in

---

*The meetings described here represented efforts by the Polish Communist government to counteract the then-widespread agitation, chiefly by students, for reforms and greater freedom. The attitude of East German leaders was one of sympathy and support for their Warsaw counterparts.

Szczecin declared, along with the chairman of the teachers union, that they oppose all efforts to resist the power of the people.

✹ W. Weinholdt—Pioneer Leader, FDJ Secretary, Teacher

I think I'm a typical example of the kind of person that's emerged thanks to the victory of Socialism in Germany.

I grew up in a home for orphans in Berlin/Neukölln. I was born in 1933, and I stayed at the home until 1945 and then trained as a gardener.

What was it like at the orphanage? What sort of upbringing did they give you?

Let's not talk about that.

Why not?

Nothing special happened at the orphanage. I worked as a gardener, and then when the GDR got its own army, I joined up and trained as a noncommissioned officer for four years. Then for two years I worked as leader for a youth club, and then I passed a qualifying exam and spent two years in administration with the district council in Ludwigslust. At the same time, I was taking a course to be a Pioneer leader, and a correspondence course for my teaching credential. I took my teaching exams in February 1966.

Where?

Partly in Schwerin and partly in Berlin.

When did you get married?

I was married in 1955.

What's your wife do?

My wife is a sewing-machinist, and also a trained Pioneer leader, like myself. We had our first child after one year of marriage. The second after three years, and the third after five.

Where does your wife work?

She works at the laundry downstairs. Everything we have here we've worked for ourselves—three rooms and kitchen, bath, TV, furniture—we didn't inherit anything. I'm a teacher now, and a Pioneer leader.

When did you come to Neustadt?

I came to Neustadt as a Pioneer leader in 1962.

What does a Pioneer leader do?

In the summers we go to Pioneer camp. My hobby is collecting Pioneer badges from all over the world. I've got badges here from Poland, Czechoslovakia, Yugoslavia, and the Soviet Union, of course. Here's one from Albania, and one from China. I'd love to get one from Sweden.

What do you do at camp?

At camp we exchange addresses. We have a great deal of correspondence with the Lenin* Pioneers.

Do the children who join the Pioneers get better grades?

The children who join the Pioneers are not always the best students by any means.

Do all Pioneers go on to the FDJ?

Most of them do. It's mostly only the ones from religious homes who don't go on. Next year we won't have any Christians at all, so we hope the continuation will be 100 percent.

What's your opinion of Youth Dedication?

Youth Dedication, which takes place at Easter, is a solemn affair. It's the big step from the world of the child to the world of the adult. The young people prepare for it by going out into the factories to talk to workers and supervisors, so they can get an idea of what awaits them in their working life.

Isn't there some military training too?

The FDJ goes back to the Fascist tradition, but its purpose is to build a defense against Fascism. The young people also get to hear lectures on the meaning of life, that

*I.e., Soviet.

is, on whether labor is a constraint or a necessity, and lectures on problems of love and sex. They are very interested in these lectures.

❄ Arithmetic Problems from a Second-grade Textbook

119. The sugar refinery is expecting 42 freight cars today, but 20 extra cars arrive. How many freight cars must be unloaded?

120. The collectives in the neighboring districts deliver their sugar beets to the refinery in trucks. Today the Schöndorf LPG sent 34 trucks to the refinery, and the Sommerfeld LPG sent 30 trucks. How many trucks carried sugar beets to the refinery?

* * * * *

430. The Pioneers are standing in formation. On one side there are 40 Pioneers, 10 in each row. How many rows are there on this side?

431. Fifty Pioneers have been invited to the Pioneer House. Ten Pioneers come from each school. State the question and the answer.

432. In a parade there are six Pioneers in each row of marchers. The Pioneers in the first ten rows are to carry flags. How many flags will be needed?

433. The next ten rows are made up of 50 Pioneers dressed in gymnastic uniforms. How many Pioneers are in each row?

❈ Hermann Kuhn
and the FDJ

They can't keep me from watching Hamburg. I want to know something about the world, and so I have to watch Hamburg. Nobody watches Berlin around here. Walk through town and look at the antennas—they're all pointing the same way, and it's not toward Berlin. They don't want us to watch Hamburg, but they're such a bore about it. A couple of years ago the FDJ drove down the streets with a loudspeaker and urged people to turn their antennas. On a few houses, they climbed up and turned them themselves. The next day there was one man who climbed up and turned his antenna back to Hamburg again. They ran his name in the *Schweriner Volkszeitung*.

We can only get one channel from Hamburg. In order to get the other one, you need a special relay attachment, but they only make them on the black market. Right now there are two boys in Ludwigslust making them, and they travel around selling them. The police are after them. If you're at someone's house where they're getting the second channel, don't tell anyone about it.

❈ Heinrich Lübke, President of
the Federal Republic, Speaks on
Television—From Hamburg, March 1

Esteemed Ladies and Gentlemen:
The attacks that have been made on me for some time now have been intensified during the past few weeks. They originated in East Berlin and were intended to

defame the presidency, and thus the entire Federal Republic, in the eyes of the world. These accusations have since been taken up by others, by people who, though not Communists, oppose the present political order in the Federal Republic, or by people who have allowed themselves to be misled.

I have been accused of disloyalty. It has been maintained, further, that during the war I planned and built concentration camps. These allegations have already been repudiated by the federal government, and disproved by the publication of the documents in question.

I have taken no legal action, because I know that those who spread these charges against me desire nothing more than to instigate a trial that will drag on for years.

I turn to you personally, because I consider it my duty to defend the office of president of the Federal Republic, and because I am of the opinion that one must complete a task once it has been undertaken.

I previously belonged to the Center Party, and from 1931 I was a member of the Prussian Diet. On April 1, 1933, several organizations, including the Deutsche Bauernschaft,* of which I was the managing director, were dissolved by the Nazis, and I was myself arrested, but soon freed. On February, 5, 1934, I was again arrested, and was held for over 20 months without its being possible to bring any action against me.

The charges made against me by the National Socialists were refuted. Nevertheless, the Soviet Union has revived these Nazi charges and is disseminating them in the Federal Republic of Germany.

During the war every person who did not become a soldier was required to work. I was employed at the Schlempp Architects Bureau in Berlin, which, shortly after the outbreak of the war, was assigned to operate

*"The German Peasantry."

under the General Construction Warden for the Reich Capital. Neither the Schlempp Construction Group nor the Architects Bureau ever planned or contributed to the planning of any project having the character of a penal or concentration camp. Those who defame and accuse me have known this for a long time. So that they will not succeed in misrepresenting the truth, I have taken this opportunity, ladies and gentlemen, of speaking to you in my own behalf. . . .

✖ At Home After "Operation Snowflake"

Where were you last week?

I was on maneuvers—"Operation Snowflake."

What kind of maneuvers was that?

The Pioneers and the FDJ.

Why were you having maneuvers?

On account of the 50th anniversary of the Soviet army, and the 25th anniversary of the liberation of Volgograd.

How many of you were there?

There was over a hundred of us.

All from the same class?

No, not from here. Most of them came from Bützow.

What did you do?

Oh, we had service caps with the Soviet star, and wooden rifles that we made ourselves.

Who led the maneuvers?

I don't know. But there was a Comrade Lieutenant Colonel from the People's Army, and three other men. And there was a girl from the seventh grade who was the commander.

What'd you do?

First, I helped with the leaflets in the morning.

What'd they say?

"Comrades in arms! We at the Central Command Staff say to you: Give all of your strength for the liberation of your home."

What'd you do then?

Then we got our battle orders, and then we got our direction of march.

Who gave the battle orders?

Jutta, the commander. Then we marched with the Red Flag up in front, and the orders were to advance to the area where the enemy was hidden.

What were you supposed to do there?

We were supposed to take up our positions and wait for the order to charge the enemy.

Why couldn't you just attack right away?

There were mines, and destroyed bridges. You could see the first mine field from a long way away—it was just balloons. In order to clear it, we were supposed to remove them without breaking any.

Then did the battle start?

No, then we took up new positions and passed out leaflets and made notice sheets to paste up, one for each company, and then we got sausages. While we were eating, the Comrade Lieutenant Colonel came up and said the enemy was going to be surrounded by all three companies. We had radios to keep contact with the other companies.

What time did the attack start?

Two o'clock.

How did you do it?

Two companies attacked from the front, and the third attacked from the rear.

Did you really fight?

We just yelled "Bang," and they surrendered. That meant the battle was over, and the enemy had been wiped out. We took their flag and put up our own—the Red Flag.

Is that how it happened at Stalingrad?

Volgograd. We call it Volgograd.

✿ Lissi Bedau, After School

We had Pioneers this afternoon. We rode out to Turkode on our bicycles to look at the cow barns. I like to do things like that. I don't plan to spend the rest of my life taking care of cows—I mean, not if I can help it—but everybody ought to see the cow barns. At school we talk a lot about agriculture, but it's all theoretical, so to speak. If a cow gives 4,000 liters of milk per year, and production is to be raised by eight percent, then how much milk will the cow give next year? That's the sort of thing we figure out at school, without asking the cow, so to speak—I mean, whether it's reasonable to ask a cow that already gives 4,000 liters of milk to give an extra 320. What do you do with a cow like that?

✿ Werner Bahlke, on Switching Parties

When I went to the teachers college in Neuholster, I studied mainly Latin and English, but I hadn't yet decided to become a teacher. You had your choice. It was an Aufbau school, where gifted children of poor parents could go. The teachers were middle-class democrats, I think; I can't remember any Socialist teachers from that time. But of course we dealt with Marx in history class.

My father was a small farmer in Brentz, and I went back to Brentz as a teacher after my release from the POW camp in Norway. The workers were astounded when I could quote Marx. I wore a tie, so I was obviously not a worker myself. "I learned it in school," I told them. It was a question of making a quick adjustment in order to adapt yourself to the new social order. For some people it's been easy. Other people still haven't managed it after 23 years.

As soon as I came to Brentz, I started doing political work, in the school and in the community. At the same time, I wanted to go on with my education in my own field, which was primarily history.

This is an interesting district here, around Neustadt. There are traces of various Stone Age settlements. I usually make excavations during the summers—I have contacts with the institute in Rostock, and I'm hoping my work will lead to a doctor's degree eventually.

While I was in Brentz, I didn't have much time for that kind of thing. That's why in 1956 I applied for a transfer to Neustadt, and since coming here I haven't taken such a lively interest in party work. But I'm in close touch with what's going on—my wife works at the Rathaus, she's Thiele's secretary. I'm active, but I don't want to have too many assignments. Life and strength have their limits. Right at the moment we're trying to get meeting rooms for the Culture Club. We meet once a month, have a lecture and discussions. We usually meet at the Körner, or at the Veterans Club. But in Ludwigslust the Culture Club has its own quarters, a place where the intellectuals in town can get together. I go there every Wednesday. We ought to be able to fix up something in that beautiful old fortress of ours.

I'd like to put in a museum there too, where we could show the history of the area from the earliest finds right up to the present. That's another problem—all the town records from the war and all the newspaper files from the Nazi period are either destroyed or have just disappeared. There just aren't any. And if that period is to be documented at all, we have to act quickly. I've assigned my students to interview the older people in town before they die and take their knowledge with them. I've run around myself and sat for hours talking to veterans. I've been asked to do a brochure about the town, something to give to tourists in the summer. It's nice to be able to show that there's a Socialist tradition and that there've been Socialist heroes even in a little place like Neustadt.

The teaching itself takes more than the 35 or 40 hours of actual class time, plus the Pioneer afternoons. I'm teaching the ninth grade now. You can't come unprepared to the students in those classes. They've got plenty to cram in, and they work long hours.

The new constitution not only guarantees every student a tenth-grade education, but everyone gets vocational training too. Without some kind of professional training, you can't make it in today's world.

✖ LPG Farmer Rudi Hoffs, on Education

You know what I like most of all? That every child is going to learn a trade. Without professional training you can't get anywhere nowadays. Now me, 53 years old and all, I'm taking a correspondence course in cattle-raising, even though I already have a certificate that shows I know all about poultry.

✖ Evald Schröder and His Poultry

Evald Schröder's wife runs the post office in Hohewisch, which is a 20-minute walk from Neustadt, east along the lake. Hohewisch is a little village, all of whose farmers now work at the Lewitz State Farm. Evald and his wife have one daughter, 17. For the house and 200 hectares* of land, the family pays a rent of 25 marks a month.

*Equal to 494 acres.

"It's like a gift," says Evald.

Because of a leg injury, Evald is on sick leave from the tannery, where he's a brigade leader. Once a week he goes to be looked at by the factory doctor, and in between he sees a specialist in Parchim, who also uses him as a messenger to the X-ray lab at the Stift Bethlehem in Ludwigslust. At home in Hohewisch, he farms on a small scale. He has a horse and two cows, but he mainly raises poultry—six different kinds laying altogether 35 eggs a day. He has a contract with the HO for delivery of the eggs, which provide him with an extra income of 100 marks a month. He raises pigeons, which he can sell for 30 to 35 marks apiece, and he also has pheasants, partridges, gold pheasants, wild and domestic ducks, and geese. On the poultry alone he earns about 2,000 marks a year. He gets eight marks for a hen.

His annual salary from the tannery has varied during the past few years, from 5,500 to 6,000 and up to 7,000 marks. His wife gets 490 marks a month. The 17-year-old daughter has just started her first job—secretarial work at Hydraulik Nord, where she makes 350 marks a month. She gives 100 marks of that to her mother for her room and board.

✪ Evald Schröder, on His Wife's Job

I do my job, and I say what I think when there's something I don't like. You can't be apathetic, you have to speak out. Most people forget that, that they have the right to speak out. I do it at the factory, and I do it in the postal collective.

This post office belongs to a collective of 20 offices. On Sundays, I take out the mail instead of my wife. Legally, she has a five-day week too, but she doesn't get a five-day week. There isn't anyone who can take her place. But on Sundays I do the delivery, and so I get to attend the postal collective meetings.

A postmaster has to contract to sell so and so many copies of *Neues Deutschland* and so and so many copies of *Bauernzeitung.** There isn't a single person in Hohewisch who buys single copies of *Neues Deutschland*, but we aren't allowed to send them back. They figure we ought to buy them ourselves. And at the postal collective they pushed it through that each post office should take at least one copy of *Bauernzeitung*. We did it for one year, but nobody bought it. It's too boring. All that's in it is like how many potatoes different collectives succeeded in producing. We paid for it for one year, but now we send it back. . . . No, we're *not* allowed to, but we do it anyway. What can they say? They can't make us buy it ourselves, and you can't sell a paper like that.

There is one that people do ask for, and that's *Magazin*. It's very good, even has some sexy pictures. But we only get one copy of that, no matter how many we order, and we'd like to keep that copy ourselves. But making us buy *Bauernzeitung* and *Neues Deutschland*, that's something you have to protest about. But people don't dare speak up, even about as simple a thing as that. They just sit there and stick up their hands every time there's a vote. They don't know exactly what it is they're voting on—they just think it has to be that way.

All the same, there are things they can't make you do, and things they can't keep you from doing. My brother is a border guard at Boizenburg. They've lived there a long time, and I like to go visit them. And I'm allowed to do that, but it takes one hell of a long time to arrange all the papers. It's only a few miles away. And it has happened that they've refused permission. And it's also happened

*"Farmers' Journal."

that it takes such a long time before the papers come back, with all the proper stamps and everything, that I just go without them. What can they do once I'm already there? They can't chase me away. Last summer his kids were here for a two-week visit, and then my daughter was going to go there and stay for a couple weeks. But they wouldn't let her. That made me mad as hell, and I went to the mayor, but either he couldn't do anything or else he didn't want to. The average guy can't get anywhere.

✺ Fashion Report From Paris*

After taking up my skirts for the fifth time in a row while still at home, and thinking that now they would surely do, I had hardly stepped from the train in Paris before I felt slightly old-fashioned. In a word—skirts are even shorter. The knee, which isn't exactly the prettiest or noblest portion of the anatomy, has come into the fashion spotlight, and seems to want to stay there—at least until next fall. Then, the prediction is, the point of view represented by the former mistress of French fashion, Mademoiselle Chanel, will carry the day, and the knee will disappear beneath the hem—if, that is, a woman doesn't want to be confused with her daughter or granddaughter, and if fashion doesn't want to become a caricature of itself. In the papers recently, Mademoiselle Chanel unleashed a furious attack on the high fashion designers, who, she thinks, basically hate women and expose them to ridicule in skirts that are too short, in miniskirts even, that in extreme cases hardly cover the seat. And a serious daily paper has entered the debate with the question, "How far will miniskirts go?" and the answer, "As far as men want them to."

For the time being, men seem happy with them—at

*From May issue of *Magazin*.

least in Paris—and gaze with obvious pleasure at the very young, very well-built girls who populate the local streets in their miniskirts and minicoats and low shoes. But I saw many heads shake, and many contemptuous smiles directed at those feminine creatures who roam about like figures straight out of the funnies. Their minibrains don't tell them what the limits are.

✵ Toni Rehmer, 33, Back on a Visit

I used to see a lot of my old friends when I came to visit in the summers, but now I spend very little time with them. I just come to visit my parents. My husband is in Frankfurt-am-Main—we have four rooms in a suburb. Everyone is so envious when I tell them about it.

I was educated as a chemical engineer, and there was no trouble getting a job when I went over. I had a very good education. It would have cost a lot of money in West Germany. Now I don't work—I have the baby. Over here all the women have to work, of course.

While I'm here, I'm required to spend at least five marks a day. I don't need to spend five marks a day. I live with my parents, after all, we're their guests. We only get to come once a year. I have friends from other districts who get to come home twice a year, in the summer and again at Christmas.

We always send a package at Christmas, and my parents send us sausages from Schumacher's. Actually, it's against regulations to send meat, but around Christmas you can get away with it. They don't have time to do so much checking. When we call up to thank them, we always say, "Thanks for the cakes from Schumacher's."

They listen in on telephone calls. Yes, we know they do —sometimes it starts to buzz. We send cigarettes and cigars to Papa, nylon stockings to Mama. We do that once a month. And then we send coffee, too.

The West German cigarettes are better. You've probably noticed that if someone offers you cigarettes, he always brings out the West German ones.

We usually put some magazines in the Christmas packages, too. That's against the rules too, of course, but we use them as packing. Then they get passed from house to house. I'm sure a lot of that kind of thing comes over at Christmas. The November and December issues of *Der Spiegel* are read in every house in Neustadt.

Grete Fischer, her mother: There isn't much sense in them, either. It's almost all about sports. That's the West for you. Once a friend of ours came over. When he came through the door, he unbuttoned his coat, and around his stomach he had a whole bundle of West German magazines and propaganda leaflets.

"Get out of here," I said, "or else throw them straight in the fire. I don't dare have you in my house."

A returnee: I moved to West Germany. Then I discovered I was going to have a baby. So I came back again to get married.

✖ Majoll Elliger, 28, on Her Sister's Coming for a Funeral

My mother was buried last week. Now we have to take care of my father. He's in bed in there—there's not much left of him, either.

It was Mother that took care of him, up to a few months ago when she got sick, or rather when it began to show how sick she was. It was awful how she changed in such a short time.

When they put her in the hospital in Ludwigslust, she already knew she didn't have long to live. She knew it, the doctors knew it, and the doctors told us, but we still didn't want to believe it. It still came as a surprise, this whole situation.

Father is so bad he hardly noticed that Mother was gone. It doesn't make any difference to him who it is that comes and makes his bed and washes him and changes his clothes. I used to say to Mother that we might just as well try to get him into a home. I'm not sure we could have done it, but we could have tried. But Mother didn't want to. Now we'll have to try to arrange it anyway.

I just can't handle it. I have two children, and I also have to try and earn a little something. My husband's a forester, but he only makes 450 a month. I get 20 marks a month for each of the children, which is what pays the rent. And now we only have my father's pension—160 marks. He pays 30 marks of that for rent, and that leaves 580 marks a month, net, for five people. Out of that we spend 200 or 250 a month for food—food is cheap, thank God—50 marks for cigarettes, and my husband gets 75 marks for pocket money. It's not really too much—I can't forbid him to go to the Körner for a cup of coffee or a cognac now and then. So that leaves just over 200 marks to swing everything else on. That's less than ten marks a day for five people. I was just sitting figuring it out.

I make most of the children's clothes myself, but I can't sew out of thin air. And they have to have shoes. We just won't make it if I don't get a job.

My sister came to the funeral from Düsseldorf. She went over in 1953—there was no trick to it then. She's married too, but she doesn't have to work. They live in a big modern apartment right outside Düsseldorf. Her husband is an engineer, but I don't know how much he makes. I've been told time and time again, and every time I'm just as astonished at how much it is. But I never remember it. You can't load down your memory with that sort of thing—I'd only go around brooding about it. Here comes my sister in a pretty new fur coat, mink, even her black dress for the funeral was in the latest Paris style. She has a big case full of cosmetics—one powder for the morning, one for the afternoon, one for the evening, one for night, a lipstick for every dress, day creams and night creams, and she's got God knows what all pencils for her eyes—and drops for her ears, I almost said. Sure, you can say it's ridiculous and luxury and nonsense, but still there's a certain difference between that and what I get along with, and it's not especially pleasant the way everyone talks about how young she looks compared to me, and I'm five years younger. I'm already starting to look like an old woman.

And you should have seen the way she eats! But why does she have to eat so much when she doesn't have to work? It's too bad, but I don't have anything in common with her any more. When she was here, now, you would think we would have helped each other out with a whole lot of things. But it was me who had to do everything. She didn't know anything about how to arrange a funeral, she said, just as if I *did*.

The only thing she knew how to do was sit and smoke fine cigarettes. I thought it was the mother of both of us we were burying, and I thought we ought to get some financial help. But she never thought of that. She came here to stand by the casket and cry very prettily. She came and acted as if she'd come to a foreign country, came and felt sorry for us because we don't have an enamel bathtub but have to take our baths in the zinc tub out in the laundry room, felt sorry for us because we don't have an indoor toilet and have to have a pot under the bed at night, anyway when it's this cold.

She felt sorry for me because I haven't had a new dress since last summer. Do you know what I did for a funeral dress? I sat and remade Mother's old black dress. I sat up half the night and worked on it while my sister sat there and smoked and drank cognac with my husband.

I don't like to speak ill of my own sister, but I don't live like she does, and it's not my fault. The only advantage she has is that she was born a few years before me. I'd like to live like she does, too, of course I would. It's more comfortable. She's never had to think about Mother and Father. She'd send packages every once in a while with coffee and cigarettes and nylon stockings for me, and then everyone would always say how thoughtful she was. And when Mother talked to people, it was always about how well her daughter was doing in Düsseldorf, what a wonderful life she had. It was always her she was proud of. But me, who just went along and emptied the pots and counted the pennies, I just did what was expected—a child should take care of his parents, because the parents took care of the children when they were little.

I don't want to speak ill of my mother—we could talk to each other, and we helped each other, but it was always my sister in Düsseldorf who was remarkable.

Sometimes I thought of skipping out myself. But it doesn't pay to even think such things nowadays. But they can't help it if people do it anyway, once in a while, take their children and disappear, and get married again, to some engineer in Düsseldorf.

✪ Evald Schröder
and His Brother Alfred

It was on a payday, many years ago. My brother Alfred was a soldier at the border. They were all sitting and drinking in a tavern, and my brother said, "Come on, boys, let's take our carbines and beat it over the border."

It was the kind of thing you say without meaning it. None of his friends took it seriously. But there was an officer in the place and he heard it and reported him. He was sentenced to four years in prison. We didn't know a thing about it—it wasn't a public trial. They sentenced him right away and sent him to Bautzen. Even Papa didn't know anything until he got a letter from Bautzen.

So Papa wrote directly to Pieck,* and asked if there might not be some mistake in the ways things were handled. Two weeks later, Pieck wrote back that he wanted to talk to Papa, and so Papa went to Berlin, and they held the hearing over again. They questioned Alfred's friends at the tavern too, and when it was all over, they let him out, and he went back to Boizenburg, to the same post again. You've always got to remember that you've got the right to protest.

Alfred: Once I wrote to Ulbricht. It was about an apartment I had a claim on. The mayor couldn't do anything, and the district government in Ludwigslust couldn't either. Three weeks after I wrote to Ulbricht I had an answer, and after a month I had the apartment.

You just have to watch out for the little functionaries—they're not very bright. One time the party secretary came to me and said I shouldn't go around with my brother Evald . . . Evald here, across the table from me. I'm a party member, and Evald isn't. The party secretary didn't think Evald was good company for me—as if he could influence me politically, as if the likelihood that I could influence him wasn't just as great, as if we couldn't hang around together across party lines, as it were. Why, it's fantastic.

Evald: They often get after me to join the party. They think a brigade leader should be a member. After the 17th of June, they almost managed to get me into the factory militia at the same time. . . . No, nothing in particular happened here in Neustadt on the 17th of June. There were just three tanks that drove up, one outside the entrance to the tannery, one at Hydraulik Nord, and one in the square.

*Wilhelm Pieck, president of the GDR for many years until his death in 1960.

God knows where they came from. But I don't think the workers had organized anything.

Alfred: I was working in the shipyard in Rostock. Several days before the 17th of June, we saw some tanks down by the harbor, and we couldn't figure out why. Nothing much happened there, either. It was only in the really big cities.

Evald: After the 17th of June, we were all questioned. They came and got us from our machines, one by one, with two armed soldiers, and took us to a little shed, and the soldiers stood there while the party secretary cross-examined us. So there were a lot of people who applied for party membership—that was the whole idea. They wanted me to join the factory militia. We were supposed to be sworn in in Ludwigslust on Sunday. On Saturday I went to my doctor and got put on sick leave. Otherwise they would have got me for sure. It was just like Hitler's time, but they didn't get me to join then, either. I wasn't in the Hitler Youth, even.

Do party members get better jobs?

Well, you can't say in general. Sometimes. You don't get to be a factory manager or a school principal unless you're a party member, that's clear enough, but . . . after all, a supervisor *is* also responsible for his workers' political education. I could have gotten somewhat further if I'd been a member, but I don't miss it. Even as a brigade leader I have rights. For example, those of us who do the heavy work at the tannery get 12 days of vacation—or so it's been, up to now. But the law says men who do heavy physical labor are supposed to get 15 days vacation. At Hydraulik Nord they get 15, and their work isn't any heavier than ours. I wrote a letter to the party secretary, pointing out that in light of the heavy work they do, tannery workers ought to get 15 days too. I know he can't arrange it all by himself, but it's his responsibility to refer the matter on to the factory management. He didn't do it. He just came to me and told me it couldn't be done. So I wrote to the factory managers, and if they can't do anything, they have to pass it on to the district government. And if they don't do it, then I can write to the district government and point out that neither the factory managers nor the party secretary bothered to take any stand on my letter. And if the district government doesn't do anything, why then I can write to the regional government, and if the regional government doesn't do anything, I can write directly to Berlin. But to do all that you've got to be stubborn and have plenty of time to write letters. And that stubborn I'm not, and I don't have that much time to write letters, and so instead I told the factory managers that if they don't do something, my brigade will stop paying its union dues. That made them sit up and take notice, so now the whole thing is up before the district government anyway.*

You have to insist on your rights all the time. You can't let them push you around.

⌑ ERNST THIELE, ON THE 17TH OF JUNE

We're still paying for what happened on the 17th of June. The people didn't know what they were doing, they were too impatient. If the authorities hadn't been forced to make the concessions they made, things would be much better now. And there's a lot of things that are still wrong.

---

*The Free German Trade Union (FDGB) represents the interests of the workers, including nonunion members, within the factory. It safeguards the workers' personal, material, social, and cultural interests, ensures the workers' participation in management, protects their right to equal pay for equal work, and their right to education, vacations, and free time. The FDGB is not a government organ. The law sets working hours at a maximum of 45 hours per week. Every other Saturday is free. Fourteen days' notice is required for all dismissals, and the factory can give notice to a worker only with the union's permission. Particular protection from dismissal is given to invalids, pregnant women, people who were persecuted by the Nazis, TB patients, and selected members of the factory's technical staff.

⊠ ERNST THIELE, IN A LETTER, OCTOBER 1968

The fight for freedom will end in victory some day, even for the Negroes in America, although certainly not under a capitalist regime. Students are often spontaneous. They have to be, because older people are often too self-satisfied. Contentment means repose, standing still, which is to say, going backward. Progress can only go forward, not backward, as in Czechoslovakia.

⊠ Hermann Kuhn in the Purchasing Department

I have to be at work at six o'clock, at the tannery. I'm in the purchasing department. It has its problems. If I need to order something, I have a big thick book I can look it up in. It tells precisely where I can order it, it tells where everything in the whole republic is manufactured and stored. It's a marvelous book. But the particular thing I need is never there. And if it is there, it almost always turns out to be a lie.

I write a letter and order an item in Leipzig. Four months later I get a reply—confirming the fact that the firm in Leipzig has received my letter. Why don't I call? It takes almost as much time to call, and besides, they need a written order anyway. Last fall I wrote out an order to a firm in Leipzig, and at the same time I wrote out another one to a similar firm in Rostock. Three months later I got answers from both places—exactly the same answer. I'd sent the letters on the same day, and I got answers on the same day, and the content was the same. That is to say, with the difference that the company in Leipzig suggested I go to the company in Rostock, while the company in Rostock suggested I go to the company in Leipzig.

Then I tried to send an order to a firm in Berlin by teletype.

A week later the teletype answered that they would forward the order to Jena. So after another week I called Jena to see if they'd got the order, but they hadn't. So then I call up a colleague of mine at another tannery and ask him what they do. He tells me they've had the same order in for six months now. After another month the little package finally comes. Where from? From Rostock. The order went from Berlin to Jena to Rostock.

There isn't any competition. Nobody bothers. But of course that isn't the whole explanation—there just aren't enough paper-pushers in this country. There's a big short-age of paper-pushers all over. That's really the explanation that comes closest.

But of course then you have to ask why there aren't enough paper-pushers, and that question isn't so hard to answer. It's because there's such a disproportionately vast amount of paper work in this country. You can hardly do anything without having to fill out a form. And so then you have to ask yourself why this country has so many forms to fill out. And that isn't hard to answer either. It's because everything has to be down in black and white. And so you have to ask why everything has to be down in black and white. It's because people don't trust each other. Masses of paper and labor get used up just because of that. And what's the result? Among other things, the result, to put it crudely, is that people go around with dirty asses. That's right—often around here you just can't get your hands on toilet paper. And even if you do, the quality is bad.

There was someone at the office, I won't say who, who took some order blanks home to use in the toilet. But it was easily discovered, because the order blanks are numbered right on the pad, and when the orders are entered in the ledger, they write down the number too. A few individual blanks can be put down as destroyed because of mistakes,

but not a whole series. And there was a whole series missing in the order ledger So they had an investigation. Probably the time spent on the investigation was worth more
than the paper. Anyway, they found out who'd taken the
paper, and when they'd come that far, they also had to find
out what he'd done with it. I was at the hearing, so I know
how it went. When they finally asked him *why,* he said the
order blanks were much better . . . but it went like this:
"The order blanks were better . . ."
"Better than what?" they asked him.
"Than the newspaper," he said.
"What newspaper?" they said.
"Neues Deutschland," he said.
You should have heard all the coughing and throat-clear-
ing.
So anyway, that was the end of the hearing, and afterward everything went on as before. Everybody just forgot
about it. But then one day, when we were taking our coffee
break, someone tipped over his thermos and dumped
coffee over both baskets of outgoing papers—including
some orders that were all written up and only waiting to
be taken up to the department head for his signature. So
we laid them out to dry, and we took an iron and tried to
press them out smooth. And then we sent the office boy
up with the order forms. The department head has to sign
his name and send them back to us, and we enter them in
the ledger before we send them on to the secretaries, who
type out the envelopes and mail them off. You've got to
have a system. Well, anyway—this time we only had to
wait about five minutes before one of the phones rang. It
was the boss. I answered it.
"Herr Pohl"—well, yes, Pohl had been the one. "Herr
Pohl," he said.
I pointed to Pohl, and he came and took the receiver.
"My dear Herr Pohl, this is certainly not what we
meant. You didn't have to pick the papers out again. Here-

after, Herr Pohl, what you've used as toilet paper is to be considered toilet paper."

We could all hear it, everyone in the room, and we all burst out laughing.

So the boss thought we were playing a joke on him, and he hung up. He sent all the order slips back down again, without a signature, and told us to write them all over on clean paper, and to do it on our own time.

You know, by the way, that tells you something about the quality of the coffee in this country.

✿ Frau Ursula Dunkelbeck

Mama told us later that it wasn't only the sorrow that changed her, it was also what she'd talked to Papa about. I asked her what that was, and why she never told me about it.

I was too little then, she said.

He'd told her about his life in the camp, and what disturbed her most of all was what he told her about Father Bernhard. He didn't mention it the first time he was home. Father Bernhard had been the camp informer.

Papa told Mama that during the last few weeks of his life, but it's only recently that she told me. She still doesn't really believe it. She just can't let her faith in Father Bernhard be shaken. I've thought about it a lot, and I've tried to talk to Mama about it. But she won't talk about it. She just keeps saying, "Father Bernhard was a good man." She would really have preferred to carry that story to the grave with her, I'm sure of that. But it was last winter, after we'd been watching TV.

They'd been playing Handel. Afterwards we were talking about Handel's devotion. Handel's music can express an almost ecstatic devotion. Then my husband said that there wasn't anything in the world as fraudulent as ecstatic devotion. It was in a spirit of ecstatic devotion that the German people committed genocide, he said, and they did it to the accompaniment of trumpets and kettle drums just like Handel's. Then Mama said it was committed with rifle barrels pressed against their necks.

I'd never heard her talk like that. I was amazed. It's the way people talk when they're trying to excuse it. Then she told us about Father Bernhard in the camp. She wanted to defend him, but she couldn't. That was the only time she and my husband ever really argued.

I still have a hard time understanding why he has to make comparisons between music and religion and politics. The cruelest thing of all was when he asked her if she really understood why she'd always liked Father Bernhard so much, if it wasn't because she herself had been young and full of life and pretty, and Father Bernhard had been an understanding and charming old rogue. You simply can't say things like that to an old person. Mama cried. After that it took at least a week for my husband and her to make up again.

We never mention it to Mama any more.

We never talk about music, either, and the three of us never talk about religion, not all together. I don't talk about religion with my husband, either. We used to. He wasn't nearly as against religion then as he is now. Actually, I don't think he's really against religion even now. But in those days all he thought was that we Catholics were a little odd. When we got married, we had to promise that we'd raise our children as Catholics, and he didn't have anything against that. With the first child everything went fine, to start with. We had it baptized—no fuss about that. With the second child everything went fine too, to start with. We had it baptized, and there wasn't any trouble about that either. I raised them as Catholics. I taught them their prayers, and Grandma and I told them about the faith. My husband didn't bother us. He joined the party himself. He read a lot in the evenings—he still does—and he didn't have much time left over for the children. But then it started.

One day I was talking to Father Gehrki, and he reminded me that it was about time to start sending the children to Sunday school. I knew right away it wasn't going to be easy to talk to my husband about that.

It all started when he asked me if it was absolutely necessary for me to run to church every single Sunday morning. He knew perfectly well it was. We'd talked about it before, and we'd talked to Father Gehrki about it.

He also asked me what it was I actually talked to Father Gehrki about . . . if Father Gehrki knew everything there was to know about us. We had a real scene about that one evening. He can't distinguish between a priest as a person and a priest as a servant of the Church. He doesn't understand that a Catholic priest is something completely different from a Protestant minister, which was the only sort of clergyman he knew anything about.

What makes a Protestant pastor different from the other members of his parish is really only the fact that he wears a black coat and a white collar and preaches in the church every Sunday. Pastor Smidt, for example, is just as sinful as any other member of his parish, if not more so. Why, he's practically a legend in Neustadt because of all the women he's slept with. One time he went to some sort of church conference in Halle, and shared a room with one of his confirmation students. I don't mean to say a Catholic priest is without sin. He's a human being, too. But his role in the congregation is something different from just being the human intermediary for God's message.

A person who talks to a Catholic priest isn't just talking to another human being, but to someone who, through the sacrament of ordination, has the power of grace. My husband doesn't understand that distinction.

Maybe you have to be Catholic to understand it.

What I say to the servant of the Church is something I say to the Church, not to the servant—do you see? Actually, it isn't one bit more remarkable than that what I say to a servant of the party is something I say to the party. A person who goes to talk to the mayor goes to talk to the mayor, not to talk to Herr Diederich. It would be absolutely pointless to talk to Herr Diederich if he weren't mayor. And it would be absolutely pointless to talk to Herr Gehrki if he weren't the parish priest. I've tried to make my husband understand that distinction.

But he says it's not the same thing.

It's not the same thing, he says, because Diederich was chosen mayor by the people. Gehrki chose himself, by setting out to study for the priesthood. Diederich is our own representative. We chose him ourselves to watch over our own interests. Gehrki is God's representative, and he says God only watches out for His own interests, namely, that we should love Him. That's the sort of thing we've been fighting about.

I'm not against the party at all. I couldn't be. Why should I be? I'm happy and proud that my husband is a member. I'm proud of my father's struggle, and I'm proud of my mother. They were Socialists a long time ago. Every day I *pray* that Socialism will win out. But to tell the truth, I still don't understand exactly how they can say Herr Diederich was chosen by the people. I never chose him. I know other people I'd like to have as mayor, and for that matter, I don't know many people here in town who do want Herr Diederich as mayor. We're not the ones who decide.

And Father Gehrki didn't choose himself to be our parish priest, either. He's assigned to a diocese, and the bishop places him. And he didn't get to be a priest just like that. I'm sure the theological seminary is harder than the party institute.

One evening I told my husband that our eldest son

would have to start Sunday school the next fall. I was sort of surprised when he answered as if it went without saying, or at least as if he'd never thought of opposing it. When fall came, we just marched off one Sunday morning, and my husband didn't say a thing. But as soon as we'd gone three, four Sundays in a row, you could begin to see that he was irritated, and then one Saturday night, as we were going to bed, he said, "Is it absolutely necessary to drag the children along, too?" He said he thought the children already talked like their grandmother, and he thought one grandmother in the house was enough.

I was expecting our third child.

Well, I was prepared for something to happen, but I hadn't expected him to say anything like that. I was absolutely speechless. I just reminded him that he'd signed a paper that bound him to let the children have a Catholic upbringing. He said it was blackmail, that that was the paper he'd been forced to sign before he could touch me. That's the sort of thing people say, and then they can apologize as often as they want, but you still never forget it.

I know I'm wrong to talk about my husband like this. But I too have bitter feelings I have to live with. I've talked to Father Gehrki about it—I had to. But now I'm talking to a man who's neither a priest nor a Catholic, and maybe you can defend my husband and explain him to me. He can't do it himself. I wish you were a party member too. Are you, perhaps? . . .

In order to have peace in the house, we did like this: We stopped going to Sunday school. But every Wednesday after school, our eldest boy went to the parish house for instruction. And that's how it's been ever since. For the other children too—once a week they go for instruction. My husband doesn't know about it. He thinks he won.

He thinks religious instruction only takes time from things that are more important. He says he thinks the

children should spend more time with the Pioneers in
stead. They're members, naturally. But they don't g
cially often. For that matter, it's not so often the Pioneers
have meetings in this town.

But this whole business gives me a terrible fright sometimes. It's an absolute wonder the children haven't given
it all away. They know they're not allowed to talk to their
father about it, but children can't always mind their
tongues, of course. Adults can't always manage it, so who
could expect children to?

One day he's going to find out what's going on. It's
inevitable. If not before, why someday they'll be
confirmed. Sometimes I think, well, I'll just give up the
whole fight. But I can't do it. That would be failing both
God and the children.

But I can't risk my marriage for just anything at all.

It was for my sake that he moved here.

✪ Federal Chancellor Kiesinger in the Bundestag, March 11*

Herr President, Ladies and Gentlemen:

Twenty-three years after the end of the Second World
War, this first survey of the state of the nation must still
bear the title, "Survey of the State of a Divided Germany."

It is not by the will of the Germans that this situation
obtains. Had they been able, at any time whatsoever, to
decide for themselves, or if they could do so today, the
peaceful reunification of the nation would be assured. This
is known to the whole world, West as well as East. The
right of self-determination, as urged by the people of the
world, and as formally established by resolutions of the

*Speech excerpts broadcast from Hamburg.

United Nations, cannot in the long run be denied the German people.

* * * * *

Ever since the end of the Second World War it has been the policy of the United States to promote European unity. A strong, unified Europe could lift a part of the burden from America's shoulders, and take upon itself a greater degree of responsibility for its own security. An independent Europe, joined in friendship with America, could very effectively serve the cause of world peace and build a bridge between East and West. A dependable alliance with America is ensured by the fact that, quite aside from our common spiritual and political values, we have an identity of interest in seeing that Western Europe does not fall under Soviet Russian influence.

* * * * *

The German people have followed the course of events in Vietnam with great sorrow and with deep sympathy for that country's suffering, war-stricken people. This sympathy illustrates how unbearable the very idea of war and bloodshed has become for our people. When we appraise the American intervention in Vietnam, however, we ought definitely to guard ourselves against the kind of one-sided statement that places on America all of the blame for the war, for its outbreak as well as for its development. We, in particular, have not the slightest occasion to make ourselves America's schoolmaster.

* * * * *

Whenever people from the two parts of Germany meet each other free from political constraint, this affinity between people with one language, one history, and one culture is always evident. Except for a small, weak minority, the Communist regime has not succeeded in winning over its population.

* * *

Until the day of reunification—which shall come, since no one can break the will of a great people to regain its unity—we shall use the time to keep our house in order, and to prepare our country for the coming time and world. Here our hands are not bound, here we can plan for ourselves, decide and act, and in so doing never lose sight of our nation's collective future.

✪ Karl Friedemann, on Moving Twice

It was in 1953 that we moved. . . . Why did we move? No, not for political reasons—who told you that? Well, it doesn't matter. Everyone talks so much about politics. When you get down to cases, it's not politics that decides at all, but other things. In this case, it was my mother-in-law. But you're not interested in that, surely—that's our affair. . . . No, no, it wasn't her who told us to move—on the contrary. The three of us lived here together, but in the long run it just didn't work out. We were still young, and we wanted to run our own lives. But you can't do that by moving.

It wasn't so easy to go over, either. I hope nobody thinks we were particularly welcome. Still, I was well trained, so it was fairly easy for me to get work. At first, we lived in

a barracks, but it wasn't so long before we got a real apartment, in a complex outside Düsseldorf. It was a nice apartment, and it was a good job. I made a lot of money. But
it was a big adjustment, even that long ago, big differences.
Over there they'd really gotten going with everything.
Here everything was just starting.

There's probably less of a difference now. The working
man doesn't have things too good over there, either. Actually, I think the worker's rights are better protected here.
But I've never been very active in union affairs. You have
to watch out you don't get involved in too many things.
People should mind their own business—that way you
don't make enemies. And you shouldn't talk too much, not
over here and not over there, either. We didn't have many
friends here when we left, and we didn't have many
friends over there when we came back. We've never cared
much for social life; we have ourselves to take care of. We
do our jobs—no one can ask any more than that—and it's
enough for us. You have to watch out you don't get all
involved with other people. I don't have any need to sit in
a tavern and talk, I have plenty to do as it is. We have our
house to take care of, and we have our garden. You have
to choose what you want to spend your time on and we've
decided to live like this. In the evenings we watch TV—
yes, well, mostly Hamburg. Here they make politics out
of everything. Of course, obviously, everything *is* politics.
But just for that reason it can be nice to see something else.
We usually watch the quiz show from Hamburg every
other Saturday.

But they shouldn't pester each other so much. Both sides
are just as bad, hounding each other. They can't make
anything any better that way. But I don't want to talk
politics. I'll let the politicians handle politics for me. Anyone who wants to fix things up nice for himself can do it
here just as well as over there—it's only a question of
working hard. And we do. People who don't are just too

lazy. Lazy people, and the kind of people who sit around in taverns and talk, you can find them anywhere, and they shouldn't complain that there isn't any equality. We work, both of us; we have to. Of course we could live on my salary, 600 a month, but we couldn't live as well. And then we have my wife's mother too, and her pension isn't very much. She's sick now. It was when she started to get old and sick that she wanted us to come back—she couldn't take care of the house herself. There wasn't anyone had done anything to the house since we moved. It just stood here for 14 years without anyone's doing anything to it, and it looked pretty run down. Obviously, we thought twice before we packed up again. But at least we knew what we were coming back to.

And then it's true, you know, that you want to go back to the things you grew up with. It was our own house we were coming to. When we left here, it wasn't easy. I was born in this house—my grandfather built it. We'd been here for visits in the summers, so we knew what things looked like over here, we didn't get any surprises. There wasn't much to break with in Düsseldorf. We sold our rights to the apartment and the garden, and what we had in the apartment, we took with us. But it's only natural that we hesitated, anyway. Over there you can always get the things you need, and you can't always get them here.

The prospect of changing jobs and working conditions didn't bother me. I know my job, after all, and I have the same job here that I had there, and I had the same job there that I'd had over here. If you know your job, there's no reason to be uneasy on that score. Of course the place where I work is different, but the work is the same, and so is the wear and tear. You always have to increase production. That isn't only true here. It doesn't make any difference if it's state-owned or collective or private, production always has to rise, whatever it is. It must be like that everywhere. Of course the fact is, here production is supposed to go up without any raise in salaries. That doesn't really jibe—there's no getting away from it. But on the other hand, nobody loses his job if the production plan isn't fulfilled, so it all evens out. We knew perfectly well what we were doing when we moved back. For us it's a matter of indifference what political system we live in.

I'd been over here and looked at the house to see what needed to be done, and I took the drawings back with me. Then we did our shopping there. We bought lumber, it's cheaper over there, we bought the things for the kitchen —look here, you can't get this kind of cabinet over here. And I bought all the bathroom fittings—here you can wait a year to get a bathtub or a washbowl. I bought floor tile. Now they're going to start making this kind of tile here too, of course, but it'll be expensive, and it'll be a long time before private individuals can buy it. I bought the paint there too. Everything we did to the house, we used materials we brought with us. Otherwise it would have been impossible. This TV is from there, too. You'd have to pay, for a TV like this, say, 3,000 marks here. Over there we got it for under 1,400.

We loaded all the building materials and everything we owned on a freight car. We could bring along as much as we wanted. Then the freight stood and waited while we were in the transit camp—that must have been about a week. We came back last fall. Since then I've spent all my free time getting the house in shape. If I'd thought I could get the materials here, it wouldn't have gone as fast as it has. Now I'm going to make some changes in the garden too. The brick is from here. The refrigerator, stove, freezer —we brought all of them with us. They're both better and cheaper over there. I'll put in a wall here by the stairs, so you can't see through. My mother-in-law's in bed up there. She doesn't like all the racket when I'm working—it makes quite a racket when you pound in a nail. But does that mean we should have left it like it was? She can be happy she's got things the way they are, but she doesn't always understand that. After all, she's the one who got us to come back. She was very eager to have us then—she seems to have forgotten that. Well, she's old and sick, and she wouldn't have been able to make it alone. But that doesn't mean we should only think of her. We're old ourselves now. We're not up to any unnecessary adventures any more.

✿ Church Services

Sunday, the first week of June 1967. In the Protestant congregation, the text for the day is Luke 14:16–26. Thirty-seven people present, of whom 23 are women, mostly older.

The morning service is conducted by a minister from Ludwigslust. The congregation's own Pastor Smidt is on vacation.

Along the walls inside the church hang tablets with the names of men who fell for Germany in the First World War. There was formerly a memorial obelisk in the churchyard as well, with the same names in gold. But it was defaced and pulled down during the desecration of the churchyards in June 1945, when the large family markers were also destroyed, among them the private burial chapel of the Weinaug family. But the rows of names inside the church remain untouched.

✿ Sermon, From Luke 14:16–26

Brethren, the text for today speaks of a man who was to give a feast, and sent out his servant to tell those who were bidden to come—"Come; for all things are now ready." But those who were invited began immediately to excuse themselves, and said, the first, that he had bought a piece of land and must needs go out and see it, and the second, that he had bought five yoke of oxen and must test them, and the third, that he had taken a wife and so could not come.

This is one of Jesus' parables, as told to us by Luke in his 14th chapter.

It is a parable that deals with our capacity for making excuses. We recognize the situation very clearly—a Sunday, for example, when the Lord offers a feast in his church. One person has bought a piece of land, and must go inspect it. And one person has a garden, and must tend it. And another person has bought a pair of oxen, and so forth. There are always more pressing concerns to attend to than going to the Lord's feast.

It is always possible to turn down God's invitation, for God uses no force.

But what does He offer at His feast?

He offers no land giving a rich harvest, and no oxen to help man till the soil and bring in the crop, for His kingdom is not of this earth, nor does He offer wives, for heavenly joys are not the earthly ones. What the Lord offers is not worldly gain, nor worldly pleasure. He gives no annual bonus to the man who heeds His invitation. He gives no compensation for lost earnings.

But what of that? When we go to a dinner, do we ask in advance what the host is going to serve?

The Lord has asked us to a feast. His word will still no hunger; His word will quell no earthly desire. In our daily lives, it is always this which is decisive: What advantage can I gain from this action, how can this action satisfy my needs? In our daily activity, it is always this which is decisive: What is the dividend, what are the profits? Our achievements are noted down; they are fed to computers. And according to our achievements do we receive our earthly wages for our earthly work.

Our human worth is measured according to what we accomplish, according to our labor.

And so how easy it is, when the Lord invites us to the feast, to say "Thank you, but I have more important things to do." And to add, like those who were invited in Jesus' parable, "I pray thee have me excused."

For what the Lord offers will yield no earthly gain. He gives no annual bonus to the man who heeds His call and listens to His word. And he who heeds His call and listens to His word lets his own land rest.

But, brethren, what of that? Before we go to a feast, do we ask in advance what the host will serve?

The Lord has called us to His feast. The Lord has said, "Come; for all things are now ready." The Lord's table is always set for those who will hear His call. . . .

Brethren, this Pentecost I went on an excursion with my confirmation class. We made a visit to the former concentration camp at Buchenwald, one of the places where our people committed their greatest crime. This visit was, for me and my confirmation candidates, a harrowing reminder of what men can do to other men. What language is spoken by the ashes of those who were burned in the ovens? Human beings from all over Europe were brought together and died at Buchenwald. They died and were killed by the thousands. They were burned to ashes, which were mixed with the earth, and the ground was smoothed and grass seed was strewn on the ash-mingled earth, and on this ashen soil of human bodies there grew up a grassy lawn, lovely with the tender green of Whitsuntide.

Brethren, it was in this way a people was to be destroyed, a people who called themselves God's chosen people.

Who looks for the traces of an entire people in the grass of a pretty park?

It was the deed of our own people in a Godless time. The men who did this deed were the kind of men who can find excuses. "I pray thee have me excused," said those who were invited to the feast. And so said the men who murdered at Buchenwald: "Have me excused."

They could not go to the Lord's feast—other things were expected of them. Their worth was measured according to a different scale than that used by the Lord our God to measure the worth of men. Before God we are all alike. One race of men is worth no more than another, and the man who prefers earthly gain when the Lord calls us to the feast, that man seeks earthly merit, but such merit is nothing to God.

When the servant returned to his master and told him that the invited guests said they could not come, then the master of the house became angry, and said to his servant:

"Go out quickly into the streets and lanes of the city, and bring in hither the poor, and the maimed, and the halt, and the blind."

"And the servant said, Lord, it is done as thou hast commanded, and yet there is room."

And the lord said unto the servant," Go out into the highways and hedges, and compel them to come in, that my house may be filled.

"For I say unto you, That none of those men which were bidden shall taste of my supper."

Dear brethren, even so the Lord opens His doors to His feast. He is angered at those who say they cannot come, and He closes His doors to them. But the poor, the maimed, the halt and blind on the highways and byways, those whom the world condemns, these he gathers in his hall to a heavenly feast. None of them excuse themselves. The last shall be first, and the first last. And it shall be an exultant feast, for the kingdom of our Lord is a kingdom of joy and peace and freedom. There will be no constraint, and there will be no contention. (A verse.) Amen.

LPG Farmer Rudi Hoffs, After the Service

A fine sermon anyway, but with that text he could just as well have given a marvelous Socialist sermon. But he didn't. The invited guests would be the capitalists, and the people on the streets would be the workers. It could have been an absolutely marvelous Socialist sermon. And didn't he say the people on the streets were *forced* to come to the feast? It would have been an absolutely perfect sermon for East Germany.

But it was really very good the way it was. It's been a long time since I was in church. I'm not actually a member. But it surprises me they still talk that way. And then a prayer for Israel—that certainly must be against regulations. We're supposed to be on Egypt's side. Ulbricht went and visited Nasser a couple years ago. Since then we're supposed to stick with Egypt.

It's a nasty war. Now if it's really true that it was the Israelis who attacked, then that's really bad. Clearly, you can't lay claim to a country where you haven't lived for 2,000 years. But why should they start a war? After all, it was the Arabs who had their land stolen. I can't imagine it was the Israelis who started it. But on the other hand, you never could depend on the Jews. They've done a lot of bad things. It's a nasty war.

Pastor Smidt, on Salvation

Communists and Christians were in the same camps, in the same concentration camps—Flossenbürg, for example. The Communists don't do anything to us, although our goals aren't the same as Communism's. They say materialism will triumph. But according to God's law, the Church will ultimately triumph. For that reason, a pastor can never be a Red. And I'm certain that God's kingdom will triumph in the end. No one can stop us from carrying out our missionary duty. In our parish we confirm from 30 to 40 children every year. Ministers are being trained in Rostock, so there won't be any shortage of pastors. We're working under economically strained circumstances, to be sure. But salvation doesn't depend on money.

❈ The Younger Gottliebs

Two houses from Martha Gottlieb live her brother's son, Richard, 43, and his wife Elsie, 42. They have two daughters: Margarethe, 19, and Katrin, 16. Richard Gottlieb is a highway engineer, employed by the district government. Elsie Gottlieb works at the library. Margarethe is studying nuclear physics in Halle, and Katrin goes to school in Ludwigslust, because "they have better teachers there." The house where they live is, like Martha Gottlieb's, over 200 years old. They occupy the entire upper story—four rooms plus a kitchen. The kitchen has an electric stove, a refrigerator, a stainless-steel sink, and brand-new cupboards for the china.

Two of the rooms are bedrooms. Of the other two, one is used as a combination dining room, library, and study, while the other is a living room with three deep soft armchairs and a sofa surrounding a circular table, and a TV set.

Engravings and etchings hang on the walls, one representing Goethe, the others mostly buildings, architectural pictures. Richard has done a certain amount of carpentry and painting in the apartment. He has remodeled the old kitchen according to his own plans and built glass doors to make the apartment more spacious.

From the parlor, or living room, a door leads out onto

a tar-papered roof that can be used as a terrace, with a view of the old church, from which organ music can be heard on Sunday mornings.

Richard Gottlieb's office is in Ludwigslust. He gets home around 6. Elsie Gottlieb is at the library four afternoons a week, but in addition to her library work, she has taken on the vice-chairmanship of the Neustadt Culture Club, where her primary duty is to arrange theater trips to Schwerin. A busload of theater-goers makes the round trip to Schwerin two or three times a month, and Frau Gottlieb says it is (at least in part) a very critical collection of theater-goers—Puccini's *Turandot* draws a full bus, but *Tales of Hoffman* is considered flimsy. The lyric theater is valued more highly than the modern, socially oriented stuff that the theater director in Schwerin likes to include in the repertoire.

Richard Gottlieb doesn't usually go along on the theater trips—he thinks they're a waste of time. "All too often," he says," I've come back from the theater with the feeling I could have used the time for something more sensible."

Elsie Gottlieb was actually trained as a teacher, but she finished her education in 1943, and two years later it was practically worthless. "Those first years after 1945," she says, "it was less a question of thinking about going back to school than of just pulling your life together in general."

Then she got married, and along came the children. When, later on, she wanted to go back to school, Mayor Diederich was against it and unwilling to recommend her for teachers college. "He said I was too religiously oriented, which I'm not at all, of course. That's Aunt Martha. He was confused."

She often returns to this subject—she really wanted to be a teacher. "But," she says, "I have to admit that that time I applied to go to teachers college, I still didn't have any real idea of what the new social order demanded."

❈ The Parchim National Theater's Last Evening at the Park Restaurant

An evening in March. The Parchim National Theater company arrives in a bus at the Park Restaurant, whose dance hall has been turned into a theater. The platform where the tannery band plays for the Gardeners' Annual Ball is now the stage.

The performance is at eight o'clock. Admission is three marks.

About 150 people come, most of them older. Outside, it's 14 degrees above zero, snowing, and windy. People come from outside directly into the auditorium—the coatroom is on the other side of the hall.

When the doors have been closed, the manager of the Park Restaurant, Paul Zander, claps his hands for attention. He announces that this is the last time the Parchim National Theater will visit the Park Restaurant, signaling the end of a long tradition. His announcement is met by a general murmur, which it seems reasonable to interpret as an expression of disappointment.

Zander is speaking on behalf of the National Front.*

He explains the grounds for the decision—primarily, he says, the unsatisfactory staging conditions in the restaurant: "As host of the Park Restaurant, I don't want to say anything unfavorable about this room. It makes a fine dance hall. But it just isn't a theater."

However, he informs the audience, the Mecklenburg Theater from Schwerin will continue to visit Neustadt.

*The National Front is a nationwide popular movement that works for the furtherance of Socialism, partly through its activities in economics and home economy, and partly, among other things, through cultural activities. Representatives of all social levels and outlooks work together within the National Front.

The Mecklenburg Theater gives its performances in Plattdeutsch, and comes four times a year.

In the future, the audience will ride a bus to the theater instead of the other way around—which is also more natural, as Herr Zander points out. "To experience the theater in its own surroundings is, after all, quite a different thing from doing it here."

Questionnaires will be sent out to get people's opinions as to when the buses should depart—if they should leave so as to arrive just before the performance begins, or an hour or so earlier so that people can walk around in Parchim a little first.

Feeble applause.

✪ The Woman in the Mirror

The evening's presentation is *The Woman in the Mirror,* an operetta in three acts by Theo Halton and Günther Schwenn, music by Will Meisel.

The description in the program runs as follows:

> *The Woman in the Mirror* is almost a musical conversation, and possesses an intimate and indisputable charm. It is colorful, and filled with comic situations. Happily, the operetta's music has grown organically out of the dialogue, seeming in no way to be a later addition, something inserted by artificial means, but rather developing out of the action, as if by itself.
>
> The action of the play consistently poses questions of current interest—questions about equal rights in marriage. Should a modern woman give up her profession in order to please her husband? On the other hand, should she be allowed to neglect her husband for the sake of her career? We learn in the end that a harmonious solution is possible only through mutual acknowledgment, through the understanding each partner must have for the other. One partner should not triumph over the other, the two should stand side by side as

equals. We want our production to lead the public to such conclusions. We want to hold up a mirror in which different people will recognize themselves, and give some thought to the questions posed. One definite advantage of our operetta —it takes place in the world of the artist, which always commands the public's interest. We remind you again that success, in this case success in the theater, doesn't fall into anyone's lap, but must always be preceded by hard work.

Our production, however, is intended to be light, elegant, and entertaining. It should inspire our audience with a happy enthusiasm for new tasks. For that reason, all the problems in our operetta are solved easily, and with a smile. We don't think it would be such a bad idea, either, if we now and then attacked the problems of our daily lives with a smile, and with greater joy.

✵ Neustadt-Glewe Workers Club—Calendar of Events for February 1968

✵ FILM PROGRAM FOR THE MONTH OF FEBRUARY 1968 AT THE FRIENDSHIP THEATER

Evening performances at 8 p.m. On Thursdays, Saturdays, and Sundays there are additional performances at 5:30 p.m.

February 3–4 *Nguyen van Troi*
6–8 *Thunder over the Indian Ocean*
9–11 *The Last Paradise*
13–15 *Sherlock Holmes*
17–18 *Here I Was Happy*
21–22 *Journey to the Center of the Earth and 100 Percent Price Rise*
23–25 *Jewel Thieves*
28–29 *Edgar–Kristina*

✶ FILMS FOR YOUNG PEOPLE

Sundays at 3 p.m., Thursdays and Saturdays at 5:30 p.m.
February   4 *The Secret Oath*
          10 *Kim-Dong Outwits the Traitors*
          11 *Grandfather Kilian and I*
          14 *Men in Night and Flames*
          17 *Young Rascal*
          18 *The Ogly Choir* (TV)
          21 *The Stolen Airship*
          24 *Gulliver's Three Worlds*
          25 *Decision on Tartar Mountain*
          28 *The Sea Cat*

✶ CHILDREN'S FILMS

Sundays at 10 a.m., Thursdays at 3 p.m.
February   4 *The Snow Queen*
          11 *Black Nobi*
          15 *Travel Troubles on Vacation*
          18 *The House of Cats*
          22 *Snow White*
          25 *Hurrah, We're on Vacation!*
          29 *The Adventures of Ferdinand the Clown*
The program is subject to change.

✶ THEATER

Tuesday, February 6, 1968, 8 p.m., at the Park Restaurant, the Parchim National Theater presents *The Liar*. Advance tickets at the Veterans Club.

✶ DRIVER TRAINING

February 14, 8 p.m., at the Theodor Körner Restaurant. Motor-bike test, February 14, 3 p.m., at the Theodor Körner Restaurant.

▣ CITY COUNCIL MEETING

Wednesday, February 7, 3 p.m., in the lecture hall at the Goethe Oberschule. Citizens are most heartily invited to take part.

▣ EVENTS AT THE PARK RESTAURANT

February 4 3–7 p.m. Young people's dance, with The Elgitas. Admission 2.10 marks.
11 2:30 p.m. Annual meeting of the local chapter of the German Anglers Club
18 4 p.m. Concert by the Mecklenburg National Stage Orchestra (Ludwigslust)
25 3–9 p.m. Young people's carnival. Dancing, with The Elgitas.
Admission 2.10 marks.
26 Dance, with The Terms (the Funkmechanik's band). Admission 2.10 marks.
March   2 Dance, with Club 67. Admission 2.10 marks.

▣ SPORTING EVENTS

Chess every Thursday evening at 8, at the Theodor Körner Restaurant.
Soccer:
February 10 2 p.m. Progress II vs. ASG [Allgemeine Sport Gesellschaft] Glöwen
February 17 2 p.m. Progress I vs. Güstrow Union

Freedom for Peace—for a future free from the fear of war for all men!

❈ Christa and Ulrich Allerding— Welder and Tractor Operator

Christa is 19 years old and a welder at Hydraulik Nord. Six months ago she married Ulrich Allerding, a tractor operator on the Theodor Körner LPG in Wöbbelin. They have a son, Manfred, three months old.

They live in an apartment in Wöbbelin, where Ulrich previously had a single room in the housing built by the collective. Every morning at 5:30, Christa takes the bus to Neustadt—a five-minute ride. She comes home again around 3.

They would rather live in Neustadt, they say. They've been on the waiting list for housing in Neustadt for two years and are hoping for a modern apartment, one with a bathroom.

"I've always longed for a bathroom," says Christa. "A tile bathroom with nickel-plated fixtures and a shower with a hose attachment."

Ulrich: When we found out Christa was going to have a baby, I asked the collective manager if I could have a larger place—I told him how things stood. So he asked me if Christa would be able to work in the shops at the LPG. And I said, "Well, first she has to have the baby." But they haven't had any openings for a welder since then. But things will work out by the time Hydraulik is done reorganizing and moves its shops to Parchim.

Christa: I wouldn't have any objection to changing my place of work. At Hydraulik Nord we're on an assembly line. All you have to know is how to weld, and you don't have to have any real training for that. I'm sure it's more exciting on a collective.

Ulrich: We've got a big machine pool. We get new equipment almost every year, and sometimes it's hard to get hold of spare parts. We don't only have East German equipment, we buy from England, Czechoslovakia, Poland, the Soviet Union, West Germany, Sweden. We can't keep a warehouse full of spare parts.

Christa: I know the people who work in the shops in Wöbbelin, and I know what they work with. It's a completely different thing from what I'm doing. They call it a repair shop, but they do just as much real manufacturing as Hydraulik. The difference is that in an LPG you get to figure out for yourself what you're going to make. They get in a broken thresher, say, and so they figure out what's wrong with it. There are only five workers, and they help each other out. On an LPG you know what you're doing, you can see what's happening. When I started at Hydraulik, I didn't really know what it was I was welding. It was Ulrich who told me where the hydraulic couplings go in a Trabant. No one else ever told me.

At Funkmechanik, they're going to specialize entirely in crossbar switches for telephone switchboards. They've had some informational meetings about it. Some of their personnel are going to have to be retrained, and a lot of them will have to figure on starting something completely new. It's going to be a big export item—the party secretary was talking about internationalism. I don't remember now exactly what he said, but it was partly something about the telephone as a means of communication, and partly something about our production as a means of communication. It sounded finally as if Funkmechanik was going to solve all the world's problems with its crossbar switch. And I was almost ready to make up my mind—I don't want to move to Parchim with Hydraulik.

But you said you'd like to live in a city.

Yes, but not Parchim.

Do you think Neustadt is better, then?

I grew up in Neustadt, and my grandmother lives here. I can't just leave her all by herself. If you live in Wöbbelin and get a motor-bike, it's practically the same thing.

Ulrich: And then we've got to have a sidecar for Manfred. We can all be in Ludwigslust in three minutes.

The chairman told us there'd be a two-room apartment available in three months—Uncle Alfred's maybe. He worked in the hog stalls, and he'd been living there for three years. You see, he used to live on his own farm, two miles out, but when Aunt Gertrude died, he thought it was too far away, so he made a trade with the LPG and moved into the apartment. But then he was going to be pensioned off and move back to his farm. He's 75. The collective had fixed up the house in the meantime, and he had to wait till the people who were living there moved out. It was an agronomist who was living there. So anyway, then the two-room place was vacant for us, and my old single room was vacant then too.

It's a very nice apartment. We moved into it on a Friday. On Saturday we got married. And on Sunday evening, Christa went to the maternity hospital.

Christa: I lived with my grandmother before we got married. I lived with my grandmother for 15 years. My father died in an accident in the tannery—he drowned in a vat. Just think of surviving two war fronts and then drowning in a vat. And my mother died of cancer. I was little then. I have an older brother who lives in Wiesbaden. When Mother got sick, he went to live with my father's sister in Wiesbaden—he must have been seven years old then—and I've never seen him since.

Grandma lives in her own house, or at least it used to be hers. It got to be too hard for her to keep it up, so she let the town buy it. I don't remember when—it was a long time ago. Nobody does much for the house now either, but now it's Grandma who makes the demands. Before, it was the city. She had to give up part of the house, but she was only too happy to do it—it meant less for her to do.

We live in two rooms too. I had the bedroom, and Grandma lived in the living room. And that's how we lived for 15 years, so I can't just leave her all alone. I have the feeling she's gotten older and a little unhappy just in the short time since I left home. I go and visit her twice a week, at the very least. She's 85 years old, and she has cheeks like peaches.

Naturally she thought it was strange when I said I wanted to work in a mechanic's shop, but as soon as she saw me in overalls, she thought it was funny. When I think about it, she must have had an awful lot of trouble with me. For one thing, I decided to become a welder.

"No, no," she said, "I just don't understand you. Do you think any real man ever wants to marry a welder?"

"You have to be feminine," she said.

Ever since I was 13 or 14, she'd been after me about how I ought to be feminine. At home in the living room she used to make me practice how you're supposed to curtsy and smile and extend your hand when you greet someone.

And I never got to stay out after ten o'clock. She insisted on that until one time I disobeyed her, and then she never mentioned it again. It may be I was *too* nice when I lived with Grandma. My friends were out much later in the evenings. They used to stay up at The Shooting Gallery till after midnight and dance, or down at Eichmann's on the lake in the summers. But I always had to be home by ten. I think I said I wanted to be a welder just to make her mad. The other kids went around bragging about the boys they'd met, and they'd giggle and whisper and I never understood a thing. And what's more, I always thought it was fun to make things. You should have heard what they used to say about that—you know, that I just wanted to get in good with the adults, or that I just wanted to be different.

In school they always taught us that women shouldn't just get married. Girls should have jobs, they said, and the female work force was in great demand. And there wasn't any difference in the schoolbooks for boys and girls. Is there where you live? And when we were supposed to choose a profession, there were a lot of girls that they recommended to take jobs with an LPG, out in the fields or in the barns, or else they'd advise them to learn one of the old male jobs. But the girls thought that was just silly. They all wanted to be office girls or hairdressers. What could be any fun about that? Now welding is much more of a profession, and why should boys get all the fun jobs? That's why I went to welding school in Ludwigslust, and I don't regret it. I wasn't the only girl. It wasn't so terribly strange after all.

And it was then, when I was learning about machines and I used to come home in overalls with my hands all oily, that Grandma started to like the idea.

I'd started to get breasts then too. I mean real breasts.

"Oh, Christa dear," she said, "now I can see you're a woman even in overalls."

That's the way Grandma is. She's much more open-minded than a lot of my friends. And it's not at all because she's a Socialist or a Communist—she isn't. And she never has been. I don't know what she is. But she's been a strict grandmother, who was particular about sitting up to the table properly, and about learning to cook, and taking some of everything on the table, and not leaving anything on your plate.

"You never know when you'll get your next meal," she always says.

You ought to see what it's like at the meals at Hydraulik, the way people waste food!

They should eat with Grandma sometime. She's very particular about that sort of thing. And I think she's right.

Ulrich: It was when I saw her in overalls, and her hands

all black with grease, that I fell in love with her. We met on the bus from Ludwigslust to Wöbbelin.

Christa: I usually changed my clothes and washed first, but the workclothes were so dirty I had to take them home anyway.

Ulrich: It was the 5:30 bus from Ludwigslust. It's always packed full. I had a light summer suit on.

Christa: But it was old. There wasn't much wear left in it.

Ulrich: You know, I really wonder if it's not against the law to use public transportation with clothes as dirty as the ones you had on. When we started to get off in Wöbbelin, I saw I'd gotten grease spots on my suit. It was from her overalls. That's how I got her name and address—she right away promised to take off the spots as soon as possible.

Christa: It was Grandma who took out the spots.

Ulrich: And the next time I put it on, you said I'd have to get rid of it.

Right after that, I went and did my military service. I was supposed to have done it before, but I'd never gotten any orders. Since I was a tractor operator, they transferred me right away—I mean, first they put me in the infantry, but since I was a tractor driver, they transferred me to armor.

I never had any cause to complain about military life. You have to learn to take orders, but you have to do that on an LPG too. And just like here I'm responsible for the tractors, there I was responsible for the tanks. Nobody can use a tractor unless the operator gives his permission, not even the chairman. And no captain or major can order anyone to drive an armored vehicle if the enlisted man who's the expert says no. The machinery has to function, and that's just as important here as it is there. There's no great difference. You have to be away from home—that's the difference. Well, and a harder life. Maneuvers are hard work.

Does the Swedish tank corps do the water obstacle test? You drive through a river, under water. We got ours stuck in the bottom. But you don't notice anything except that you're not coming up again, because the water up above us was absolutely black. We turned on the oxygen tanks. We put it in reverse, but it didn't move. That was the only time in my whole life I really thought I'd had it. . . .

I used to live in Dömitz, but one night they ordered everyone to move. We didn't know why. We thought the war had started. But I wasn't scared—I probably wasn't old enough to be scared. All the others moved farther east, but I went to my uncle in Wöbbelin, so I only moved a few miles. Anyway, I didn't have much to do in Dömitz, so I might have moved anyhow.

I asked them myself to transfer me to armor. I don't think they usually do that. But I was amazed how much trouble they take over individuals. Like, there was this one guy that snored—he sounded like a whole armored regiment on the move. At camp he had a separate room. And on field maneuvers he always had to sit up in the cab of the truck. That way he didn't bother the other guys, and at the same time he kept the driver awake.

Obviously you have to defend your country, I've never had any doubts about that. War is insane—we all know that well enough—but you have to defend what you've built up. I said I wasn't scared when I lived in Dömitz, but of course things did happen at the border. There were a lot of West German troop columns. I'm sure things have calmed down since the border was closed. I don't understand what it's all about, why the West German TV thinks the border is such a scandal. All countries have borders and border checkpoints. The Wall is a good thing. In West Germany, now, they're having an influenza epidemic—you hear about it on TV. But there isn't any influenza here. The

Wall's in the way. It stops all the germs. . . .

No, we don't talk much politics at work. We do our work. I'm not even interested in politics. I drive a tractor, that's my politics. We're all interested in higher production. If they want to introduce a new system in agriculture, why I'm for it, providing it means bigger bonuses for me. If I want a bigger bonus, I've got to produce more. But if they're talking about some change that won't increase production, no one's interested.

For example, we bought this Czech beet-harvester. I'm not responsible for it, but whether the machine pays for itself or not depends on how it's driven. It depends on how much gets done. The whole bonus depends on all of us together, and we split the losses, too.

Uncle Alfred told about when they first called the farmers together and started talking about collective action. They spent the whole evening talking about collective action, and then one of the farmers asked for the floor and said, "There's been a lot of fine talk about 'collective action,' but couldn't you just talk so's regular people can understand it? I mean, for example, when do we start taking up this collection?"

Now at least they know what "collective action" means.

Uncle Alfred can tell a lot of stories about when they changed over. In the beginning, they got to keep their livestock. But it was like extortion—every once in a while they'd make a check to see if people were delivering a hundred percent of what they produced. Once when the man came to count the pigs, it was my cousin who opened the door—they'd reported that they had one pig.

"Where's the pig," the man asked him.

"Up in the attic," my cousin said.

Then Aunt Gertrude came running up. "No, no," she said, "it's out here." And she took the inspector out and showed him the pig in the yard.

But there was another pig in the attic.

Everybody cheated. The inspector knew that. Otherwise people couldn't have made it. The inspector knew that too. He may well have had a pig up in his own attic.

Christa: Grandma had a goat, but they must have counted it as a pet. It didn't give much milk.

While Ulrich was away in the army, we didn't see each other more than once every three weeks, at most. He didn't have his room in Wöbbelin any more—they couldn't just let a room stand empty in Wöbbelin so he could come and use it for one or two days every three weeks. So the first time he came, he stayed at the Theodor Körner. It cost five marks a night. When Grandma heard that, she went crazy—five marks for one night! The next time, she went to Pallein's and rented a rubber air mattress for 50 pfennigs. I think she haggled over it. Anyway, it was the first time Ulrich and I slept under the same roof. Grandma slept in the living room between Ulrich in the kitchen and me in the bedroom, so there wasn't anything to be nervous about. But Grandma was nervous. I don't think she slept all night, at least not the first time.

That's how it was for about six months. Grandma always sat up until we'd gone to bed. But then there was one Saturday when they were going to show *The Blue Angel* on TV. Grandma had a cold, but she was going to sit up anyway. But she went to sleep before they got around to Marlene Dietrich. We woke her up and asked if she didn't want to go to bed, and we practically had to carry her into the bedroom. We thought we'd finally get to be by ourselves, and we did, too. But we slept in different rooms anyway.

Ulrich: It came so unexpectedly.

Christa: But after that, Grandma asked me if I was thinking of marrying Ulrich, and I said if it was O.K. with him it was O.K. with me. She said the main thing was whether *he* wanted to. A woman can always adapt, she said, but with men it's worse. And the next time Ulrich came, she asked him if he wanted to marry me. *She* asked. I'd prepared Ulrich for the question, because I had a feeling it was coming. And Ulrich said, "Yes." And Grandma slept in the living room again that night.

When Ulrich had gone, Grandma asked me if I knew anything about what men do.

"We learned that in school, and in the FDJ," I told her.

I thought she was going to die on the spot. So I explained how it was, how a doctor had come and talked to us about it, and we'd seen a film, and for that matter, we had heard it mentioned even before that.

So she calmed down, and the next time, she went to bed early—in the bedroom. And then we got engaged. Isn't that a wonderful grandmother?

Ulrich: Christa was the first for me. My friends started a little earlier, I guess, at least if you can believe what they say. Maybe they were just bragging.

Christa: Yes, I'm sure most of the girls around here begin sooner than I did. And we'd even said we were going to get married. But they started in school. You should have heard the things they used to talk about at recess.

How did you react when you found out you were going to have a baby?

Ulrich: I think both Christa and I were just happy. I was, at least.

Christa: And since Ulrich was happy, so was I.

What did the other welders say at Hydraulik?

There were some boys my own age who said some dumb things. When the brigade leader found out, he just said, "Aha!" And he said I should have told them last year when they were making up the plan for '67.

Haven't you ever thought of staying home so you can take care of the baby?

There's a day nursery in Wöbbelin. Ulrich takes Manfred there before he goes to roll call at 7:15. Then I collect him in the afternoon.

What does your grandmother say?

That a mother should take care of her children. I think maybe that's what's been such a blow to her—that I don't do what she tells me.

✿ Ursula Dunkelbeck
Continues Her Story

It was dreadful when Papa came home.

I was four years old when they came and got him the first time. I remember it very well. I don't think I'll ever forget it. Papa and I had been out in the horse pasture. We had a lot of riding horses—I think we always did have, but now we'd been assigned to breed them for the army, I think. They'd come at regular intervals and pick out a few full-grown horses, and brand the colts and fillies and count them. Once they came back with a veterinarian and examined them.

"That's no real veterinarian," Papa said. "He doesn't know anything about horses."

The day after they'd been there, Papa and I were out with the horses. I'd gotten to go riding with him. On the way home we saw the truck coming.

"Now where are they going?" Papa said.

Then they drove up to our place. I was holding Papa's hand, and it got all wet and cold. I remember that so well. And then he stopped. We just stood there a long time. Then he lifted me up on his shoulders and ran down toward the yard. I started to cry. At least five soldiers got out of the truck. They weren't the same ones who used to come and get the horses, but it was the same kind of truck. We hid behind a lilac bush and stood there looking down into the farmyard. They put bayonets on their rifles and then ran off toward the kitchen. Papa told me to stay where I was, he was going to go in. But I didn't want to. I didn't want to be left alone, and I started to cry again. So he picked me up again and carried me, and we went slowly down toward the house. He carried me against his chest, and he held one hand over the back of my neck. I was crying. "Calm," he said. "Be calm." And then I remember thinking that if Papa was so calm, then there couldn't be anything dangerous. We went right into the kitchen. One of the soldiers was standing there with his rifle and bayonet pointed straight at Mama, and the others were going around opening all the cupboards and dragging out all our clothes and ripping up the beds with their bayonets. When we came in, the one in the kitchen yelled to the others, and they told Papa to put me down on the floor. Then they shoved him out in the yard and pushed him into the truck and drove away with him.

A few days later they had him standing by the church, bound. Mama left me with the manager's wife—she was going to stay by Papa all day. The manager had five children, and we always used to play together. That day they tied me up to the swings and walked around me and pointed at me with sticks and rakes and yelled, "Traitor! Traitor!" I screamed as loud as I could, so then their mother came and bawled me out for screaming, because then everyone in the whole village would know where I was. She took me up to the attic and locked me in. In the evening, when Mama came to get me, she'd been crying her eyes out. Whenever we talked about it later, she always said that that was her Good Friday. Now she knew what Good Friday was like for the people who loved Jesus, and for the people who loved justice. From that day on, I think, and ever since, Papa's been almost a Christ-figure for her. I remember when I'd ask her when Papa was coming back, she used to say, "Be calm, my child. He shall come."

She was as sure of that as of Christ's Resurrection and of his Second Coming on Judgment Day, when the sheep shall be separated from the goats.

But it was a long time before Papa came. Just two days after he'd stood up by the church, men came with five big trucks and got all the horses. Mama kept asking them, "Where is my husband? Where is my husband?"

She stood by the trucks and kept shouting out that same question all the time they were loading the horses: "Where is my husband? Where is my husband?" I can still hear her voice. Nobody answered her. But they weren't mean to her either. I was sitting in the kitchen window. When the trucks drove off, she ran after them, shouting.

After that we didn't go around with anyone else in the village, and I didn't play with the manager's children any more. I didn't even go out and play by myself. Mama was always with me. In the evenings she sat and read to me from devotional books. She taught me prayers, and told me stories about Jesus. In the end, the good will triumph and the evil will burn in Gehenna.

When I think about it, that was a remarkable time. All I remember is a great loneliness and a great deal in common with my mother. I followed her everywhere. She was trying to take care of the whole farm by herself, but there must have been a lot she couldn't manage. I don't know how she did it. In the mornings the manager would come in, and Mama would sit and talk to him. Then he quit coming. I think after a while Mama just left it up to him to take care of everything. I think she only took care of the business side. It seems to me there were long periods when neither of us left the house. Once in a while, Czech or German soldiers would come and spend the night with us. When the Czechs came, I was always afraid. Mama would take all the food we had and put it out for them. Then we'd lock ourselves in together. I think Mama said prayers all night long.

I don't think she ever knew what was going on—she probably knew as little as I did. I don't remember that she ever listened to the radio. I don't remember that she ever read newspapers. All I remember is that we used to sit there together, afraid, and make dolls and say prayers and read religious books.

And then Papa came back. Suddenly, there he was, standing in the room, and I think Mama was just as frightened as I was. He didn't have any hair on his head. He had such an awful face. I remember I screamed and cried. Now I didn't even have Mama all to myself any more, I thought, now I'm even lonelier. It's cruel to say it, but to be honest, I felt like I was being set free when they came and took him away the next time, and by that time I was old enough to know that I couldn't tell Mama about it. That was the first thing I ever had to bear all alone. I knew it was a sin, but I couldn't confess it.

We came here. I wasn't sorry. The only thing I knew was that something entirely new was beginning. I thought we were going to get away from everything, the confinement, the fear, the loneliness. I remember people crying, and getting on the train as if to go to our deaths. On the train the adults were talking about a death train. But I wasn't afraid of dying. As many prayers as I'd prayed, God wouldn't let anything bad happen to me. And he wouldn't punish me for what I'd thought about my father. I had told about it in so many prayers. And the things they were talking about on the train made me even calmer—there were going to be long lines at the gates of Gehenna, even without me.

And I remember going down to the train, and then riding it through what was my homeland. It was like I was seeing that scenery for the first time. It was both the first time and the last time. I've never wanted to go back.

When we got here, I realized that everything really was going to be different. I went to school, and the way they taught me to hate everything in the past went right along with how I felt myself. Even for us little kids, the teacher told us that a new era had begun. And she talked about the past as if it were a time of terror. And what she said was the truth for me. And when I told Mama what I'd heard in school, she said it was the truth, and that we should thank Our Lord for it. When I told my teacher what Mama said, that we should thank Our Lord, the teacher laughed and said that we should thank the Heroes of the Soviet Revolution. That sounded like an even more powerful God.

After class, the teacher made me stay, and she told me never again to mention Our Lord in school. Now we were supposed to talk about the Heroes of the Soviet Revolution. And when I went home, I told Mama we weren't supposed to thank Our Lord, but the Heroes of the Soviet Revolution. It was strange, but Mama's face lit up and she looked so happy. She laughed, and it wasn't often I'd seen her laugh. "Yes," she said. "We should thank them too."

Mama worked hard. In school we learned all about Nazism. In the evenings, Mama would talk about Papa sometimes. She did that so I'd know that Papa wasn't one of those who'd committed crimes, so that from everything I was learning in school about the way things had been, I wouldn't also learn to hate my father.

Even I started to think of him as a Christ-figure.

In the afternoons I played out here in the yard with a bunch of other children. It was the beginning of a new time. In the evenings, when I'd finished my homework, Mama and I would sit and talk.

I did well in school. Mama and I did my lessons together. She thought it was as much fun as I did. We'd test each other, and I'd tell Mama what the teacher had told us in school. She used to say there was so much she hadn't learned when she was in school.

Then Papa came back the second time, and everything was different again.

He looked much worse than the first time.

But both Mama and I were happy that first day. He was sick, but that didn't matter—he was back. During the daytime he mostly lay in bed. At night he'd talk to Mama. There wasn't much left of our lessons and our conversations in the evenings, but that didn't matter so much, I thought; I was out playing most of the time. And then he died. I thought it was just from grief that Mama didn't talk to me so much after that. She didn't go through my lessons with me any more, either. She didn't answer when I spoke to her. The only thing she wanted to talk about was faith.

"The only thing we have is our God," she said. "The only thing we can depend on is God."

✖ A Weekend at the Körner Hotel

Saturday afternoon. Dieter Orphal sits at a table in the hotel dining room, drinking beer.

Frau Waslowski, the waitress, stands by his table. As soon as he empties his glass, she gets him another.

Dieter is wearing a double-breasted suit and rimless glasses. He has a light, barely visible mustache. During his conversation with Frau Waslowski, he changes his glasses, puts on a pair with black rims, looks questioningly at Frau Waslowski. She nods. He keeps them on.

Dieter Orphal is 23 years old and living in Neustadt temporarily, staying at the Theodor Körner for five weeks while, he tells me, he is doing preliminary work on a tunneling project at the tannery.

His actual home is about four miles from Schwerin—a two-room apartment to himself, he says, with a kitchen.

Preisstufe II

HOG *Tageskarte*

Nonstadt-Glowo, 3.3.1968

Der Küchenmeister empfiehlt:

Mittagskarte

Suppen:
Goulaschsuppe	-,80
Brühe mit Einlage	-,65
Ochsenschwanzsuppe	-,75
Tomatensuppe	-,45

Gedeck I: Tomatensuppe
Rinderrouladen, Rotkohl, Salzkartoffeln
Aprikosen   4,15

Gedeck II: Eierflockensuppe
Schweinekotelett, Rotkohl, Salzkartoffeln
Birnen   3,75

Eisbein mit Sauerkraut, Salzkart.	2,85
Schinken" Prager Art"Salzkart.	2,20
Schweinekotelett, Rotkohl, Salzkart.	2,45
Bratwurst, Sauerkraut, Salzkart.	1,65
Rinderfilet, Bohnensalat, Salzkart.	2,95
Schweinebraten, Rotkohl, Salzkart.	2,70
Ung.Goulasch, gem.Salat, Salzkart.	2,80
Hackbraten, gem.Salat, Salzkart.	2,50
Rinderrouladen, gem.Salat, Salzkart.	3,05
Schweineschnitzel, Rotkohl, Salzkart.	2,45
Fischfilet mit Mayonaisensalat	2,00
Spiegelei mit Mayonaisensalat	1,80
Brathering mit Kartoffelpüree	1,20

Kompott: Aprikosen -,65
        Birnen -,65

WBG II/10/4 DI G 104/87 1007 5

HO Restaurant—Daily Menu
Menu from the Theodor Körner:

Price Level II

HOG* Daily Menu

Neustadt-Glewe, March 3, 1968

The chef recommends:

Dinner Menu

Soups:	Goulash soup	.80
	Bouillon with trimmings	.65
	Ox-tail soup	.75
	Tomato soup	.45

Dinner #1: Tomato soup
Rolled beef, red cabbage, boiled potatoes
                    Apricots   4.15

Dinner #2: Soup with egg
Pork chop, red cabbage, boiled potatoes
                    Pears   3.75

Pigs' feet with sauerkraut, boiled pot.	2.85
Ham à la Prague,** boiled pot.	2.20
Pork chop, red cabbage, boiled pot.	2.45
Bratwurst, sauerkraut, boiled pot.	1.65
Beef fillet, bean salad, boiled pot.	2.95
Roast pork, red cabbage, boiled pot.	2.70
Hung. goulash, mixed salad, boiled pot.	2.80
Meat loaf, mixed salad, boiled pot.	2.50
Rolled beef, mixed salad, boiled pot.	3.05
Pork schnitzel, red cabbage, boiled pot.	2.45

Fish fillet with mayonnaise salad		2.00
Fried egg with mayonnaise salad		1.80
Fried Baltic herring with mashed potatoes		1.20
Fruit compote:	Apricots	.65
	Pears	.65

*HOG=HO Gaststätte—HO Restaurant
**Fried smoked ham.

During the periods when he isn't working in Schwerin, where the construction firm has its headquarters, he seldom goes home. Actually, he doesn't have anything at all to do at home.

He has no relatives there, no job there. But he lives there, pays his 15 marks monthly rent there.

He used to have a motorcycle, but he sold it in November—it got too cold to ride it. Besides, he needs a suit. He got 1,200 marks for the motorcycle, the suit cost 350—a double-breasted dark suit with white stripes, vest, pants with cuffs. He lives at the hotel with Horst, one of his workmates on the tunneling job.

Outside of working hours, the two of them don't hang around together. They prepare meals together in their hotel room; that is, they cut up some bologna or brockwurst or smoked ham, slice bread, drink a beer. Dieter usually has a sack of fruit lying around too.

They go to sleep early in the evenings, as early as 8. They get up at 5:30.

▣ A WEEKDAY MORNING

Dieter and Horst each drink a beer and make sandwiches —bologna, cheese, smoked ham again. Horst eats. For Dieter it's too early. He stuffs his sandwiches in his pocket.

Marten, the brigade leader, who lives down the hall with Kali, comes to check that they're up.

They start off for the tannery, where they arrive half an hour after the tannery workers. They wave to the gatekeeper, who already knows them, turn left, and walk along past the factory kindergarten.

They don't say much on the way. Dieter asks when Marten is going to take his vacation, but Marten doesn't answer, maybe doesn't hear.

Kali and Horst walk with bent backs and hanging arms,

Marten and Dieter straighten up with their arms swinging. Horst coughs the whole way.

Marten unlocks the tool shed.

They each take a long-handled spade. The preparations for the tunneling project consist primarily of digging. The soil is sandy and light.

Each of them hops down in his own hole. Horst lights a cigarette.

"Are you starting already, Horst?" Dieter says.

"What's it to you?" Horst answers.

"Come on, boys," says Marten. "Let's get to work."

They work in silence, Kali pushes his hat back on his head and looks at the time.

"Go ahead," says Marten. "It may get hot today."

Kali goes to get a case of beer—Grabower Brau in clasp-topped bottles. They each get a bottle, one bottle in the pile of sand by each hole.

Horst says that Lübzer Brau is better.

"So why don't you drink it?" Dieter wants to know.

Horst doesn't answer.

"You can't get Lübzer Brau at the Co-op on Bahnhofstrasse," says Marten.

About nine o'clock, Marten and Horst take off their shirts. It's the first time this year they've been able to work with their shirts off—two weeks ago they were still hacking away at frost.

They have lunch in the tannery canteen. There are two dishes to choose from: a cheap one for 90 pfennigs, and another dish you have to pay full price for, 2.30. The cheaper dish is potato pancakes. They all take it.

🕮 SATURDAY AFTERNOON

"Last week," Dieter says, "I was home with my mother in Schwerin. She's remarried. I don't get to see her because of her new husband—hadn't seen her in six months.

Her husband came in while I was there, and he threw me out."

A young man in a Beatles haircut comes into the restaurant and straight over to the table.

His name is Hans Waller. Dieter and Hans know each other—Hans works at the tannery, and they agree that they've seen each other in the canteen. Hans works in the chrome-tannery. He shows his hands, covered with brown blisters.

"When I dance with a girl, she always thinks I haven't washed," he says.

Hans is about 20. He has a white shirt with black stripes and rows of black roses printed between the stripes. He's wearing a bow tie, the ends of which he's tucked under the tips of his collar.

"This is no criticism," says Dieter. "It's nice like it is. But I think a regular black tie would look better, or maybe one of those real narrow ties, just a string."

Hans agrees. "It's not a criticism," Dieter repeats.

He immediately tells Hans, too, about his visit to Schwerin the week before. Hans listens, and answers quickly, as if to brush the subject aside.

"Listen . . . what's your name? Listen, Dieter. I was in a children's home, and one day they told me my parents had gone over to the West. That's five years ago, and if you think that was easy, well . . ."

He tells us that he got the shirt from his mother, who lives in Bremerhaven.

He asks if the others want to go with him to Ludwigslust that evening—The Elgitas are playing.

"Come on," he says. "You should see what it's like. The girls all have short skirts."

Dieter says he doesn't want to go.

"But you're coming to Blievenstorf tomorrow, aren't you?" says Hans. "There's a Youth Dance over there at three o'clock, why don't you come along?"

Dieter says that sounds better.

The train to Ludwigslust leaves at 6:32. More young people of Hans' age show up and collect around him. They're all going to Ludwigslust for the evening. They talk about spending the night, and the possibilities of arranging some way to get home.

"Aren't you coming along?" says Hans.

Dieter shakes his head. "I'm too old," he says.

"Idiot," says Hans. "You ought to see all the old men."

They agree to meet Sunday morning at 10. About six o'clock the Ludwigslust group starts off for the station. "Blievenstorf tomorrow," says Hans, as he gets up from the table.

When they've gone, Dieter says that he's already drunk too much; but he orders two cognacs.

◙ DIETER'S STORY

My father was an architect. He used to say that Schwerin was a city for architects. It's a beautiful place. He got a job with the city bureau of architecture.

From the time I first went to school, he always told me I shouldn't believe what they said—"The teachers," he'd say, "aren't any better than the rest of us."

My father wanted me to be an architect.

When I was in the seventh grade, a teacher came to our place and talked to my parents. Afterwards my father told me I wasn't supposed to say anything at school about what we talked about at home, or what we did.

I was a Pioneer, went to meetings all the time—Papa said I had to—and then I went into the FDJ. "If you want to be an architect," my father said, "you have to put up with all that other stuff too. Otherwise you'll never get into the right schools," he said. "It doesn't matter how clever you are."

When I found out I wasn't going to get to go to architectural school after all, I took the bus to Boizenburg one day. Stayed with my cousin. I was 16 then.

For a week I walked around in Boizenburg, watching the guards. I made up a schedule of when the guard was changed, watched how the guards walked their rounds, and after a week I went over.

There's no trick to it.

You can still do it today, if you want to. Today I wouldn't do it. It's not any easier over there than it is here. You have to work over there too. But there's no trick to getting over the border. They cover you from the other side, in case they start shooting from this side. You can't count on it, but you can figure they will.

I just walked across, just like that. Not a shot was fired.

The border police on the other side took care of me, sent me to a camp, and notified my parents. And they answered by demanding I be sent back.

Since I was only 16 years old, they could do that. The people on the other side don't have anything against extradition—they're glad to do it. When I got back, they had me up before the court as a fugitive from the republic. I was sentenced to ten months, and they sent me to the big prison in Bützow. But I couldn't understand why my parents had asked to have me sent back.

In prison we had a pretty good deal. I worked as a bricklayer. If you wanted to work, you could. If you didn't want to, you didn't have to. But the ones who didn't work had to pay for their keep. And the ones who worked got paid.

Good food.

When I got out, I had some nice savings to get started on.

I wrote to my parents from prison and asked them to explain why they didn't let me stay in the West. I don't know if there's censorship, but anyway the letter got there. But it was a while before I got an answer.

Finally my mother wrote, and I've got that letter here in my wallet. She said they had me brought back out of consideration for me. She said I'd acted hastily, and that a person shouldn't give in to his whims like that, because even if I had been denied the training I'd wanted, there were still many paths open to me. That's what she wrote. It was out of consideration, she said.

It seemed to me it was like somebody had dictated it to her. It didn't sound like her at all.

She wrote that she knew all too well that we hadn't always had the best relationship, like she and Papa wanted, but that I should forgive them too, because, she said, they had to suffer a great deal in the past, and when I was born, I was their hope for a new and better world. That's the sort of thing she wrote, and she promised me all sorts of help, but she didn't say how I was supposed to get it.

I don't know how parents can help their children, but I'd like to believe it.

After ten months I got out of Bützow, and Papa picked me up outside the gates. When we got home to Schwerin, Mama had fixed a nice meal. She'd taken the day off work. Papa was on sick leave. He was going to the hospital the next day.

I started as a construction worker. There was a lot of construction in Schwerin then—still is. I carried hod. I thought that later I'd learn to be a bricklayer—a trade is still a trade, after all, and it's a start. That's what Papa said too. It was actually him that helped me at the beginning.

A month later he died. It was some kind of blood disease. We knew he was going to die, but we didn't think it would happen that fast.

Mama and I did the best we could to make life pleasant for each other. I stayed home with her every evening. It went on like that for a few months.

But then one Sunday dinner, Mama set the table for three again.

And that's that.

Now I can't see Mama any more. And that's all there is to it—that's the story of my life.

Sunday morning. Dieter sits in the dining room again; it is five minutes to ten. At ten, the dining room is opened to the public, but for hotel guests it opens at seven. He and Hans have agreed to meet at ten.

Hans arrives at 10:15.

"Today, Blievenstorf," he says.

"Are you sure we've got some way of getting there and back again?" Dieter asks.

"We can always walk. I've walked to Blievenstorf lots of times."

"Not in this weather."

"Then we'll ride bikes."

Hans tells about the night before.

He had borrowed a bicycle in Ludwigslust and ridden it home. A traffic policeman had stopped him because he didn't have a light on the bike.

"But he didn't say anything about my hair. He couldn't, not a traffic cop. Boy, Dieter, they were after me at the tannery—you better believe it. But I do my job. And as long as I do my job, they can't cut my hair."

"It looks good on you," Dieter says. "That's not true of everybody who wears it that way."

Dieter asks Hans what he does with his laundry.

"I send it to the laundry," Hans answers. "Weird, hunh?"

Dieter says that when *his* clothes get dirty, he throws them away—at least the underwear: "It just wouldn't occur to me to send my underpants to the laundry."

Hans wants to show us how he lives. He has two tape recorders, he says. There's no point in having a record player, since he can't buy the records he wants. With the tape recorders, he can tape music from Hamburg and West Berlin, and sometimes he can get good sound quality on Radio Luxembourg. He thinks the Rolling Stones are better than the Beatles. A tape recorder costs 120 marks. He only uses them for music.

"Actually, I wanted to be a singer," he says. "But you can't do that here."

"Sure you can," says Dieter.

—But you have to take a whole bunch of tests, and go to a whole bunch of schools.

—Yeah, sure.

—You don't have to do that over there.

Hans rents a furnished room, right off the square. The furniture is heavy, of brown oak. There is a large table that must once have been meant for a dining table, and a bureau.

A landscape hangs on the wall—a lake, a swan, a rowboat pulled up on the shore, a cabin at the edge of the woods. Dieter laughs at it.

Hans says he likes it. It's included in the furnishings.

He's pinned up pictures of pop stars on the wallpaper, and he's hung up a guitar string on a nail. He tells how a band from Berlin was in Grabow, and one of the guitar players smashed his guitar. The string had come flying out across the dance floor.

Hans pays 35 marks a month for the room. Dieter thinks it's too much, and Hans says he'll talk to the landlady.

Dieter says it certainly isn't the landlady who decides. He thinks Hans should go to the mayor.

"Not on your life," says Hans. "That's the last thing I'd do. I'd rather pay too much."

He earns 450 a month at the chrome-tannery. As a matter of fact, he says, he was trained as a smith, but there aren't any openings for a smith.

—There are people with no training at all who make

more than I do. It's really not fair. It really ought to pay to get training.

About 3:30 they start off for Blievenstorf.

There are no buses or trains. Hans takes the bike he borrowed the evening before in Ludwigslust, and lends his own bike to Dieter. Two other boys go along, Otto and Reinhold. Neither of them has a bike, so they ride double. There's a drizzle, cold, hail.

At about seven o'clock they come back, soaked through, the whole group. The dance in Blievenstorf had been canceled. Otto is drunk. Instead of the dance, they had gone to a restaurant. Otto goes home.

"His mother never says a word when he comes home drunk," Hans notes. "He has a nice mother."

Dieter goes to change his clothes, and comes back in a high-collared jacket with flaps on the pockets.

Hans lets his clothes dry on his body in the warmth of the Theodor Körner dining room. He orders a cup of soup. It's the third time he's eaten soup today—70 pfennigs a cup.

A bright, clucking laugh is heard across the room. It's Herr Puttain. He has sleekly combed white hair and a white mustache.

Frau Waslowski has been telling him about the fools who went to Blievenstorf to dance without first finding out if there was going to be a dance. Herr Puttain has a good laugh. He orders small glasses of cognac for the Blievenstorf travelers, raises his own glass, and they all drink to each other across the room. He is singing something. He is almost always singing—a tenor.

He waves time with his right hand while he sings. Then he laughs his bright laugh. Then he raises his glass toward the Blievenstorf travelers, who bow, nod their thanks, and drink. Then Herr Puttain begins to sing to himself again.

It grows late. A young man from Parchim comes to the table—he had also been in Ludwigslust the evening before. He's missed the train and intends to take a taxi home, is only hoping to find someone to share the taxi with. Hans doubts he'll find anyone, doubts he'll even be able to get a taxi. Frau Soden has had a fare all the way to Grabow, and hasn't come back yet.

The best chance, he says, is that some Russians will come along.

Horst comes and sits down at the table too, but only for a little while. Then he goes up to his room and goes to bed. Dieter stays on.

"How long have you had that T-shirt on?" he asks the boy from Parchim.

The Parchimer has on a checked shirt, open at the neck. An undershirt is visible in the opening, noticeably dirty.

Dieter says, with a smile, "You're a regular pigpen."

He criticizes the Parchim boy's narrow-legged pants: "I think you'll find that narrow-legged pants aren't in any more. You're not supposed to wear bell-bottoms any more either. Pants are supposed to be wide, all the way down."

To Hans he says, "I'm not talking about you, Hans. You're a Beatle."

Hans says to the Parchim boy, "Listen, you know your T-shirt really is pretty dirty."

The boy from Parchim tries to make fun of Dieter's jacket: "You're Chinese, of course."

Dieter laughs. The boy from Parchim takes a long sheath knife out of his back pocket and lays it on the table.

"Cool it," says Hans. "Put the knife away."

To Dieter he says, "Go get Horst."

Dieter gets up without saying anything and goes up to his and Horst's room.

Frau Waslowski watches him leave. He hasn't paid. Hans explains that he is coming right back, that he's only gone to get his buddy.

It's at least a quarter of an hour before Dieter comes back, alone, and sits back down at the table.

Herr Puttain is still singing.

Dieter sits silently for a long time. When Hans asks him about Horst, he says Horst didn't want to come.

After another silence, Dieter takes out a knife.

He lays it on the table in front of him, with his right hand around the handle and his left around the sheath. Very calmly, the boy from Parchim takes out his knife again, and holds it in front of him the same way Dieter is holding his.

Reinhold looks narrowly at the two knives.

"They're equal," he says.

"Come on, Dieter," says Hans. "Put away the knife."

The boy from Parchim draws his knife out of the sheath, which he calmly puts back in his pocket. Dieter quickly pulls his own knife out, and the sheath falls to the floor. Reinhold picks it up.

"You guys are crazy," says Hans. "Put away the knife, Dieter."

"No. I'm ready."

"*I*'m ready."

"He'll kill you, Deiter," says Hans. "And it'll be just as bad if you kill him."

A large, powerful man is standing behind the boy from Parchim. He bends down and gets a grip on the boy's right wrist. The boy's hand slowly opens, and the knife falls out.

While this is happening, Dieter gets up and leaves.

"Hide the knife, Dieter," says Hans.

The big man says nothing. He takes the boy's knife. Everything has happened very quietly, no commotion at the tables on either side. The big man sits calmly down at his table again, doesn't even appear to tell his companions about it.

On Monday, Dieter's brigade wasn't supposed to start work until 1:30.

At about 9:30 that morning, Dieter and Hans happened to run into each other on Breitscheidstrasse outside the hotel. Dieter was on his way into the hotel. Hans suggested they eat together, but Dieter said he had some errands to do first.

Three-quarters of an hour later, Dieter was tottering around in the hotel corridor. He gave the chambermaid a letter addressed to a Vera Mayer. The chambermaid thought he was behaving oddly. After handing her the letter, he went back toward his room, sat down at a table just outside, crossed his arms on the tabletop, and rested his head on his arms. He was sweating heavily. The chambermaid opened the door to the room, where Horst still lay in bed. On Dieter's bed lay empty foil wrappings from sleeping tablets. Obviously, he had poisoned himself.

"Didn't you notice anything?" the chambermaid asked Horst.

"No," he said.

An ambulance was called from the Stift Bethlehem in Ludwigslust.

"How many did you take?"

"Twenty," said Dieter.

"What a dumb thing to do," said the chambermaid. "I'm sure he didn't have to do that."

"Come on, Dieter, pull yourself together," said Horst. "What kind of nonsense is this?"

After a while, Dieter fell asleep. The chambermaid, without hesitation, ripped open the letter. She read it to herself, then aloud:

When you get this letter, I will no longer be here. In half an hour, I will no longer be here. We will never meet again. It is by your own choice, and my departure is irrevocable.

"Dear God, what does he mean? Didn't you really notice anything?"

"He asked me for two marks to buy beer with. Then he came back, and I noticed he was sitting and writing. Come on, Dieter, wake up! What are you trying to do?"

Dieter slept. It took 45 minutes for the ambulance to come the 5½ miles from Ludwigslust.

The ambulance driver: "Is anyone going along?"

The four men who'd carried Dieter to the ambulance turned to Horst:

"Are you going along?"

"I have to start work at 1:30. I won't have time to get back. Who's going to pay for my lost time? And for the trip back? No, I'm not going."

Hans had been waiting for Dieter at the Stadt Hamburg, where they'd agreed to meet, since ten o'clock. He found out what had happened about an hour later.

"I was on Dieter's side. He could have died yesterday, but he was saved. I think I can say I saved his life yesterday. I wonder if it was what happened yesterday that did it, or if it was that thing with his mother."

Hans was supposed to start his shift at one o'clock, but he didn't go to work. He drank three cognacs, one after the other.

"No, I'm not going to work today. They can't fire me. As long as they keep me in the chrome-tannery, I'll stay away when I want to. When I work, I'm a good worker— you can ask the brigade leader."

No one in Dieter's brigade went to work, either. They carried Kali up to his room about three o'clock. Marten was already in bed.

✿ Horst's Story

Believe it or not, I'm from Hamburg. Lived on the Reeperbahn, had a wife, had three kids. Or my wife had three
kids. My folks had a place—still have. Do you know the
Reeperbahn? If you ever go there, say hello from me, from
Horst. You go along the big street from downtown, then
down to the left, up the hill—there on the corner on
the left, that's my father's place. Not a big place, but we
made do. I helped my folks out. You can see I'm strong.
Look at that hand, buddy—What that didn't do before
it took hold of a spade, *boy.* Excuse me for speaking English.

You know the Reeperbahn, it's an international market-
place. I stood out by the street and hustled the customers
in, and then threw them out again. I was better at throwing
them out than in. Take a look at my mug—I'm no beauty.
You see the scar on my cheek, well, don't think I'm afraid
of knives. But it's better if you use your hands. I've never
tried to mark anyone for life. You push in somebody's
nose, that's an accident, but you cut up somebody's face,
you're marking him for life. I'm not talking about Dieter
now, but people that carry knives can blame themselves
for what happens. See here on my arm—that was a knife
too. What do people want with knives? It's only chicken-
shits carry knives. Back home I didn't even carry a stick.
I had my hands, see, and they were enough—you better
believe it, *boy.* Forgive the English. You understand English. You can't imagine the things these hands have done.
I'm 30. Lived in the Reeperbahn all my life, up to three
years ago. I had my first woman when I was 11. Woman,
girl, she was a pro, of course. But I didn't pay her. Never
paid. See, I'm Catholic. You don't pay for that kind of
thing if you're a Catholic.

Are you Lutheran? I don't have anything against Lutherans. But my papa used to say, "It's the Lutherans we live on." He had some girls, too, you know—girls, whores, Catholics got a discount. That's what you call faith. Dieter didn't have any faith. I'm not going to talk about Dieter, but he didn't give a shit about God. You got to watch that. He didn't have any respect for life. You just don't kill yourself, that's a mortal sin. You know that well enough. It's his own fault if he dies. If he wants to kill himself, he can. It's not my responsibility. But I'm not going to talk about Dieter.

What do you think it's like, living in the Reeperbahn? What do you think goes on at night? I've got three kids, and they'll grow up just like I did. You hear a shot in the middle of the night, and they carry out a body. The next morning, *boy,* you go to school at 7:30. The teacher thinks you're dumb. I'm not dumb. Am I? It's just that you're thinking about something else.

My wife's from Stuttgart. That is to say, to be exact, my wife *was* from Stuttgart. There's a difference—I don't have a wife any more. Papa was the one who found her. He was going to take her on, but since I was 17, he thought he'd let me test her out for a while first. Nice father, hunh? Then we got married. The wife stood behind the counter and I was at the door, hustling 'em in and throwing 'em out.

But it seems that wasn't enough for her. You know, it was still an honest job, and business was good. You have no idea how much you can make on the side. Look at my hands, *boy.* One day I found out my wife was making a little extra on the side too. Look at these hands. Believe me, I took care of him with these here hands—in the neck. There's a difference between killing yourself and killing somebody else. I was mad as hell, you understand, and I didn't know what I was doing. But, *boy,* I don't regret it.

I got to the border before they found out, but the West German police came and got me from the border camp. Then I sat in prison for four years.

Boy, you're shaking. What are you afraid of? Give me your hand—my God, you're weaker than Dieter. Deiter thought he was something, thought he was better than the rest of us. But he was a worker too, and he'd been in jail. I don't say anything about anyone just because he's been in, but Dieter was in for ten months—you know why? National security. They couldn't trust him. I don't care about politics. I didn't come here for political reasons. When I came out of prison, I just didn't know what else to do. Papa'd said I couldn't come back to the Reeperbahn. So what was I supposed to do?

✖ Dieter Recovers

On Tuesday, a week later, Dieter got out of the hospital. He came back to the hotel in Neustadt in the afternoon. The next day he was going on to the mental clinic in Schwerin for observation.

Now I'm not allowed to drink beer or schnapps or coffee or tea—the old pump won't take it.

The hospital was fine. They pumped my stomach and did two transfusions. Along about six in the evening I came back to life, just in time for evening prayer.

They had evening prayer every day. A nurse would come and say a prayer by the edge of the bed.

My mother came for a visit last Thursday. I talked to the doctor the whole morning, and the whole afternoon I talked to my mother, and then it was time for evening prayer again. Say, who was it opened the letter? Do you know?

The doctor was great. But he thought it was because of some girl. Why do they always believe something else than what you tell them? Why should it have anything to do with a girl? When Mother was at the hospital, she sat and talked about how I had a duty to my country. Her husband's in the party. Because I ran away that time, he calls me a Fascist and a traitor. I could report him for that.

You know, it wasn't my fault I didn't get to go to school to be an architect. It was my parents, and what they taught me to believe. They taught me to object every time my friends in the party would come up with even the simplest statements.

I was in the Pioneers and the FDJ, and it really was a new life. And now they tell me I'm a Fascist. It's really too much. You know, I tried to kill myself once before—I probably never told you about that. That was when I was still in school. At recess one day, there was one of my classmates who said my father was a Fascist. He wasn't. He had been, but there weren't many people's fathers that hadn't been. I don't see why he said it was *my* father that was a Fascist. Wasn't I supposed to defend my father? That's what I did, even if I didn't know what I was defending.

Later, when I talked to the principal about my education, he said I couldn't ask the state to invest money educating a person who'd shown so little respect for his own life. It was too big an economic risk from the state's standpoint, he said. But don't you think it's the other way around? Don't you? I'm worthless now. What do you think it's like to stand there day after day and shovel dirt with Horst? Or Marten and Kali? Well, Marten's O.K. But they're still pretty simple people. I tell myself I won't despise them. So should I feel guilty when I do anyway? It all comes from the idea that no one is worth more than anyone else. If I'm not worth any more than they are, then I'm not worth anything. That's what I told the doctor too. He won't report me.

Dieter went down to the tannery to show Marten his sick leave papers and his letter to Schwerin. Work on the tunnel stopped; a hearty welcome, joking invitations to Dieter to take a shovel.

"When are you coming back?"

"I'm on sick leave another week."

"That's a good deal."

"I'd like to start working again."

"Yeah, sure."

"Say, Marten, what did you do with the knife? Did you give it to the police? That's what I heard."

"You must have heard wrong. I didn't give any knife to the police."

"That was Herr Stiefel, the hotel manager. He came and searched the whole room," Horst reports. " 'Where's the knife? Where's the knife?' he kept asking me. I never said anything about the knife."

"You must have misunderstood. We never said anything."

"Did they come and ask all of you questions?" Dieter asks them.

"We never said a word," Marten says.

"Not a peep," says Kali. "The collective's got to stick together."

"Aren't you going to stay at the mental hospital afterwards?" Marten asks him.

"I don't even want to go there," says Dieter.

"You'll have a good deal there," says Marten. "Lie in bed and sleep."

"I haven't slept for five nights."

"Didn't they give you any sleeping pills?" Horst asks. They laugh.

"Come on boys, let's get to work," says Marten.

B. Ablieferungssoll tierische Erzeugnisse

Erzeugnis		*)	*)	Mindestablieferung in % bis			
				I. Quartal	II. Quartal	III. Quartal	IV. Quartal
1. Lebendvieh insgesamt kg	*1236*						
davon: Lebendvieh ohne Schwein kg	*507*			25%	50%	75%	100%
Schwein kg	*729*						
2. Geflügel Gänse, Enten od. Puten kg	*6,5*					30%	100%
3. Eier nicht unt. 45 g je Stück **) kg/Stück	*1289*			30%	85%	95%	100%
4. Milch, mit einem Fettgehalt von 3,5 % kg	*4809*			30%	60%	85%	100%
5. Wolle natura kg				bis 15. Dez. = 100%			

Schlachtvieh, Milch und Eier sind mindestens nach den in den Quartalen festgelegten Ablieferungssätzen anteilmäßig in jedem Monat zu erfüllen. Wolle ist spätestens 14 Tage nach der Schur abzuliefern.

Die an Stelle von Wolle festgelegten Austauschmengen sind im Ablieferungssoll von Lebendvieh bzw. Milch enthalten.

Gegen diesen Ablieferungsbescheid kann nach der Verordnung innerhalb von 10 Tagen nach Aushändigung beim Rat der Gemeinde Einspruch erhoben werden.

Gegen die Entscheidung des Rates der Gemeinde über den Einspruch kann innerhalb von 10 Tagen, nach der Zustellung, Einspruch beim Rat des Kreises über den Rat der Gemeinde erhoben werden.

Die Entscheidung des Rates des Kreises ist endgültig.

Die Einlegung eines Einspruches entbindet nicht von der Verpflichtung, die Ablieferungen zur Erfüllung der Pflichtablieferung termingerecht und in voller Höhe vorzunehmen.

Neustadt-Glewe, am ....*12. 12.*....... 195*8*

Siegel

Der Rat der Gemeinde

[signature]

Bürgermeister

B. Obligation for Delivery of Animal Products					
Product		Minimum delivery in % for			
		1st Quarter	2nd Quarter	3rd Quarter	4th Quarter
1. Livestock, total kg.	1,236 (2,725 lb.)				
of which: Livestock except hogs kg.	507 (1,118 lb.)	25%	50%	75%	100%
Hogs kg.	729 (1,607 lb.)				
2. Poultry Geese, ducks, or turkeys kg.	6.5 (14 lb.)			30%	100%
3. Eggs not under 45 g. each kg./number	(1.59 oz.) 1,289	30%	85%	95%	100%
4. Milk, with a fat content of 3.5% kg.	4,809 (10,406 lb.)	30%	60%	85%	100%
5. Natural wool		by Dec. 15 = 100%			

Delivery obligations for animals for slaughter, milk, and eggs must be filled *each month* in proportion to the quotas set down for each quarter. Wool must be delivered within 14 days of shearing.

Quotas assigned in place of wool are included in the Obligation under animals or milk.

According to regulations, a protest against this order may be lodged with the municipal council within ten days of receipt.

A protest against the decision of the municipal council on the initial protest may be lodged with the district council within ten days of delivery of the municipal council's decision.

The decision of the district council is *final*.

Submission of a protest does in no way absolve the obligation to complete delivery in full, according to the time schedule listed above.

Neustadt-Glewe, Dec. 12, 1958   The Municipal Council
           Seal   Diederich
                                                          Mayor
[At the end of the fifties, the authorities pursued
a vigorous campaign to induce farmers to join collectives.]

❈ The Case of
Friedrich Lemke

Friedrich Lemke is the last member in Neustadt of a large clan whose other members, singly and in pairs, all moved to West Germany between 1948 and 1959. But Friedrich himself has never given a second thought to the idea of leaving home.

Six months ago, Lemke was brought into court in Ludwigslust. The affair had begun with someone's report that, on the way from the fields to his stalls on Petersilienstrasse, Lemke had beaten his cow with a willow switch, hollering "Hurry up, Henrietta! Hurry up, Henrietta!," followed occasionally by a more muted but still quite clearly audible, "Or I'll beat you as red as the party!"

According to the complaint, this was considered an inappropriate remark, since it implied whipping within the party. Moreover, Henrietta was not only the name of Friedrich Lemke's cow, but also the name of Commissioner Brentzler's wife. The latter, at the monthly meeting of the Party Women's Society shortly before, had expressed herself so forcefully on the subject of those townspeople who had not yet taken a political stand in favor of the party, that news of it had reached even Friedrich Lemke's ears, which were otherwise exposed to few of the town's many rumors and reports. Frau Brentzler's utterances had, indeed, included such information as to betray the fact that Commissioner Brentzler was not altogether silent in his own home about certain observations he had made in the course of his duties.

All of this naturally accelerated the course of justice in the Lemke case, which might otherwise have seemed comparatively harmless, at least to those who knew Friedrich Lemke, his past, and his general way of life. (All the information here comes from separate but concurring sources.)

Immediately after the war, Lemke married the widow of his second cousin, who had been killed in action. She was characterized by an aristocratic bearing and fine manners—which made the marriage even more surprising than it was already. For everyone had grown accustomed to looking upon Friedrich Lemke as an inveterate recluse, having nothing in common with the rest of the Lemke clan except certain arrangements for the cultivation of the family lands.

The degree to which he differed from the rest of the family, even in appearance, was, at its greatest, comparable with that of his half-brother, Frans-Günther Lemke. But even they differed in different ways—Frans-Günther primarily by virtue of a still-legendary corpulence and a thin, pale voice, in which, to be sure, he did not differ from the women in the family, but which definitely distinguished him from the men, of whom he was one, and from what was considered normal for that sex. Friedrich's outward dissimilarity consisted of a general boniness that marked even his face, not least of all his nose—and of a clubfoot.

The Lemke family with the exception of Friedrich, was

regarded as belonging to the town's social and intellectual elite. One was a judge, one a doctor, another was the conductor of the theater orchestra in Schwerin, still another was the curator of the museum in Ludwigslust and also a writer in the Low German style of Fritz Reuter and the local district. Frans-Günther had risen quickly to a high position at the Rathaus. Finally, they all owned small pieces of land here and there on the outskirts of town, as well as some forest.

But of all the Lemkean splendor, only Friedrich now remained.

The others sold their houses and forests when they left, and the money still lies in the bank in Ludwigslust, to be put at the disposal of any one of them who comes to Neustadt to visit. But so far, none of them has come to visit, and as far as Friedrich knows, none of them is thinking of coming to visit before Friedrich's funeral, or unless it should become possible to take their money with them to West Germany.

But they did not sell their land. The major part of it had already been under Friedrich's supervision for some time when, in 1953, the family council, in Friedrich's absence, entrusted to him complete responsibility for all the family lands within the borders of Neustadt.

Then, once a year, Friedrich sent a financial report to Frans-Günther in West Berlin, who always answered promptly with a glittery Christmas card, postmarked in February.

Friedrich Lemke now has nine such Christmas cards.

Friedrich remained the last private farmer in Neustadt.

As recently as a year ago, he still had, at his place on Petersilienstrasse, five sows, a bull, three cows, and two horses, in addition to poultry. He took care of everything himself: drove his slaughter animals to the slaughterhouse in Ludwigslust in a horse-drawn wagon, plowed and harrowed by horse, sowed by hand, spread fertilizer by hand. That he succeeded in holding on to his land when land reform was pushed through was considered a miracle. What was also a miracle was that he was able, with the agricultural methods he used, to fill the production quotas that were assigned him in his capacity as landowner, despite his efforts to remain an outsider. But he worked and he slaved.

As time went by, things became even harder. It didn't matter how impressed the town government was by his production results—personal sympathies cannot in any case be allowed to affect production plans. It was immediately after a mild warning on the completion of such a production plan that Friedrich was reported for having beaten his cow and for having loudly and publicly defamed the party. "That is to say," he says, "they didn't care so much about the cow. It's probably all right to flog a cow with a willow switch."

It was, in any event, the remark about Henrietta and the party that brought on the investigation through which the whole course of Friedrich Lemke's life was placed on record. He was, and always had been, interested only in agriculture. Under the Nazis, too, he had had no other interest. He very early chose the life of a recluse, isolated from the family that so happily contributed to his isolation by helping him acquire the house on Petersilienstrasse. He was a man of few words, "as if the animals were sufficient for him," according to the inquiry. He was seldom seen at the Körner. To the extent that he drank—and he did—he drank at home.

Out of the whole house he had chosen a single room for himself which, besides the kitchen, was the only one he kept for his own use. The rest he turned over to the pigs, chickens, and cats. Except for the years of his marriage, that was the way it had always been. The war had not caused him any inconvenience in that respect.

His clubfoot naturally exempted him from service. On the other hand, the clubfoot was, in a way, the cause of his having once before conducted himself in such a way as to give rise to a police report. But on that case there are no documents.

It was the day Fräulein Mattis, on Grosse Wallstrasse, was taken away, never to return. Fräulein Mattis was about 30, and lived with her mother in the same house as Thiele the shoemaker. Up to her 20th year she'd been like most girls. But there then occurred a drastic mental transformation as a result of which she could no longer work, no longer go dancing with her friends—an illness that the doctors judged incurable, a mental disease. No one had said she was never coming back. But people knew it, people figured it out. Why else do ten armed men come to collect one defenseless girl?

Friedrich Lemke was an eyewitness to this incident.

He disappeared for a whole week afterward. No one saw him, though there weren't many who gave the matter a second thought, aside from the neighbors, who had to come in and feed the animals and milk the cows when they bawled so loudly that the evening peace and quiet of the whole Kietz neighborhood were threatened. And the neighbors—the old Gericke couple—didn't tell anyone either, until later. They had grown accustomed to so many odd things that they took care not to make any fuss about them: "We thought, 'Well, he'll come back, or else he won't come back. We'll find out, all in good time.' "

After a week, Friedrich turned up at the foot of the Rathaus steps, facing the building.

No one remembers now just what he said, not even he himself any more. He recalls that two policemen took him into the Rathaus, and that it was not until his half-brother Frans-Günther intervened that he was allowed to go home. It is known, however, that he gestured with his clubfoot and asked to be sent to the same place Kätchen Mattis had been sent to, and—most importantly—it is known that what he said on that occasion was much more serious than the few words he let fall about Henrietta much later, for which he was held legally to account. This fact was even noted by the court, with some embarrassment, according to many witnesses. But there was no prospect of Frans-Günther's influence entering into the present case.

In point of fact, that influence appears to have been once very great. At the same time, however, it was this incident at the Rathaus that occasioned the final break between Friedrich and all the other Lemkes in Mecklenburg. For, in spite of everything, it was still a burden to have a man like that in one's family.

Perhaps, it is suggested, this affair also illuminates—in part—the background to the marriage into which Friedrich entered in 1947 with his second cousin's pretty widow, Mari, nee von Stein. "That was at the time of all the great atonement and rehabilitation, when people would commit any insanity at all in order to look respectable," as Elfriede Gericke puts it.

Mari von Stein had originally been a church soprano and had once performed in the cathedral in Ulm. During the last years of the war she had served in an entertainment detail, stationed principally in Berlin itself. According to reports, she is supposed to have sung for Mussolini once at some kind of soiree. Meanwhile, her husband, a major, was fighting and falling to tank fire in the environs of Leningrad. It was this woman who came and married Friedrich Lemke, and moved into one room on Peter-silienstrasse with the bulls, cows, horses, pigs, chickens, and cats.

She is described as of a thoroughly good and cherishing nature.

But after only a year and a half, she had cherished Friedrich enough. He didn't want to be cherished, would not be cherished—so goes the story. He wanted to work, and he had massive amounts of work to do.

When, now, Friedrich Lemke was brought into court for his remark about Henrietta and the party, the story of his life became his defense. No one could accuse him of being a deliberate political incendiary or propagandist. He was a man who, when he said anything at all, said just precisely whatever occurred to him. That what occurred to him was not altogether judicious was, in the final analysis, another matter. Henrietta Brentzler herself was not completely judicious in what she said.

The public prosecutor was of the decided opinion that Lemke's statement, however regrettable, was nevertheless entirely innocent. To treat this man as a political criminal, he maintained, would cast ridicule on the efforts of a constitutional state to fulfill its obligations to its citizens. On the other hand, he had to insist that Friedrich Lemke was not the ideal citizen in a Socialist society. He had always, in a spirit of bourgeois proprietorship, defended his right —to this day, indeed, his undeniable right—to protect his property, and even if he had so far succeeded, thanks to an astonishing capacity for work, in meeting whatever production demands could be placed on his property, yet we also had to realize that his holdings constituted an inefficiently operated production unit, which, under other circumstances, would undoubtedly have produced greater yields.

"His land," declared the prosecutor, "constitutes a small portion of our republic's total area, and we must realize that on this portion, up to now, the strivings of the Socialist society have not borne fruit, in that the owner of this piece of land, by opposing the inclusion of that property in a larger production cooperative, has also opposed the efforts of the republic to exploit the inner resources of the nation to their utmost extent.

"We must ask ourselves," he went on, "what the motive

has been. We have determined that we cannot treat Lemke as a political incendiary. There is, however, another matter that must be clarified. I would not go so far as to characterize Herr Lemke as standing in opposition to the goals of the Socialist state. However, this does not preclude the possibility of his having lived and acted in a manner which, if practiced by many, would delay the development of the Socialist state. It has been to the detriment of the republic, and—I think the court will agree with me on this point— it has been to Herr Lemke's own detriment, that he, in contrast to hundreds of other former small farmers in Neustadt, has declined to perceive the personal advantages he would have gained by accepting the invitation of the Turkode LPG and merging his farm into the collective. A hundred other former small farmers could have borne witness to Herr Lemke of the advantages. We can only conclude that Socialist thinking has never reached him. We cannot condemn him for that reason. He has the right to believe what he wants. He has the right to hold whatever views he wishes. And we can also understand, from the picture we have been given of Herr Lemke's hermit's life, why it is that he has not yet been convinced, of the easier working conditions, on the one hand, and of the economic advantages his former colleagues have enjoyed, on the other.

"The character testimony has also stressed that Herr Lemke suffers from a dependency on alcohol. Without in any way wishing to imply a connection, I think it is our duty, rather than to judge, to render assistance. I propose that Herr Lemke be submitted to a medical examination, which will determine his need for care in a home for alcoholics, and if the period of care should stretch over an extended period, that the Turkode LPG should temporarily take over the cultivation of Herr Lemke's land. . . ."

The court made its decision in accordance with the public

prosecutor's proposal. Friedrich Lemke spent five months in a home for alcohol-damaged persons, and came back completely rested, feeling in the best of health.

It was fall, and for the first few days he just walked around town. His land and his animals were in the care of Turkode.

He had been out to look at the land. It looked fine. The sows had been taken to the slaughterhouse, as well as the cow—which gave him 3,000 marks as starting capital. The horses had been taken out to Turkode, where they had been well cared for, and Friedrich had gone out and fetched them back to their own stall. He paid nothing for the help. They had promised that whatever profits derived from Turkode's use of his land would be put to his account. He had been to talk to the LPG chairman, who had naturally offered him membership in the collective. It would mean that he'd begin work at 7 in the morning and finish at 5, get 2 days completely off if he would do field work, 12 days vacation, and after working hours not have to worry himself about anything.

"You're not getting any younger, Herr Lemke."

"No, I'm not," Friedrich answered.

Now Friedrich Lemke has sold his lands and his livestock—except for one horse, which he hitches up in the mornings when he starts out for Turkode at 6:30. He comes home in the afternoon, with horse and wagon, at about 4:30. He then goes up to the Körner for a while and has a beer.

"Ha!" he says. "I thought this was a workers' state, this place. Ha!" he says again. "Does that mean that the workers are only going to work at half-speed? What are all these people doing who are sitting here?"

On Sundays he goes out to the hogs for three hours, to feed them and get some food for himself.

"One day," he says, "I went out to have a look at my

own fields. Just think, I couldn't find them. After all these years, not to be able to find your own land, just simply because you don't have any land any more."

He tells about life where he was, the life of luxury. But he is a man of few words. When he sits at the Körner, he is mostly a listener.

This year he has not sent an account to Frans-Günther, and has not received his February Christmas card.*

✪ Unanimous: Condemn Political Provocateurs With the Utmost Severity

Warsaw (ADN/SVZ), March 15, 1968—"The voices of the workers of Warsaw and the nation are unanimous: Help the students who devote themselves honorably to their studies and want to use their political understanding to help the Polish people; but condemn with the utmost severity those who, for their own interests or simply for the sake of dissension, incite other students to disorders." This

---

*Elected jurors, with the same privileges as the salaried judges, take part in the proceedings of courts of the first instance. All judges are elected for a term of four years by the relevant body of people's representatives. Special courts or political courts do not exist. In criminal trials, authorized representatives of the collective where the defendant is employed or resides are allowed to participate. These authorized citizens can appear as either public defenders or public prosecutors. At present, 65 percent of the cases in which the occurrence of an offense has been established are brought to court, while 35 percent of accused persons must answer to the charges against them before independent conflict or arbitration commissions that are chosen in the factory, collective, housing development, etc., without any trial's taking place.

is the appraisal of *Trybuna Ludu*, on Wednesday, of the results of the just-concluded nationwide workers' meetings at which sharp protests were raised against the riots instigated by a small minority of students in Warsaw, and at which full support was assured the leadership of the Polish United Workers' Party.

✪ Diederich, Thiele, and the District Prosecutor in Ludwigslust

Broadly speaking, there is no crime in Neustadt. The most recent political verdict dates more than ten years back. The prison in Neustadt has been closed down, as has also, for several years now, the one in Ludwigslust—though this is the result of prison centralization. The closest prison now is in Bützow.

According to Mayor Diederich, Neustadt has no drinking problem. According to Deputy Mayor Thiele, there *is* a certain drinking problem just in the month of March, when annual bonuses are distributed.. According to the district prosecutor, the drinking problem is the only big problem. According to the district chairman for the HO, it is from the sale of alcohol that the HO restaurants in Neustadt earn their greatest profits. He asserts with particular satisfaction that there has been a steady shift in consumption from foreign cognac to the German variety, which is also cheaper—70 pfennigs for two centiliters.*

✪ Commissioner Brentzler

It hasn't always been a pleasant job—that I'll have to admit. I've been commissioner now for 20 years. It wasn't easy at

---

*Two-thirds of a fluid ounce.

the beginning. A lot of the actions were difficult. We were forced to search homes, for example. It was essential if we were going to make anything of our country—every possibility of underground agitation had to be crushed. You can appreciate that. You lost a lot of friends in the midst of it all, and we undoubtedly made a few mistakes. But better too many actions than too few.

✸ REMARKS ON A STAY IN PRISON

I believe the happiest day of my life was the day my family and I were let out of prison in Ludwigslust. That was shortly after the 17th of June.

They'd made a raid here at home. We used to be among the well-to-do, and I suppose they thought they'd find something. But they didn't find a thing—there wasn't anything to find. I suppose it was because they were mad they'd made a mistake that we landed in prison. I just can't tell you what the raid was like! My grandmother was still alive then, and they put her in prison too. But we were only there for a month, then came the 17th of June. When we got home, the house was full of flowers.

✸ To Bicycle Owners

Ludwigslust (SVZ), March 16—The German Insurance Administration informs us that reports of missing bicycles are increasing, and issues an appeal to all bicycle owners to insure their vehicles, and to provide them with a lock for parking. Only in such cases is insurance protection valid in the event of loss.

✪ From the Songbook for the Ninth to Twelfth Grades

LPG Song

WORDS: HELMUT PREISSLER

*Das Gut, auf dem uns Herrn und Ochsen quälten
gehört nun uns, mit Gutsherrn ist 's vorbei.
Die LPG, die wir uns selber wählten,
die machte Faust und Herz und Hirn uns frei.*

*In unserm Staat sind wir die Gutsbesitzer
mit Herrenhaus und Stall und Wald und Feld,
sind Festsaal- Park- und Büchereibenützer
mit Feierabend, Urlaub und auch Geld.*

*Im Dorf wird 's nie mehr Hass und Zwietracht geben
der Grenzrain ist gepflügt, die Staat geht auf gemeinsam leben
und gemeinsam streben
da türmen Frucht und Garben sich zuhauf.*

*Wir werden nie mehr dienen
Gemeinsamkeit gibt Kraft.
Uns dienen die Maschinen,
wir herrschen und verdienen
durch die Genossenschaft.*

Literal translation:

The estate on which the masters and the oxen tortured us now belongs to us, the landowners have had their day. The LPG, which we chose ourselves, makes us free in hand and heart and brain.

In our state, we are the estate owners, with manor house and stable and forest and field. We enjoy the banquet hall and park and library. We have free evenings, vacations, and even money.

Hate and discord will never again be found in the village,

the space between fields is plowed, the state (or the budget) is devoted to communal living and communal striving, and fruit and sheaves will tower up in heaps.

Never again will we be servants, community gives us strength. Machines serve us, we rule and benefit through the collective.

✪ Berthold Dunkelbeck, Home From Ditching

I've been out working in the drainage ditches all day. It's hard work, and wet and cold. But we have to get the pipe down before the end of the month, so we don't have much time. We all worked ten hours today. It's way too much —you don't have the strength to do anything afterwards. I come home here, my wife is tired, the kids are tired, we sit around the table and eat without having the energy to talk. Every muscle in my body aches.

On days when the pressure's really on, you just have to follow the plan. Everything is mapped out. Ditching isn't such simple work, as a matter of fact. The soil is difficult out here. It blows away easily. We've made calculations and taken random samples of the soil consistency, and by and large they hold up. But if there's going to be any point in ditching, why, it's got to be done so it'll last a few years.

You have to be reminded what that kind of work is like. Then you can appreciate it better afterwards. It's not the workers' fault if their labor is badly invested. The man chosen by the workers is still only human, after all. He can make mistakes, and he has to have the right to make mistakes—that's all too easy to forget when the mistakes have serious consequences. And even when they don't.

In the days when the supervisors belonged to a different

class from the workers, their mistakes were proof of the shortcomings of the higher class, and of the shortcomings of the capitalist system. Now, supervisors still make mistakes—that's inevitable. And it's still true that when a supervisor makes a mistake, the first thing the worker wants to know is: How did that guy get to be supervisor?

So the worker thinks there must still be something wrong with the system, even though it's a workers' and peasants' state. And what's the consequence of workers' being disappointed in their representatives? Well, I think we can safely predict that reactionary ideas will gain ground as a result of disappointments in relation to the party, since the party is the most left-wing element we have. Of all our parties, it's the SED that stands furthest to the left. Just like in West Germany, there is no alternative further to the left than the alternative already offered by the government position. But the difference is, first, that this is a Socialist party in a Socialist country, and second, that there is no possibility of organizing demonstrations in the part of Berlin that's on this side of the wall. None at all. That situation is worth talking about. You could say it's a limit on the freedom of expression. But it's also insurance. We don't dare forget what happened in 1953, and even if it was 15 years ago, the fact remains that in this country, Socialism wasn't accomplished by means of an internal revolution, not originally.

As a supervisor and party member, you're constantly being reminded that you're a representative of the Socialist system. You're continuously watched, you continuously have to watch yourself, to see that you're a good supervisor, to see that you're a good worker, to see that you do the right thing by your position.

In the SED's party program, there's a whole list of instructions on how a party member is supposed to conduct himself, but when you just read them in a book, they seem like the purest nonsense. You don't understand what all those different precepts mean until you discover that they're not even adequate as descriptions of what's *really* required. It obviously won't do to sit in some tavern and get drunk, or to run around chasing other men's wives. It's a question of always knowing exactly what you're doing and saying. If you do something stupid, then right away everyone says "Well, just look at the kind of people who join the party." That's how people react, and that's how they draw their conclusions. The levels of tolerance aren't very great. The party watches its members, and so does everyone else.

✺ Advertisement Page in the Schweriner Volkszeitung, March 21

Youth Dedication

A big day for young people.
And a fitting gift for the music lover:
the DUO Record Player. Two speeds
and the Stereo-Mono-Crystal system
make this phonograph outstanding.
Price 120.00

Best wishes and practical gifts,
from the shops of HO and the Co-op—
to those on the road to life.

Linugran

This highly valued health aid will give
your bowels an education in regularity.
Even chronic constipation can be cured.
Linugran is an organic laxative.

Needed at once

Bran.

Seed potatoes and silage offered in exchange.

Life in Bloom LPG

Göhlen, Ludwigslust

Prophylactics

(Best Gold Label) 3 doz. 12.00 Add. inf. discr. supp. in plain env.

S. Hennig, 9216 Siebenlehn/Sa.

Carl Zeiss Jena

Center for construction of
scientific equipment in the GDR

In order to accomplish the mission assigned our plant in the scientific-technological revolution, we require, at once:
Workers
for our mechanical manufacture division
(shift-work) as
lathe operators, milling-machine operators, grinders, and drillers.

We offer these workers:

—Newly constructed apartments. Good board and lodging until occupancy.

—Moving expenses, travel allowance and per diem in accordance with regulations.

—Salaries in accordance with the rate schedule for general machine production.

—Company-owned vacation homes.

—Excellent chances for advancement.

Applications from agricultural and construction workers, or from workers employed at VEB Klement-Gottwald-Werke, VEB Elbe Shipyards Boizenburg, and VEB Fliesenwerke Boizenburg, cannot be considered.

Hello! Hello!

Joy in the garden! 10 gladioli, golden-yel., price level I, 3.85; 30 gladioli, salmon, pr. lev. II, 4.85; 30 gladioli, clear red, pr. lev. III, 6.35; 30 gladioli, mixed, 2.65; 5 lrg.-leaf begonias, 2.15; 20 Jap. dwarf dahlias, mixed, 12.00; 5 lrg.-leaf dahlias, 1- and 2-colors, 10.00, 12.00, 15.00; 30 fringed carnations, 5.25; 30 country carnations, mixed, 7.50; 5 cactus, favorite assortment, 12.30; 10 heaven's ladders, 40 cm.* leaves, 6.00; 10 large blue thistles, 8.00; 10 rose carnations, 20 cm., 8.00; 3 broom, dense-spiked, 8.10; 10 blue cornflowers, 10.00. Beginning March 18. Retail sales Mon. to Fri., 9-4 only. G. Riebecker, Quedlinburg, K.-Liebknechtsstr. 36.

The high-tension electrical equipment plants of the GDR

will present, on March 28 and 29, 1968, in
Magdeburg, at the
HO New World Stadium Restaurant, a
Production Sales Fair
featuring: cables and wires, thermostats, relays, metering apparatus, transformers, rheostats, high- and low-tension equipment, metal goods, closed-circuit equipment, and other products for electrical installations.
The Sales Fair will be open continuously from 8 a.m. to 4 p.m.

For sale or exchange

for grain or fodder, 50 tons* of fodder beets.
Glückauf LPG, Perleberg

Personal

Am 28 years old, 1.70 m. tall, seek simple girl who loves agriculture. Poss. marriage. Reply 6011 DEWAG.

---

*16 inches.
*Fifty metric or "long" tons, equal to approx. 55 "short" tons; 1.70 m. (meters) =
   5' 7"; 100 kg. = 224 lb.

Wanted, before June 30, 1968

330 young pigs.
100 kg.* grain offered for each.
VEG Saatzucht, Karow.

Choosing a Career at the Schröders'

Evald's daughter: Yes, I'm in the FDJ. . . . No, it's not compulsory . . . Well, maybe it's sort of a voluntary requirement, because the teacher said it would be easier to get the job you want if you've been in the FDJ, so I joined. I've been to meetings twice. But I didn't get to choose my own job anyway. When we went into the seventh grade, we had to fill out a questionnaire about what we wanted to be. I put down "secretary." But when they came to school from the district government to talk about career choices, they still wanted me to go to an LPG. They wanted me to be a cattle worker. I didn't want to, and I said so. So then they came here to talk to my parents. . . .

Evald: They came here one morning and said my daughter wanted to be a cow tender. "A cow tender?" I said. "Why, she never said any such thing! I don't believe it," I said. "I've got two calves out here, and she's not one whit interested in tending them. She's afraid of them."

"Yes," they said. "She said she wanted to be a cow tender."

They didn't know we had a telephone—there aren't many people who do. So I called the principal and asked to speak to my daughter, and she came right home. They just looked blank. They couldn't go on insisting she'd said she wanted to be a cow tender. So now, instead, they said they needed people on the LPG's.

Daughter: And I was willing to take it, I mean, I would have been happy to take office work at an LPG. But they wanted me for the cows.

Evald: She didn't want to. So they said in that case she wouldn't get any job at all. They thought they could threaten us that way. But I told them in that case she could just stay at home. You know, I figured it wouldn't matter if she just stayed home for a year. When she's 18, no one can keep her from getting a job anyway.

Daughter: Can't they?

Evald: No, then you're not under the Youth Administration any more.

Besides, we know well enough there's a labor shortage. There isn't any risk of unemployment. For one year she could have just as well stayed at home. We had plenty of money. But instead, we sent her to a private school in Ludwigslust—it's the only private school in the whole Schwerin region. An old woman runs it. There's a long waiting list, but my daughter got in. She went there for five months and learned stenography and typing. It cost us 700 marks. She rode her bike over and back, twice a week, and the rest of the time she helped out here at home. As soon as she finished the course, she got a job at Hydraulik Nord.

Daughter: The first thing they asked was whether I'd been a member of the FDJ.

Evald: How much vacation do you get?

Daughter: I don't know. A whole lot, I think.

�֍ Conversation Between Dr. Köstlin and His Son

But, Papa, it's obvious everybody isn't the same. Nobody's forcing you to think so, either. It's just that you're making value judgments on the things that make them different. For example, you think intellectual strength is worth more than physical strength.

—But that's what our dear Ulbricht thinks too, my boy.

—Well, surely we're not going to let Ulbricht decide our values for us. For that matter, you've got your terms turned around. When you say the workers stole from your grandparents, you're completely forgetting it was your grandparents who stole from the workers in the first place. It's really way back then that the revolution began.

—Now, come now, my grandparents really weren't thieves.

—Your great-grandparents then.

—You mean the sins of the fathers . . .

—Yes, that's exactly what it's all about.

—Why, you've just *learned* all this, precisely the way we learned the catechism and the race laws.

—Come on, Papa, you really have to admit there's a certain difference.

—I envy you, son, and I hope you're right. . . . Rainer, do you think something like what happened in Czechoslovakia and Poland could happen here, I mean, among the students?

—No, absolutely not.

—Why not?

—If there are reactionary elements in this republic, why they aren't among the students in any case.

—You say, if there are any reactionary . . .

—Well of course there *are*, but not among the students.

—But what if the student revolts in Warsaw and Prague aren't reactionary at all, but Socialist? What if they're really stages in the development of Socialism toward Communism?

—That sounds very pretty, but I think they must be reactionary.

—But the books say that the path of Marxism leads through criticism and self-criticism.

—Yes, but not reactionary . . .

—But the Czech writers have stated quite clearly that they're not opposed to Socialism at all. They don't want anything but a Socialist society.

—Have they developed that far in Prague? . . . In any case, I don't think it would be possible to have student revolts here. There are too many weapons here.

—I've heard they have tanks ready in case anything should happen in Leipzig—at least in Leipzig.

—It's possible. We've even asked our teachers why there isn't any freedom of the press in this country.

—You agree there isn't any freedom of the press.

—We asked them why it took such a long time for the things you hear on the Western radio and television to get into the papers over here, and the teacher said it was due to the fact that reports have to be checked more carefully here. There's no point in just regurgitating a great mass of canards like they do in the Western media. . . .

—But free criticism . . .

—We *have* criticism. . . . Where's today's *Schweriner Volkszeitung?* Look here, here's a report on the inspection of milk production at the Bernhard Quandt LPG in Muchow. Listen to this extract from the inspector's conversation with the milkers:

"Question: How are the shifts organized?

Answer: We don't have any carefully worked-out shifts.

Question: How high is the daily quota?

Answer: I don't know. Nothing's ever been said about that. . . .

Question: Are the cows arranged in production groups?

Answer: Yes, they're changed every month."

Then there's the summary of the whole conversation:

"Production flaws were ruthlessly exposed. Comrade Szameitpreiksch characterized the primary deficiency in these words: 'There has not been an adequate effort to introduce the Socialist system of production according to the Neuholland model.' In the course of the discussion it was established that not all the milkers had taken part in the planning discussions for 1968."

That's criticism!

✿ Karlheinz Schröder, Evald's Brother

Karlheinz Schröder lives with his wife and three sons in a barracks building on Brauereistrasse. Occupation: truck driver; his wife is a bookkeeper at a Co-op store. The eldest son, 19, is a bricklayer at the Kurz Concrete Works; the second son, 13, goes to school and has, for the last four years, been a member of the Neustadt boxing club. The youngest son is two years old.

Karlheinz was formerly a traffic policeman in Ludwigslust, where he still does extra work, and where he usually has his dinner. He served as a Vopo* for eight years, and is a party member, as is his wife. Their eldest son is a candidate for party membership.

The parents share their bedroom with the youngest child. Over their bed hangs a picture of a winged angel, resting its chin and chubby arms against a cloud. The two older boys share the second bedroom. The eldest brother's side of the room is dominated by a bookcase, with books chiefly about the history of German Socialism and economic development in the GDR since 1950. The 13-year-old's side of the room is dominated by pictures of pop bands, exclusively East German. He says his friends have more pictures than he. He says his friends also hear more pop music than he does: "They watch the Western TV— 90 percent of them watch the West."

"In the beginning, I tried to fight it," says Karlheinz. "But it doesn't do any good. Young people have to have

*Contraction of "Volkspolizei"—"People's Police."

their own interests. I can't appreciate that music myself—
it's just noise. But I let him have his way. But Western TV,
no, not in my house, never. Never."

The 13-year-old is both district and regional boxing
champion in his weight division. He goes for training
twice a week. He doesn't belong to the Pioneers, because,
he says, the Pioneers don't do anything, not in this town.
The eldest son goes to the party institute once every two
weeks—two hours each session. The classes are held in
Ludwigslust. As a bricklayer, he often has occasion to take
part in voluntary National Construction Work. Both he
and his father do four hours of fire-fighting practice every
other week.

"This is the best fire brigade in the whole Schwerin
region," says Karlheinz. Frau Schröder goes to the meetings of the party women's division once a month. The
family's total net income is 1,000 marks a month. A short
way from the barracks they have a small garden, mainly for
vegetables. They have so many chickens they get a feed
allotment from the HO.

Karlheinz Schröder goes to work at 6 in the morning
and comes home around 5 p.m. Frau Schröder takes care
of lighting the fire, since she doesn't start until 8. The
eldest son works from 7 to about 6. The middle boy takes
the youngest with him in the mornings and leaves him at
the Klara Zetkin Nursery, not far from school. He is left
off about 7:30, and his mother picks him up around half past
3.

—No, you know, I really wouldn't want to just stay
home. I've done that a few times, and I just get all cross
and out of sorts.

In the evenings the whole family usually watches TV
together. After a working day you're really not up to much
more than that, says Karlheinz.

The 13-year-old has a great deal of homework. The others
often go to bed about 9 so as not to disturb his schoolwork

by watching TV. When there's a feature film, they stay up a little longer, but even then it depends on the boy's lessons.

The two older boys usually go to the Youth Dance at the Park Restaurant on Saturday or Sunday afternoon—the 13-year-old mostly to listen to the music. But the eldest boy likes the music too: "It's more fun at the Youth Dances since they started that music. And," he adds, "the short skirts."

He has no plans for getting married. Nor has he put his name on the housing list: "There are 400 names on it already."

On Sunday mornings in the summer, the whole family gets up at five o'clock to go out to the garden.

✪ Klara and the Future

The formal garden looks much like any other baroque garden. But between the well-clipped hedges, soccer goals have been set up, and the side paths have been made over into a track for running. School children are having their physical education lesson, the boys shot-putting and the girls practicing their sprinting starts.

The castle itself is the party headquarters.

When you come in through the huge doors, you are met by placards inscribed with the biography of Klara Zetkin. The old royal furnishings still stand in the castle's rooms. In one of them there is also a ping-pong table. In another room, another Klara is strolling around—she wears slacks and a white blouse with lace, and her hair is in a ponytail that reaches the middle of her back. She is probably about 25.

She asks for the key to the hall of mirrors. She has come from another town to see the castle, the garden, the church, the waterfall. She says her parents came here on their honeymoon. Now they are both dead—her mother several years ago, her father only a few months before.

—Papa should just have seen it. He would have seen his old Ludwigslust. He'd sit there and talk about the culture and refinement of the old days, and Ludwigslust was the symbol for all of it. It was the only castle he'd ever seen. He was a furniture dealer. But quite likely he suffered over having to sell that Co-op furniture. I feel sorry for him, I guess.

She is a textile worker herself, and she has a fiancé, a carpenter at the furniture factory. Her stroll through Ludwigslust is a constant argument with the surroundings. She views the armorial embroidery with contempt. She looks at the design on the furniture upholstery and recognizes the swastika where none is in fact visible.

When some other visitors stand in front of two pots in the garden and one of them tells the other that in 1945 the Russians broke two other pots that had stood there, and that it cost thousands of marks to replace them, Klara says it is insane to replace a couple of old pots.

The loudspeakers, which are attached to lampposts but hidden by the trees, start to churn out some light dance music. All the old houses seem to shake. A voice announces something over the loudspeakers. A jet plane sweeps over, just above the rooftops. What's happened? What is it?

Klara laughs.

"There's a meeting tonight," she says. "My fiancé says if we could just learn to adjust the loudspeakers, things in this country would be much nicer."

At the café she orders a large piece of chocolate cake with extra whipped cream. She says her fiancé doesn't like her to eat whipped cream, because it makes her too fat. He always says you can see the difference between East and

West on the girls. The West German girls look like seven lean years—don't they have any food over there?—and the East German girls look like seven fat.

Herself, she just thinks the West German girls who come to visit in the summer look stuck-up. "And then they say they have a larger choice of boys. I wouldn't want to have their boys. All they can talk about is cars."

Her fiancé has been in the party for a year. She will probably join too, by and by. They met at a youth congress three years ago, and they will eventually be married. But it's fine the way it is, too.

They usually get together on the weekends. But this weekend he's doing some volunteer work—building benches for the outdoor theater. He often does such things. "As a carpenter, he's very useful in the work of building the republic."

Still, doesn't it rankle just a bit that he gives so much time to the republic? After all, he doesn't get any pay for his volunteer work. Couldn't he be thinking about saving up money for a family?

Klara chooses not to understand the question. She dismisses it by calling it a capitalistic way of reasoning. "If you carry that to its logical conclusion," she says, "you wouldn't send any help to the oppressed people in Vietnam either. But then you don't, either," she adds.

"In West Germany, they send help to Israel, but why do they do that? It's a well-calculated combination of bad conscience and egotism."

She tells me that her father had been a member of the former party: "Oh, you should have heard him when he got started. It was like the rights and wrongs of the world depended on the fact that he got a grenade splinter in his back outside Leningrad."

She laughs.

"He wasn't easy to live with. When I used to come home in my FDJ shirt, he'd try irony. When that didn't work, he'd say that the Hitler Youth was at least German, but this was treason. And then it didn't help any to explain that the FDJ was something completely different, that the FDJ worked primarily to protect peace."

After her father's death she moved out of the apartment where they'd lived. Now she has room and board right in the neighborhood of the factory. Her fiancé also has room and board. It gets a little tiresome sometimes. But this summer they're going to go camping together up near Rostock.

What are her dreams?

"I hope," she says, "that my children will one day be able to grow up in a republic that lives in peace. I hope the children I have will live to see the final triumph of Socialism."

What does she mean by "the final triumph of Socialism"?

"I mean a world where no one dreams capitalistic dreams any more, a Socialist world, where people acknowledge each other, and themselves. . . . Isn't it awful here in Ludwigslust? What a monument to pretense and depravity!"

Then she orders another portion of whipped cream.

✖ Three Cheers for the Party

SVZ, March 7, 1968—The members of our Socialist youth organization today celebrate the 22nd anniversary of their society, the Freie Deutsche Jugend. The young comrades have prepared for this day with many new achievements. They have assumed obligations that will do them honor. The young FDJ comrades at the Leussow LPG will support their collective by taking over the work in the area of soil improvement. The young comrade Peter Neper, of

Grabow, will become a soldier, along with many of his contemporaries.

On the birthday table are also several applications from apprentices at VEB Funkmechanik in Neustadt-Glewe— Brigitte Zöllig, Carsten Bruhns, and Karin Stapel. They ask to be accepted as candidates for membership in the German Socialist Unity Party. All three apprentices will complete their training this year and will be received into the community as full-fledged workers. They have used their training period well. They have learned to understand what Socialist cooperation means, that it is necessary for every citizen in our nation to be always prepared for new tasks. They have learned to use their heads and their hands. Political discussion has strengthened their determination to become valuable members of the working class.

The parents of the three young people have had an essential part in this decision. Through careful upbringing they have implanted in their children confidence in the policy of our party and our Socialist state. Parents, teachers, guardians, instructors, and the Socialist youth organization have again and again answered all the questions of children and young people about the meaning of life. Socialism and young people go together, and the best of them, like Brigitte, Karin, and Carsten, declare their faith by aligning themselves with the like-minded, by joining the vanguard of the working class and a working people. Brigitte, Karin, and Carsten have pledged their loyalty to the revolutionary tradition of the heroes of the working class and their Marxist-Leninist party. It is their desire to take their place alongside their experienced comrades, to continue the struggle, and with youthful élan carry it to victory.

Today, on the birthday of the Socialist youth organization, we wish to congratulate these three young people, and all other young people, for their decision. They, like many other citizens, have once again given us proof that

281 | MEN OF OUR TIME

the Freie Deutsche Jugend is the forge of cadres for the party of the working class. May Brigitte Zöllig, Carsten Bruhns, and Karin Stapel always be found where new paths are being blazed.

✪ Men of Our Time

No task
is too great
for him

SVZ, March 12, 1968—One of many men returned to their posts in the elections of the German Socialist Unity Party is Comrade Otto Kunze.

Otto Kunze, now 47, became a member of the German Communist Party* in 1945 in Neustadt-Glewe, and began his political work as local party secretary at IG [Industriegewerkschaft] Metall.

He was raised in the spirit of proletarian internationalism, and even before the Fascist collapse he sought contact with such good comrades as Max Zeise, Karl Mumme, Robert and Otto Schröder, and Gustav Eisermann. These comrades became his models.

At the beginning of the fifties the party assigned him to study at the district party institute. Since then, he has held various posts—as staff member in the district government, as a member of the political section of the former Wöbbelin Machine-Tractor Station, as city councilman in Grabow, and as party secretary at VEB Bama. Things have not always gone smoothly over the years, and Otto Kunze has often found that carrying out party decisions is no simple matter. But he has always learned and grown from the tasks assigned him.

*The Socialist Unity Party was subsequently formed by a forced merger of the Communist Party and the old Social Democrats.

Comrade Kunze is now in his second year at VEB Funk-mechanik and has good relations with all the members of the tool-and-punch brigade. The respect these comrades feel for him is demonstrated by the fact that some of them come to him to confide their personal troubles.

"Since Otto came to us, he has performed outstanding political work, no time of day and no task is too much for him"—such is the judgment of Party Secretary Otto Kurr. What's more, the work, in a party group that includes two skilled trades, is not at all easy. But with the support of the party collective, even problems that look difficult can be solved.

This is the motto by which work in the party group is guided: Great are the goals in the years of decision. It is not only a question of doing well in the competitive plan —the group is also eager to fulfill all the conditions neces-sary to achieve for the collective the official title "Collec-tive of Socialist Labor." We wish them all success in attaining that goal.

✖ Berthold Dunkelbeck, on Solidarity

I was selected to be a party member. To be perfectly honest, I didn't look at it as a particularly revolutionary event in my life. I know there are some people who look on the day they're accepted as candidates as a turning point in their lives. But it wasn't like that for me. I guess it seemed to me that the demands made on a party mem-ber weren't any greater than the kinds of demands I al-ready lived up to, as far as anyone could expect me to. What jolts a lot of people is that the interests of the party and the state have to come before personal interests. I didn't find anything upsetting about that—it only meant I'd be working more for communal production and less for private profit. It seemed to me I was doing that already.

What's more, I didn't really see the difference. If you work for the state, you work for yourself. I think that's completely logical. As far as the party work itself goes, it might mean you have to give up a few evenings with the family in order to spend them on party work instead, or in my case, even that I'd have to sacrifice some of my study time; because even if studying does serve the party and the state to a very substantial degree, still there's no point in denying that it gives me greater personal benefit than working on various committees, where the result of the work has a much less obvious influence on my personal life.

But becoming a party member meant something else, too, from a purely personal standpoint. There are a lot of other party members who married girls from Catholic homes, just like I did. But they don't seem to have had the same problem. Or maybe they were stronger than I've been, or maybe their wives' Catholicism was more superficial. My wife is a strict Catholic, and I respect her deeply for it. Her faith means a great deal to her. There are other people it's meant less to, and they've left the Church, since they haven't found the two ideologies compatible. I'd like to think they are compatible—but I'm not sure of it. Sometimes I'm full of aggression toward everything Christianity stands for, and I have a hard time not showing it. At the same time, you have to look at the practice of religion as a fact, and instead of fighting it, you have to try to look at it and figure out how it can best be used to serve Socialism. I think the law on religious freedom has already made that very concession. There's no point in being too dogmatic about Marx. After all, Marx's society was different from this one. But I have to admit that deep down I can't decide whether a Communist society will be realized faster with the more or less active support of religion, or if it would go faster if we fought it. And I have to admit that my uncertainty on that point has created problems in my own marriage. The government hasn't actually taken any

stand. They're being very careful. It's a controversial subject even for them.

There's supposed to have been some harassment of
Christians and churches 10 or 15 years ago. But today the
Catholics are getting a building permit to put up their own
church here in town. There isn't enough housing, but still
they're putting up a church. . . . You ask why. Well, quite
simply because there are so many Catholics around here
these days, and building a church for them makes them
favorably disposed, or even positively disposed. It's not
impossible there's also a little blackmail behind it. Because
whatever you may say about the party's consideration for
the Christians, still you can't accuse it of being especially
friendly to religion. The party headquarters in Neustadt is
in pretty bad shape. There aren't enough nurseries. The
Rathaus isn't exactly a source of pride, it looks by and large
the same way it did under Hitler—well, I don't know—but
I don't know either that they've done much to it besides
minor repairs. The schools are inadequate. But a Catholic
church comes before everything else. It's a propaganda
church for the party.

Inside the party itself there's by no means such a positive
attitude. The Church is more of a necessary evil that you
don't quite know what to do with. And however much
people talk about religious freedom, you can't get away
from the fact that most party members are outright enemies of religion, and they'd like nothing better than to just
get rid of the whole clergy. Now under these circumstances, it's perfectly obvious that a party member who has
his house full of prayers and incense isn't going to get off
scot-free—particularly since in all the other families where
one person has been a Catholic, the family has always been
de-Christianized in favor of the party. It would never cross
my mind to try anything like that. But I can tell you quite
frankly that I was exposed to a lot of needling from various
other members. It doesn't do any good to try to explain

that my wife and her mother are possibly just as good Socialists as a lot of party members. It doesn't do you any good to argue like that. It only sharpens the antagonisms. And there's a rule about unity—even though it wasn't me that started the argument. I could have reported the accusations and the needling to the party leadership, since they were breaking the rules too. But after all, I couldn't be sure they'd support me. Inevitably, it led to unpleasantness here at home too.

Three winters ago I went to the party institute in Ludwigslust. Maybe you remember, it was a terrible winter. I used to take the five o'clock bus, and one afternoon it was already snowing so hard and so slippery that it took us almost an hour to get there. Then I used to take the 11 o'clock train home. There aren't very good connections between Neustadt and Ludwigslust in the evenings. After classes, several of us used to go to the Hamburg Hotel and drink coffee, or sometimes to the Mitropa. We'd sit there and get warm and wait for our buses and talk. There were only five of us from Neustadt, a few from Wöbbelin, some all the way from Dömitz, but their bus left earlier. That night there were only three of us from Neustadt, and one of them was staying over, because he had to be in Ludwigslust the next morning at 6 anyway. The other two were a nursery school teacher and myself. The others must have run into trouble with the snow before they even got to the bus.

Anyway, the two of us went to the Mitropa, so we'd be close to the station. We had a couple glasses of cognac to warm ourselves up a little, and then when it was time we went out to the train, which was standing there waiting. It was cold, no heat in the cars. The storm was still going, a terrible wind that cut right through my fur coat. You could hardly stand up straight. It was the same way when we got off in Neustadt. She lived in about the center of town, and we were both frozen by the time we got there, so I said yes when she asked me to come up and get warm before I went on home. It's really quite a ways out here, and so it wasn't so unusual, all by itself.

I don't know why I'm telling this in such detail. Maybe I'm trying to excuse myself. Anyway, as it happened, I didn't go home afterwards. I didn't have any desire to go home. I slept there on the floor overnight. I didn't sleep in her bed. At 5:30 she went to the nursery, but I couldn't leave right at the same time, naturally. It was dark, of course, but the streets were full of workers on their way to the tannery. And every time I thought about getting out of there, I was too afraid of being seen. I knew well enough that if I was seen coming out of her door, it wouldn't make a bit of difference *how* much I swore that I hadn't slept in her bed with her. I didn't dare go out later in the day, either. There were neighbors, and they'd be pretty surprised to see me come out of her door, when they knew she hadn't been home since 5:30 that morning. So I stayed in her apartment. In the meantime, my wife had gotten in touch with the station to see if all the trains had been running. It never occurred to her, of course, that I might have done something like spend the night with someone. I think the whole town knew I was missing. That kind of news always gets around in a town like Neustadt, no matter how awful the weather is, no matter if the roads are impassable.

When the girl came home from the nursery, she was really frightened to find me still there. Things had gone so far by then that the longer I stayed away, the more mysterious it got. So I finally gathered up my courage and went home. There sat my wife, along with her mother, crying, and the children were crying, and my wife and her mother had their prayer books out and I had a hell of a time explaining where I'd been. It wouldn't have been so bad if my wife had been alone. And it wouldn't have been such a big deal, either, if things had been the way they should have been between my wife and me. She would have believed me when I said I just slept on somebody else's floor. We'd always believed each other—that's the only way you can make a marriage work. On the other hand, if everything had been the way it should have been, I never would even have slept on somebody else's floor. But that's something else again. Anyway, the fuss here at home wasn't the worst part. The situation around here was bad enough already, and it might even have been easier to repair the damage after all that—although I can't be absolutely sure of that either. But no, the worst part was what happened to my standing with the comrades in the party.

Since my wife had reported my absence to the police, it was their business to find out where I'd been. They can't be satisfied with just knowing I'd turned up again. I told them where I'd been. I knew perfectly well what that might mean, but to try to lie would have been even worse. The truth always comes out. And I was prepared for the fact that no one would believe I hadn't really slept with the girl in her bed. The truth never comes that far out. In itself, there shouldn't be anything so shameful about spending the night under someone else's roof. But the upshot was that the girl got the reputation of having loose morals, and so she was declared obviously unfit to be in charge of raising children. I don't know if the parents of the children got mixed up in it—I'm sure some of them did. But officially, that is to say, inside the party, they said our behavior had damaged the party's reputation, and thereby made it more difficult for the party to carry out its work. In her case, that meant they didn't think a girl like her could be expected to be able to assert any authority in questions of child-raising. What was unfortunate for her was that the job of nursery school teacher is one of the most popular. There's no shortage of nursery teachers—girls wait in line for that job. So it wouldn't be any loss to the national economy if they kept her from practicing her profession for a time.

And they asked her to move away, because they considered it impossible for her to resume her profession in this town. And when she left, she took a warning from the party with her.

I got a warning too. But they couldn't dispose of me without more far-reaching consequences, since I was more important for production. They let me keep my job, but I had to pay a fine for the damage I'd done the party. They gave me extra party assignments too. And I was pointed out as a whoremonger. Obviously that didn't make my marriage any easier. When I asked the party secretary if it really would have been so terrible if I *had* slept with the girl, he just laughed and said everybody makes a little slip now and then. But the trouble this time was that the whole thing had drawn so much attention, and that it had been with a nursery school teacher.

So it wasn't because of the thing itself—which never happened—that we were punished, but because of what other people made of it, because of other people's fantasies.

You can't imagine how many spicy stories go around about Pastor Smidt. But no fewer people go to his sermons because of that. On the contrary, all the old women fill up the church to lap up what he has to say, and to look at him. A clergyman becomes more interesting if he shows a little interest in this life too. And if a party member spread false rumors about him, he'd have to answer to the highest court. The highest court, that's the people, in this country. Listen to the masses!

Now you might suppose the whole thing was cleared up, once I'd done all the duties they assigned me. And that's the way it should have been. There's even a law in this country that says you can't keep bringing up something a person's already paid the penalty for, without being liable to punishment yourself. But I never paid any legal penalty. And the thing I'm supposed to have done wasn't actually a crime, it was just something that wasn't really fitting for a person like me. And of crimes in general, you know, you can always say they're committed in a rash mood, or something like that. But once you've been labeled an adulterer, why then, obviously, you have to live with it for the rest of your life.

I know what people say about me. I hardly dare tell a woman how to clean the floor in the hog stalls; I'm afraid someone will report me. I hardly dare *hire* women. . . . Well, O.K., you can laugh if you want to—maybe I'm exaggerating. But you know what I mean, anyway.

In actual fact, I live practically like a monk.

And so that's how well I know what it means to let the interests of the state and the party have precedence over your own.

✿ Hermann Kuhn,
on Sharing a House

It's awful coffee we have here, and expensive, too. Sometimes when we sit here together in the evenings, the railroad man and I, we joke a little. "Just think," we say, "if our wife would at least send us a little West German coffee once in a while."

He's a rather uneducated man, and his only real interest is his stamp collection—he's one of those collectors the republic is full of. But I won't say anything against him. On the whole, we get along very well. He takes care of the fire and getting fuel and the handy-man jobs, and I take care of the garden and the cleaning. He gets to make his own bed, and he's the one who takes care of the pigeons too.

Once I tried to teach him to play chess, but it didn't

work out. When he always lost, he got tired of it. That's how primitive he is.

We don't do much cooking, except every other Sunday —that's when I take care of Sunday dinner. I usually try to find something nice. Last Sunday we had venison. Then it's I who treat him. On the other Sundays, he treats me. He usually takes me to the Körner, and we take turns paying for the schnapps.

Sometimes I've thought I should get myself another woman. But it isn't easy when you start to get my age. You can't move about quite so freely any more. For a 20-year-old, it's right and proper if he's out chasing girls. You can forgive a 20-year-old almost anything. But when you get to be my age, people keep more of an eye on you. I'm not actually so old, but most women of the right age are already on pretty firm ground, so to speak. If a man my age tries to get his hands on young game, he's immediately viewed with suspicion. And then it may mean something, too, that I have a past in the SS. There isn't anybody really cares about that, but it's still not a first-class dividend for a young girl. A few years ago I went out with a girl from the office, a real pretty girl, daughter of a farmer in Brentz. It started one Women's Day. We'd been partying all evening—we may have been a little drunk. But the remarkable thing about this girl was that she got me to give up my sense of resignation. I told you how it was when my wife and I found each other again. I couldn't any more, I mean, you know, I couldn't do it any more. I accepted it as a fact. After that, I didn't bother to be interested in it any more. I learned to look at life with different eyes. I got used to not looking at women as possibilities for sexual intercourse. And if it sometimes happened that a woman looked at me as if she—well, you know well enough how women look at a man, you're still young—why, I'd start to shake with fright. But with this girl it wasn't like that.

She didn't seem to feel there was anything to worry about, and she gave me the feeling there wasn't anything to worry about either. She gave me a kind of security which I actually never even experienced with my wife. But then one time we were sitting eating together in a restaurant in Schwerin—we were going to the theater—and she took my hand and stroked it, and she said, "Sometimes I wonder what these hands have done."

That was all she said. I asked her who it was had told her.

"No one," she said. "Nobody said anything. But tell me. You have something to tell."

She wanted me to tell about it. Someone must have said something to her. "Well, whoever it was," I thought, "sooner or later I'll have to tell her. Sometime I'll have to explain those seven years at Seven Oaks." I told her more than I told my wife.

"I'm not a murderer," I said. "I've never murdered anyone. I wasn't convicted of murder. I was convicted of mistreating anti-Fascists."

And what is an anti-Fascist, according to that terminology? If you could see a list of the verdicts, you'd understand. The ones who'd murdered people got the stiffest sentences. But there's a difference between one murder and another. There's a difference between murdering a Communist and a Social Democrat, and between murdering a Social Democrat and a Christian, and between murdering a Communist and a Jew. It's the same way with mistreatment. When the person who was mistreated wasn't a Social Democrat or a Christian or a Jew or a Communist, then he was called an anti-Fascist, simply because of having been subjected to mistreatment by a Fascist. They don't ask into the cause of the mistreatment, but only who did the mistreating. Anyone who wore the SS uniform was a Fascist, that's clear. I've never denied it. I never denied the mistreatment either. But what kind of people was it I flogged . . . yes, I flogged people. They were Polish partisans, and for sure they weren't God's best children. They earned their lashes. I still think so today. I wouldn't be afraid to say so right out on the street.

I told this girl everything—we never got to the theater that evening. But after that, I wasn't allowed to touch her any more. She didn't say so, she just withdrew. I asked her, but she said it wasn't what I thought.

The railroad man has had girls now and then too. Once he came home with a girl from Parchim. The worst thing about that was that we almost became enemies. I thought the girl was cheap, and I told him so. I didn't think it was the right way for him to honor the memory of our wife. If we were going to have girls, they ought to be worthy of her memory. That sounds ridiculous, of course—she abandoned us, after all. But think about it. You have to understand her. Would *you* be able to live in the same house with three *women* at the same time? I understand completely why she disappeared.

✿ Vacation Plans

Kurt Gericke's sister Anna comes to visit once a month. She comes from Rostock, where she works as a nurse in a shipyard. She comes partly in order to see her best friend from her school days, Toni Brandt, who lives with her mother in a two-room house on Grosse Wallstrasse.

Toni works in a shop; bonuses were handed out a week ago. The shop manager had decided that the bonuses would not, as prescribed, be distributed according to merit. According to Toni, the manager said that system only created dissension. But Toni thinks it's also unfair to distribute the bonuses evenly. She's just gotten a bonus of

900 marks, but if merit points had been counted, she figures she could reasonably have expected 1,500. She wanted the money for a vacation trip with Anna. They usually go on FDGB trips. A couple of times they've gone to the Klink vacation village near Müritz.*

Anna doesn't know yet what the bonuses will be like at the shipyard, but she has savings. They're getting together to plan this year's trip. Toni tells how a family invited her to go with them and camp at different places along the Baltic. But she said no.

Hanging on the wall in the room where they're sitting are pictures from a trip to the Harz Mountains.

They talk about whether they should repeat their trip to Wernigerode. Anna has brought along some brochures from the FDGB travel bureau in Rostock.

"Do you remember the first trip we took?" Anna asks.

"You mean the Hitler Tour, the one to Marseilles."

"His trips were better," says Anna.

"Be quiet," says Toni.

She goes to the window and looks out.

"Do you remember the trip to Norway?"

"We didn't even get to go ashore that time."

Toni Brandt's mother comes in—she's been sitting asleep in the next room. They tell her they're planning their trip for next summer.

"The last time *I* traveled was ten years ago," she says. "I was in Berlin with my sister. That was before the Wall. My sister and I went walking in Treptower Park—it was so pretty. They'll never see us there again."

---

*A 13-day visit at one of the FDGB's vacation resorts costs 50 marks for a union member with a monthly salary of up to 500 marks, 62.50 if the monthly income is up to 750 marks, 75 marks if it is up to 1,000. Every vacationer gets a 33½-percent discount on train travel once a year.

❈ Else Pesatzke, Office Worker, 40, on Internationalism

Communism is Internationalism. That means you have to get to know the whole world. I work in an office and write up invoices, and you don't exactly get to know the world that way, anyway not in the sense of Internationalism. Every summer I take a trip. I save for it all winter. The most fantastic was the one to China; we flew to Peking via Moscow. I'd like to make that trip again, but now you can't do it any more. We traveled around in the vicinity of Peking, went out to the Great Wall of China, and we went to the Ming graves, which are surrounded by beautiful mountains and rivers, and we went to the Ting-Ling Mausoleum, which was built underground by the 14th emperor of the Ming Dynasty. What unbelievable culture and wealth there was in that country!

I always buy postcards on my trips. And I take along a camera too, with color film. Then I paste all the pictures and souvenirs into scrapbooks. See here, I've got 13 of these scrapbooks from my trips. . . .

Here's my Chinese trip. Here's the Cloister of the Azure Clouds at the foot of the Western Mountains—look how the pagoda towers rise up against the mountain peaks. And this is the Pagoda of the Diamond Throne. From Peking the tour went all the way down to Canton. That's where they do ivory carving. We went around in an ivory factory that was 300 years old. . . . See, this is one of the girls who worked there. They do a great deal for the culture of the workers in China, you can't deny that. You see it in Canton.

Then we went by bus up to Hangchow. Did you know that Hangchow is called "The Paradise of the Earth"? Here's the grave of Yeu Fei, and the Golden Dragon

Grotto, and the Pagoda of the Six Harmonies—look . . .
The things you learn and the things you experience on a
trip like that! But we didn't have to learn how to eat with
chopsticks—that wasn't required.

I've made 13 trips, and I've made 13 scrapbooks like this
one. One time I went to Leningrad and Moscow. Once I
went to the Black Sea for a vacation on the beach. Once
I went to Yugoslavia, once to Albania. I usually travel with
a close friend of mine. Her hobby is learning *The Internationale* in the language of the country we travel to. She
knows *The Internationale* now in 12 languages. But, you
know, she couldn't learn the Chinese. Well, for that matter, she wouldn't have much use for it now.

Once we went on an art trip to Poland. I liked Cracow
a lot. Once I was in Czechoslovakia. I wanted to see Prague
and the Moldau, but mostly Kafka's Prague. When we
came back, I gave a lecture to our women's club on Kafka
and Prague.

❀ Ernst Thiele's Summer

I usually spend my summers down at the lake, but I didn't
get much of that this year. In July I had visitors from
Canada—six people who stayed for ten days. And right
afterwards, two more people, my brothers from West Germany. Then my uncle came from British Columbia and
stayed for ten days. That was very interesting—I got to
know Canada as a cold and purposeful country. At night
we'd sit up and talk economics and politics till 2 in the
morning, although none of us wanted to talk about politics.
We did some sailing too. And we went and looked at the
fortress, and up in the Rathaus tower, and to the school.
My uncle hadn't been here for 32 years. He watched us
take in a big harvest in a week. "Boy," he said, "we can't
do it any faster than that in Canada."

I haven't had much time for my stamp collection, either. And I've had a lot of work at the Rathaus. We haven't had a bookkeeper in the finance department for six months. Compared to industry, we pay lower salaries at city hall.

✿ Beach Director Arnold—a Winter Evening at the Einheit Café

Have you been down to the lake? Now they're going to put up street lights on the road down, and they're going to put up a new bus stop too. It's about time they did something down there, a lot of it's deteriorating. It used to be splendid, once upon a time. But the restaurant isn't well run—there isn't anyplace down there you can really eat. The Eichmanns ought to be able to arrange that, but they don't do a very good job. The swimming season runs from May to August. In the winter I have other work to do. There has to be some planning, you know, and then I help out with other things too—party work. In the summer, people come here to the beach from all over. You see a lot of foreign cars, mostly Czechs and Poles. In the summer I don't even count the West Germans as foreigners, there are so many of them, in their big fine cars. But we ought to have more to offer them. There ought to be some sort of tent movie house down there. And I think we ought to have a theater. But not the dull kind of stuff the Parchim National Theater puts on. They ought to put on plays in Plattdeutsch. People like that, it's the sort of thing they understand. The choice of plays in Plattdeutsch isn't wide, though you could take something of Fritz Reuter's. But it wouldn't have to be that. We could translate Goethe's plays into Plattdeutsch. People like that sort of thing. Faust would be very good in Plattdeutsch.

✹ Werner Bahlke, on Plans for the Summer, and Dreams

Come summer, I'm going to buy a car. My son's an engineer at the Wartburg factories, and, among other things, he's involved in testing new cars. Before they start manufacturing a new series, they test some of the cars, drive them for a few months, and afterwards they sell them cheaper, and often as not to somebody who works there, who gets a discount too. So that's why my son can buy a car for me. I've got two aunts in Rostock who are looking forward to it. But most of all, I need it in the summer, when I'm working on digs here in this area. I don't take any long vacation trips. I used to use a motor-bike. That was good too, but a car will be a little more comfortable, of course. . . . But let me tell you the vacation trip I'd like to take.

I'd like to travel that stretch from Oslo to Gothenburg, Karlstad, Östersund, Kiruna, and Narvik.

I was in Norway during the war—got there first on September 15, 1941. I traveled that stretch from Oslo to Narvik four times as a courier. It was a fantastically beautiful trip. In Gothenburg they put the cars on a siding, and the Swedish Red Cross gave us food. In Östersund they cleaned the coaches, and the Swedish officers gave us a meal. We had good German cigarettes to give in exchange. I was a captain—yes, and a Nazi. I had to be, as a teacher. We built fortifications on the Swedish border, and over on the other side the Swedes built fortifications. Then we'd meet in the woods—it was all very *gemütlich.* They gave us chocolate, and we gave them cigarettes and French cognac. What will happen if there's a war between Germany and Sweden, we'd ask ourselves. And then we'd

298 | THE OTHER GERMANS

answer, "That depends on which one of us finds out first. If I find out first, I'll kill you. If you find out first, you'll kill me."

But our relations with the Swedish officers were excellent. They could speak German, almost all of them, and a number of them had studied electrical engineering in Germany. Our relations with the Norwegians were good too. You always have to keep on a good footing with the population. Toward the end of the war, the morale got a lot looser in some other companies, but not in mine. It was like with the Russians here. But I became personally acquainted with a lot of Norwegians. There was a resistance movement. When they'd sabotage something now and then, our officers would get mad. But I always tried to tell them, "'It's not as if we were guests here." One night, when we'd just been sitting talking things over with our local contact, one of our boats was blown up. "Who could it be?" we asked ourselves. It seemed to me that the person who could have done it most easily was our contact. "Impossible," they said. "He's a quisling, after all." Later, when I was a prisoner, the contact came and said hello to me one day—he was wearing a Norwegian major's uniform.

When I retire, I really am going to make that trip.

✺ The Constitution Meeting—Thiele's Presentation

Ernst Thiele has before him a copy of the document that has been distributed to each family—the constitutional proposal.

—I don't need to read from it. Everyone knows the proposal, everyone has read it. There are some points that have given rise to discussion. There is also one point that is *not* included, but which has also given rise to discussion —namely, in the whole constitutional proposal, not a word is said about the right to strike. Since the beginning of the workers' movement, the right to strike has been considered self-evident. But now that we have a workers' and peasants' state, we discard the right to strike, the workers' old weapon. But we don't need to concern ourselves at any length with that. The right to strike is a right that the workers' movement won for itself under the conditions of capitalism. The development of the GDR has made it superfluous. Today, the industries are owned by the people, by the workers themselves. The workers don't merely have the right to collaborate in decision-making, it is the workers who make the decisions. Why should they go on strike against themselves? An article in our new constitution on the right to strike would be self-contradictory.

The constitution contains several other points that mark our progress. For example, it no longer says only that the citizen has an obligation to work, as it did earlier. Today it says that every citizen has the *right* to work. Obviously these two articles, on the right to work and the obligation to work, come to the same thing—and yet there is a difference. It's as Comrade Ulbricht says, that in our country, democracy stops neither outside nor inside the factory gates.

I'll go on to the next point.

In the past we've always talked of the equality of women and men on the labor market. Today, this equality has been achieved. Now the constitution says, "Men and women have equal powers and an equal station before the law." As you can see, that's an alteration that's been made so that women will not acquire even greater legal rights than we men. But we needn't speak more of that. It is true, all the same, that men still occupy most of the leading positions. But that state of affairs will be altered.

Liebe Einwohner
des Wohnbezirks IV Neustadt-Glewe

Am Donnerstag, dem 29. Februar 1968 um 19.30 Uhr findet im VEB Hydraulik Nord im Rahmen der Nationalen Front eine

Einwohnerversammlung

statt.

Thema: Aussprache über den Entwurf der neuen sozialistischen Verfassung der DDR, über Fragen des Volkswirtschaftsplanes der Stadt Neustadt-Glewe und andere Sie interessierende Fragen.

Hierzu laden wir Sie herzlich ein.

Wir würden uns freuen, auch Sie zu dieser Versammlung begrüßen zu können und rufen Sie auf, bei der Entscheidung über unsere neue sozialistische Verfassung aktiv teilzunehmen.

Es spricht der Genosse Thiele

Weiter nehmen teil:

Herr Helmuth Martensen, Vorsitzender der CDU
Genosse Wilhelm Warnecke, VEB Hydraulik Nord
Genosse Heinz Pröwer, VEB Hydraulik Nord
Genosse Wilhelm Naecker, VEB Lederwerk

Stadtausschuß der Nationalen Front   Rat der Stadt

Ecker   Diederich

Heuberg's Buchdruckerei Neustadt-Glewe 3-10-2 Dt G 101-0/68 2009

**Dear Residents
of Neustadt-Glewe Residential District IV,**

On Thursday, February 29, 1968, at 7:30 p.m., a

Residents' Meeting

will be held at VEB Hydraulik Nord, under the auspices of the National Front.

Subject: discussion of the proposed new Socialist constitution for the GDR, of questions on the economic plan for Neustadt-Glewe, and of other questions of interest.

We heartily invite you to attend.

We would be happy to see you at the meeting, and we urge you to take an active part in the decisions concerning our new Socialist constitution.

This notice is from Comrade Thiele.
The following will also take part:
Herr Helmuth Martensen, CDU chairman
Comrade Wilhelm Warnecke, VEB Hydraulik Nord
Comrade Heinz Pröwer, VEB Hydraulik Nord
Comrade Wilhelm Naecker, VEB Lederwerk

Town Committee for the National Front   Mayor

Ecker   Diederich

Then we have point number 36, and we shall discuss this more extensively later on this evening. It says, "Every citizen has the right to housing for himself and his family within the limits of developing availability. The state is obligated to effectuate this right by increased housing construction, by maintaining the available housing in stable condition, and by public control of the just disposition of apartment space." That's what it says in the constitutional draft, and it means that the state takes upon itself the obligation to increase the number of dwellings through methodical construction, but it also means, as before, that there is a continued need for each individual's active cooperation in solving the housing problem—those who have dwelling space must help to solve the problem for those who have none. We must all join in this effort, and we all know this. . . .

ON CONSTRUCTION PLANS

Let's have a look at the construction plan. Five separate buildings are going to be built, two of them by the city, all of them out on Strasse des Friedens. Repair work will be carried out to a value of 80,000 marks, of which 44,000 will represent by volunteer efforts. This will be at Breitscheidstrasse 11—Fritz Sass's house—at Kleine Wallstrasse 13 and 12, at Rosenstrasse 9, 10, and 14, at Ludwigslusterstrasse 23, and at Gartenstrasse 6—all of them private dwellings.

On public property, work will be done to a value of 45,400 marks, of which 4,900 will be voluntary. This will be at the savings bank on Breitscheidstrasse; at Grosse Wallstrasse 10, to a value of 470 marks; at Kronskamper Weg 13, where the chimney is cracked; at Burgstrasse 19, 800 marks; the party headquarters will be repaired at a cost of 2,900 marks—a furnace needs to be installed, the roof is cracked, the half-timbering is decaying in places; at Breitscheidstrasse 31, 60 marks' worth of repairs will be done;

at Schwerinerstrasse 13, work will be done worth 1,150 marks—the ceiling is cracked in three rooms. At Wabeler-strasse 5, a great deal of repair is needed, at a cost of 7,200 marks—among other things, toilets will be installed, indoor toilets—and new floors are needed in the entire building. At Breitscheidstrasse 14, nine rooms need renovating.

The day nursery will be enlarged at VEB Lederwerk. The cost of this work, 35,000 marks, will be borne by the tannery itself. Renovations will be carried out in 21 apartments belonging to the tannery. The sports field will be fenced—the fencing will cost 3,000 marks. Here at VEB Hydraulik Nord, the paint-drying installation will be rebuilt, and warehouse space will be constructed—at a total cost of 87,700 marks. At VEB Funkmechanik, the production area will be increased with two sheds. At VEG Lewitz, the driveway to the administration building and the workshop area will both be paved with concrete. Moreover, a day nursery will be established.

Streets and sidewalks will be improved. From Brauerei-strasse to Bahnhofstrasse, 210 square meters* of paving stones will be laid. The work will be donated by workers at the tannery, and the materials will be supplied by the town. Cost: 2,300 marks. On Qverstrasse, in front of Funk-mechanik, 150 square meters* of paving stones will be laid. The work will be carried out by Funkmechanik—cost: 2,200 marks. Wasserstrasse–Seestrasse will be paved with 120 square meters* of concrete slabs. The work will be done by the FDJ. On Thälmanstrasse, the street lights will be replaced with modern neon lights at a cost of 29,300 marks. On Seestrasse, on the way down to the beach, 18 lampposts will be erected at a cost of 25,000 marks. The work will be organized as a youth project by the local FDJ leadership. A new bus stop will be installed at the public

*210 square meters = 251 square yards; 150 square meters = 179 square yards; 120 square meters = 144 square yards.

beach at a cost of 600 marks. A new boat-building facility will also be constructed. At the camping area, the space for trailers and campers will be enlarged. Up to now it's been against regulations to use house trailers down there, but it's happened anyway, we know that—it's been reported. But it seemed to us that the trailers were so well hidden away that they could just as well stay.

In connection with the planned housing construction along Strasse des Friedens, which is planned for completion in 1972, there are also plans for new shops, and the problems that arise in this connection must be solved during 1968. New stores have to be opened here in town, too. The dairy store on Breitscheidstrasse is inadequate to the needs of the town, and a new one is planned for Rosenstrasse. And for Liebssiedlung and along the lake, we're planning shops of the same kind as those near the tannery.

Because of the introduction of the five-day week, larger demands will be placed on our restaurants—and for this reason we will have to establish increased cooperation with the food-preparation kitchens in Ludwigslust. Perhaps not everyone here knows that no restaurant in Neustadt, and none of the school kitchens and none of the factory kitchens, peels its own potatoes. Potatoes are delivered from Ludwigslust already peeled. That's one of the ways we save on labor.

The major proportion of the shops in town are still small or medium-sized, and even though we realize how uneconomical this is, we won't be able to alter the situation within the next few years.

One new shop will open this year—a game and poultry shop, on the square.

And then we have a section of the plan that deals with youth, but since I see there aren't many young people present, we can skip that section.

✪ Discussion Follows

Werner Bahlke: For several years now, we've been talking about this new construction project on Strasse des Friedens, and there have been waiting lists for that housing for over four years. Now we discover that the project won't be completed until 1972. A whole series of questions come to mind in connection with this matter. The project is immediately adjacent to the tannery, and the idea is that the housing should, first of all, be put at the disposal of the tannery employees. But at the same time, there's going to be a change-over in the tannery's production, in connection with which the tannery is going to be enlarged. The change-over figures to be completed as early as 1970, and the number of workers is expected to increase by several hundred. And we have two more large industries in town, both of which find themselves in a state of rapid growth. A production change-over is also being undertaken at Funkmechanik, one that will place that factory in a position of international competition. That will also require additional manpower. We already have a waiting list of about 400 people for housing, and now the largest housing project in Neustadt has been set a long time off. The housing situation is bad, and as far as I can see, it's only going to get worse.

Another thing about the project on Strasse des Friedens: The buildings constructed there will make up a small suburb to Neustadt. Now it's already been said that shops are planned for that area, but the plans are not yet completed. It's important that we be told when the plans *are* completed, so that we can take action to see that the needs of such a project are properly provided for. It simply won't do for us always to be told that the plans aren't ready yet, and then one day they start work without our ever having seen the plans. The needs we have to consider in a project like the one on Strasse des Friedens are, namely, that from the very outset we must plan for an area that will function autonomously. It isn't enough just to put up a few shops. Our school is crowded, and a new school building is planned for completion in 1970. But this one large school construction project shouldn't rule out an additional school project—that is, one on Strasse des Friedens.

We can't afford to invest a great sum of money in a project that, when it's finally completed, will prove to have been built for an era that's already past. The Strasse des Friedens project should also include plans for day nurseries and kindergartens. Such institutions are already to be found in that area—at the tannery. But they won't accommodate a whole new housing development, even if they're enlarged, and even if the development is, to begin with, primarily intended for tannery workers. And in the long run, it's inconceivable that an entire section of the city should be reserved for tannery workers. We mustn't plan ourselves into a city of categorized sections. At an early stage, we have to ensure that the Neustadt of the future will be a more fluid society than that. We have to make sure that the housing development on Strasse des Friedens will include the institutions I've named, and that the entire environment will be shaped in such a progressive manner that we won't be suddenly left with a development that amounts to some sort of terribly expensive emergency housing. That also means that the planning will have to consider such things as artistic adornment and the distribution of parks. I mention these things now, because I want to make sure that we will have an opportunity to see and express our opinions of the plans before it's too late. It has happened, unfortunately, that entire housing developments have been put up without paying any attention to the wishes of the people most nearly affected by the project.

Thiele: These are important questions. It's true we won't solve the housing problem with the buildings now planned for Strasse des Friedens. But the problem, of course, is the same problem we've had to struggle with ever since the founding of the republic, and that is that we always have to think first of the country's production capacities. The economy of the nation is still such that we always have to give production the upper hand. The production change-overs at the tannery and Funkmechanik are both of the kind that will contribute to exports. The tannery is changing over from pigskin to artificial leather, and Funkmechanik is going to specialize in rheostats for telephone apparatus, of a kind that are already produced in Leipzig, and from Leipzig already exported to, among other places, the White House. There are some things that just aren't made anywhere else. In addition, there's going to be another production change-over here in Neustadt, namely, at Hydraulik Nord. Within a few years, Hydraulik Nord's main plant will be transferred to Parchim. The buildings here will become primarily office buildings. That means that some of the labor needed for the change-overs at the tannery and Funkmechanik can be shifted over from Hydraulik Nord, and so they won't have to be supplied exclusively by new residents. That means that the housing situation needn't become as bad as Herr Bahlke has predicted. But it's true that it's already critical enough. It's also true that up to now, housing construction has been all too much neglected, and I don't need to describe the reasons for that at any greater length than I've already done. But the idea has always been that once we get a good start on production development, then housing construction can begin.

Willy Köstlin: But construction is going on in other places. It's only here in Neustadt that housing has fallen so far behind.

Thiele: Construction *is* going on in other places, yes, I know. But there has been construction here too. I think it's an exaggeration to say that Neustadt is far behind. We aren't. The housing shortage is nothing peculiar to Neustadt, unfortunately—we can't say that it is. If that *were* the case, we could make greater demands. And you'll have to admit that even if we know that the project on Strasse des Friedens isn't enough to solve our housing shortage, still, it is a beginning to large-scale construction, and it is a beginning to the solution of this problem. You can't improve unfortunate conditions by magic. And even if the housing situation should worsen, which is possible, it won't worsen as seriously as it would if the Strasse des Friedens project weren't carried out. We should understand that too. But then comes the question that Herr Bahlke raised, the question of a voice in the planning. The planners have consulted representatives from the tannery and representatives of the town. This constant contact between the town and the planners in Ludwigslust will continue, of course, and obviously those who've been promised housing in the project will be allowed to express their opinions of the plans, and present their wishes. . . .

Bahlke: But can we be sure that won't happen when it's too late?

Thiele: The idea is not to operate as if this were a sham democracy, at least not as far as I know!

Bahlke: But this is a matter of concern to more than just the representatives of the town and the people who are going to live in the project at the beginning.

Thiele: Well, we're discussing it here too, and Strasse des Friedens is on the other side of town.

Frau Schultz: We're talking here about new construction programs, and we've also heard about what's going to be done to some of the old buildings. And I don't doubt the buildings that are going to be repaired according to the plan are in need of it, too. On the contrary, I'm sure they need repairs badly. But I would like to discuss the priorities. We have one part of town here in Neustadt, the part I live in, Kietz, that looks frightful. But the plan doesn't include very many of those houses. A few years ago we had the experience of seeing a house simply collapse. In one instant, a whole family had no place to live. We remember that, yes, and we laugh at it a little, because we hardly thought anything like that could happen, that the roof could simply fall in. That time, things were all right, I mean in the sense that no one in the house was injured. And I don't want to predict further accidents along those lines, because I really don't believe they'll happen—housing inspection these days is better than it was then. But the other houses in Kietz were built at the same time as the Schallers' house, and equally little is done about them, and I don't understand why the accident that did happen didn't lead to a more complete program of repairs than was actually carried out.

Thiele: The houses in Kietz have been inspected. The older buildings belong to the category that can no longer be considered adequate housing, and we have to reckon with a complete renewal of the area sometime in the future— and we can't wait too terribly long either. But the condition of the buildings, and the future reconstruction, mean that at the moment we can't invest too much money in temporary repairs, except for those that are necessary to keep those houses in a habitable condition. Now that's not a very grand ambition, and not very satisfactory to the residents, but the situation is such that we can't allow ourselves any short-term projects. To put the houses in Kietz into really satisfactory condition would cost just as much, if not more, than it would to build new ones.

Köstlin: As long as we're talking about Kietz, I think in any case we should take notice of *one* thing, and not wait any longer before we take some steps to correct it. I'm thinking of what can't simply be called a scandal, it's much worse. I'm thinking of the pollution of that stagnant arm of the river. It's impossible to describe what that water looks like, and I don't need to, because everyone knows, and nothing is done about it. It isn't enough that that part of the river looks like an open sewer, in the summer it stinks too.

Besides, all of Kietz is water-logged. We can't avoid drainage work, which will have to be done whether Kietz is rebuilt or not, and I doubt that it has to wait until the reconstruction has been started.

Thiele: It's true, the water is unsanitary, and it stinks, and there are children who play beside it. Whether or not all of Kietz is water-logged I don't know, but the area *is* largely swampy. Drainage work is absolutely necessary for solving that problem. It has to be done, and I also think it would save us certain expenses in health care. For the time being, I can say that the department for water problems has already taken note of the situation, and they're investigating the possibility of diverting the water, but according to what I've heard, there are certain difficulties on that point too. We can't just let the water in that little arm of the river out into the mainstream of the Elde, which is already polluted by the runoff from the tuberculosis sanitarium, just as it used to be by the waste from the tannery. Great errors have been made in this area before, and we're not without our share of the blame. Errors like that are hard to correct. The only thing I can assure you of is that we recognize the problem and are trying to find a solution.

Hermann Kuhn: Since new paving stones are being laid on Wasserstrasse down to Seestrasse, why not take up all of Wasserstrasse and put down concrete paving?

Thiele: That ought to be done. But we're taking it a little at a time.

Bahlke: Isn't there enough concrete?

Thiele: Oh, there'd be enough concrete if there was enough money.

Bahlke: But since Wasserstrasse is the main thoroughfare down to the lake, it's a heavily traveled street. Wasserstrasse is still paved with cobblestones, which, as a historian, I can certainly appreciate. But there's a torn-up pathway in the middle of the street that's used by both bicycles and pedestrians, and as far as possible, by cars too. We can't get away from the fact that it's a traffic hazard.

Herr Wallau: But if we're going to talk about traffic hazards, surely it's more important to do something about the corner of Breitscheidstrasse and Wasserstrasse. At least the cobblestones make the cars drive slower.

Bahlke: Not at all. I live on Wasserstrasse, and I've never yet seen any car drive down that street slowly. Drivers always go too fast.

Thiele: Well, then, what should we do about it?

✪ In the Mayor's Office

—Were you threatened?

—I told him he was drunk, so then he wanted us to go outside and settle it.

—Yes, I've heard about it, I've talked to people who were there. When we've got a foreign guest in our town, we don't want him threatened by any of the citizens—that certainly doesn't make a favorable impression. I'll find out who it was. There were a lot of people there, and I've only talked to a few of them so far. But you know you should also realize that it's hardly to your advantage for people in town to be saying that you sit in the town taverns and talk to drunks. I know you were talking about things it's not proper for a citizen of our republic to talk about.

—I agree with you. And I told him I didn't think there was any point in listening to him, since he was drunk. That's what started the argument.

—Would you recognize him?

—I can't go around and talk to people if I'm going to act as an informer afterwards.

—Informer? . . . What did he look like? Do you know where he lives? . . . Frau Schultze, who is that walking around out there?

Frau Schultze (through the door): Comrade Brentzler.

—Why doesn't he come in? Does he want me for something?

—Comrade Brentzler!

Comrade Brentzler comes in in his police uniform and says hello.

—What were you doing out there in the hall?

—Well, I didn't want to interrupt.

—Perhaps I should go now, so *I* don't interrupt.

—No, not at all, sit down, sit down. We don't have any secrets. That isn't the way we do things here.

—No, that's not the way we do things here.

—Well, Comrade Brentzler?

—Well, I just wanted to give you some information about a matter I can't do anything about, but I thought you should be told what's going on, anyway. You know Meyerholtz on Rosenstrasse?

—Yes, of course.

—Well, you see, things aren't as they ought to be in that house. There's a girl who goes there to visit him almost every evening. It's the neighbors, the Steiners, who say she comes almost every evening. She usually comes around ten o'clock, and she often doesn't leave before

about four in the morning, in time to catch the first train
to Parchim.

—How old is she?

—Twenty-three.

—How old is he?

—Thirty-two.

—What does his wife say?

—Yes, well, she doesn't seem to care much, because
young Brandt comes to visit her. When Meyerholtz is on
the day shift, he comes in the afternoons, and when Meyerholtz is on the night shift, he comes in the evenings.

—How old is he?

—Seventeen.

—Seventeen? Good God, and he goes to Frau Meyerholtz?

—Yes, that's what the Steiners say, and the Brauners,
who live across the street, and I've checked it out. It's true.

—How does young Brandt manage about his work? His
foreman at the tannery, that must be Meyer. . . .

—No, he's moved over to the chrome-tannery. There's
nothing unusual about his work.

—What is this girl from Parchim? What sort of work
does she do?

—She's been to secretarial school, she says—I've talked
to her. She's got the idea she wants to move to Neustadt.

—What? She wants to move here? That'll have to be
stopped, any way we can. We certainly don't want that
kind of person in our town. It'll have to be stopped.

—Yes, of course. I just wanted to tell you so you'd know
how things stood—I mean, in case an application should
arrive.

—Good, yes, I'm glad to know it. It's just the kind of
story we don't like to hear. You'll go on keeping an eye on
things?

—Of course.

—You see, Herr Holm, we have our little dramas here too, but then that kind of thing happens everywhere, of course. Things like that happen where you live, too, don't they? . . . Have you talked to her employer, Comrade? How is her work?

—Yes, I've talked to him. He's not particularly pleased with her. She seems tired and sloppy.

—We'll have to keep her from moving here. A person like that certainly wouldn't do the town any good. Well, Herr Holm, things like this happen where you live too, of course?

—Of course.

—Problems like this happen everywhere.

—Comrade, these are the kinds of problems we'll always have.

—Of course. Don't you think so, Herr Holm?

—Yes, of course.

—Well, Comrade, that's all I wanted to tell you. Here's her name.

—Fine.

—So I guess I'll be going.

—Yes . . . Herr Holm, this kind of thing has nothing to do with the way society is organized.

—Of course not.

—We'll get hold of that fellow you talked to at the Hamburg, I promise you. He'll feel the consequences.

—I'm afraid I have to go now, Herr Mayor. I have to meet someone at three o'clock.